MW01620217

Signs & Relics

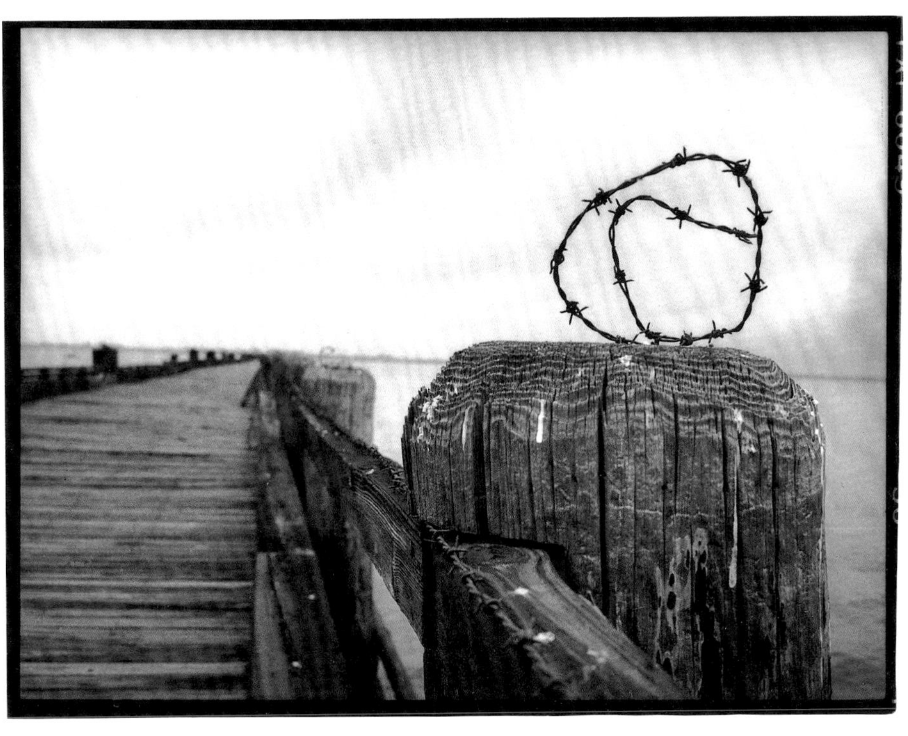

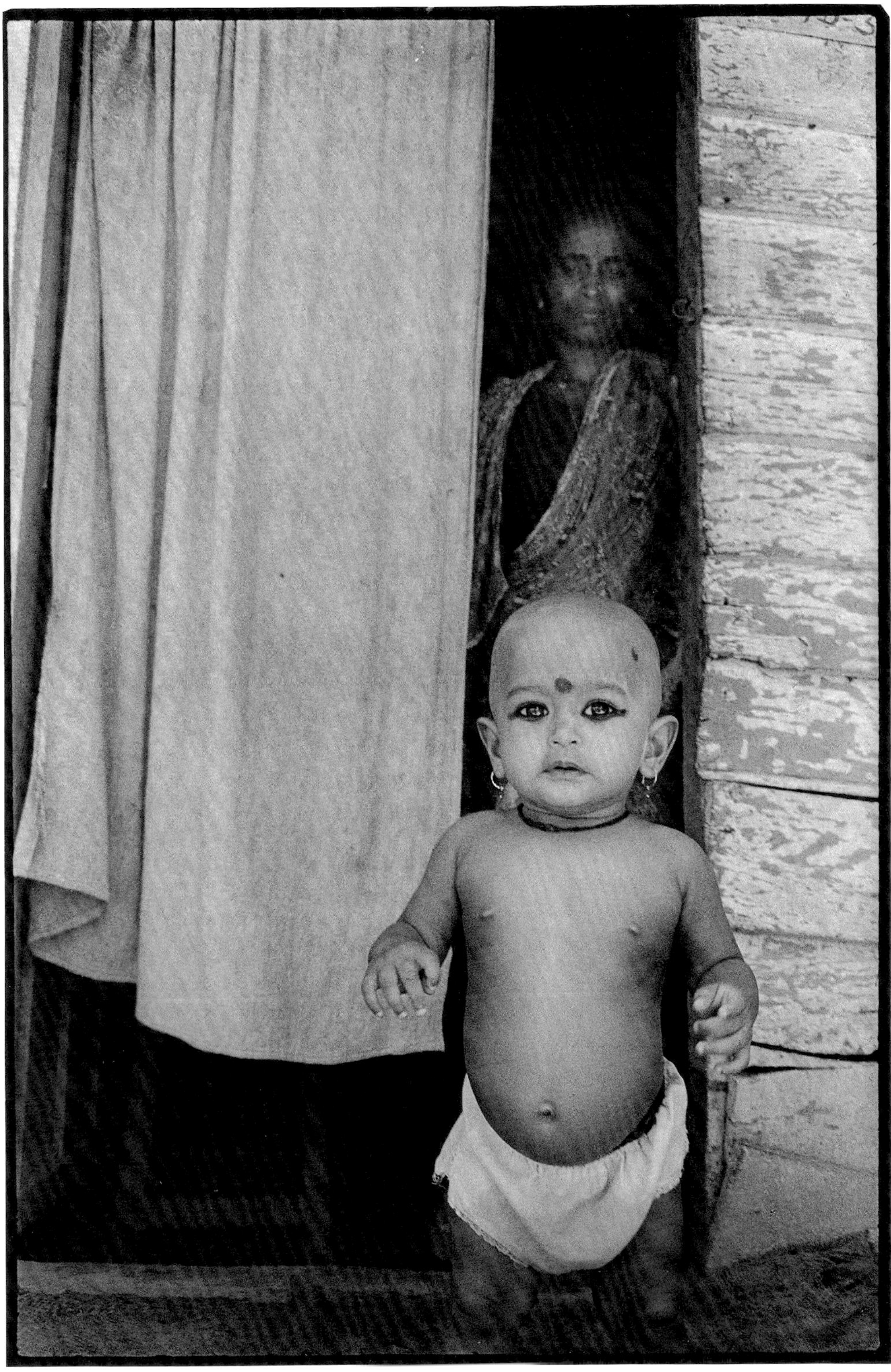

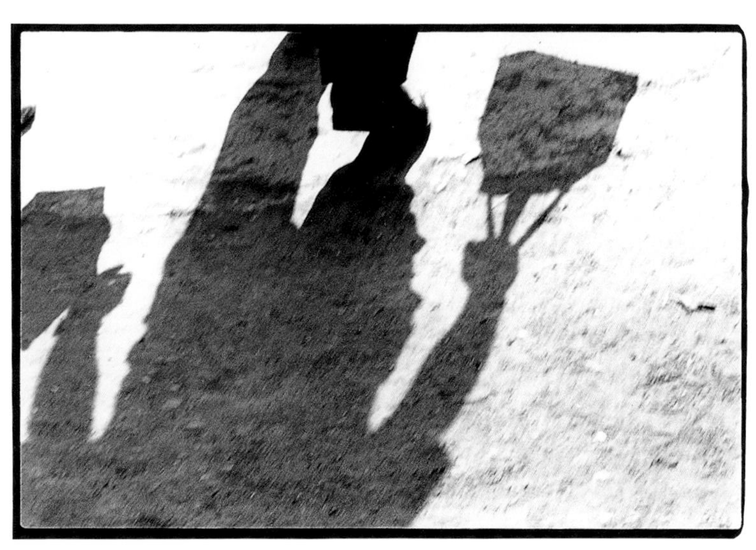

Signs & Relics

SYLVIA PLACHY

foreword by Wim Wenders

THE MONACELLI PRESS

First published in the United States of America in 1999 by
The Monacelli Press, Inc.
10 East 92nd Street, New York, New York 10128

Library of Congress Cataloging-in-Publication Data
Plachy, Sylvia.
Signs & relics / Sylvia Plachy ; foreword by Wim Wenders
p. cm.
ISBN 1-58093-057-3
1. Photography, Artistic. 2. Plachy, Sylvia. I. Title: Signs and relics. II. Title.
TR654.P5343 1999
779'.092—dc21 99-10690

Printed and bound in Singapore

Design: Carl Lehmann-Haupt and William van Roden

contents

Let me tell you:
Whoever came up first with that saying
"a picture is worth a thousand words"
didn't understand the first thing about either one.
I wonder who that was.
Anyway, he (or she?) keeps finding followers who keep recycling that notion.
Impossible to eradicate it anymore.
Which is sort of saddening, like any other misconception or prejudice.
It has become one of those nonsense mantras
that you can just as well turn into their opposite.
A word can be worth a million pictures, too, if you know what I mean.
In my book, they're definitely not even half as smart as they think,
those picture-worth-a-million-words people.
Don't compare apples to . . . light bulbs.
Pictures and words have nothing in common, period.
You can compare one picture to another, fine.
You can have them relate to each other in a common context, all right.
You can put them on a string like laundry on a line.
You can shuffle them like cards before a game.
As long as you don't think of them as words, okay?
So far, so good. End of dogma.
Until I actually saw somebody have pictures do the equivalent to what words do
when you put them together and turn them into a poem.

"Picture poems?"
Amazing. I didn't even know they existed until a while ago,
until I saw Sylvia Plachy's book *Signs & Relics*.
(I would have bought that book anytime for its title alone.
I'm a sucker for good titles. Again: the power of words!)
It had me . . . looking at pictures in a whole different way.
Actually, I must admit, it was more like . . . reading.
It showed me that photographs can do all sorts of things that I never thought of.
That they can rhyme, for instance! Who would have thought of that!
Or that they can build up to a punch line, like good jokes.
Or that they can tell a family saga that covers generations, like great novels.
Or that they can be riddles, pamphlets, metaphors, and prayers.
I finally put Sylvia's book down and realized in amazement
that photographs can cover all the good word territories.
I found myself thinking: "A picture is worth a thousand words."
Hey! Wait a minute! — Wim Wenders

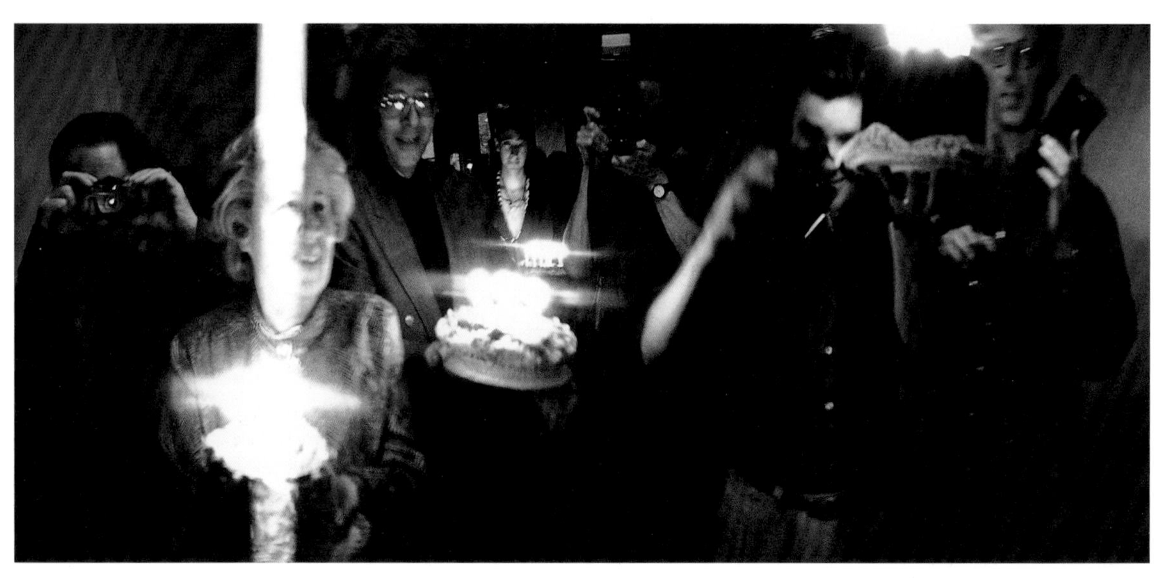

beginning

Years ago, I was briefly blinded by a migraine in the eye. As I sat in the library, a brightness crowded out most of the room. Dumbstruck, I continued to sit and wait, anticipating something, perhaps like a deer in the headlights. The end?

The cemetery is glazed with ice; dried acorns lie in its frozen grip. Like some flower child, a hungry squirrel holds in his paw a chrysanthemum meant for my mother and then gobbles it down. It's cold. We make do with the yellow flowers: the squirrel, my mother, and I.

It was my mother who taught me about signs and superstitions: "Knock on wood" for good things, "Don't say it" for ominous things, "Pull your ear" if you sneeze while there is talk of death. But beyond the broken mirrors, itchy noses, and lucky pennies, she looked for meaning, for a connection to the unseen world. A cloud, a change in the breeze, a butterfly could be a messenger with a secret to decode.

Yet when I was eight, and X-ray technology had finally reached Budapest, my mother refused to look at my chest X-ray, saying "A mother should not see some things." I wonder, was it respect for the privacy between my ribs or dread to look past my lung and see the skeleton?

It was Halloween when I saw the tumor in my mother's skull. On the monitor, in mocking Day-Glo colors, the MRI was an omen more final than a ruptured lifeline.

The white line in front of my mother on a photograph I took at my fiftieth birthday party, before I blew out the candles, had a technical cause. As the lens on my panoramic camera took its usual three-and-a-half seconds to revolve, someone popped a flash and it left a streak on the negative. To me, it looked like a light saber, but not to my mother. "I was crossed out," she said. "I won't see another of your birthdays."

In the final days, my mother had few pleasures, though she had no pain. Mostly she slept. When she woke, she'd say cheerfully "Szerbusz, kis Pici." Was it "Hello" or was it "Good-bye, little one"? It's the same in Hungarian. Once she looked up from her bath, surprised to see me. "I never thought," she said, "when you were a baby and I was bathing you, that one day you'd be bathing me."

I stood by the kitchen window during one of her naps and I saw a woman's profile: a wet spot left by the rain on the wall of a building. I hurried to catch it before it evaporated.

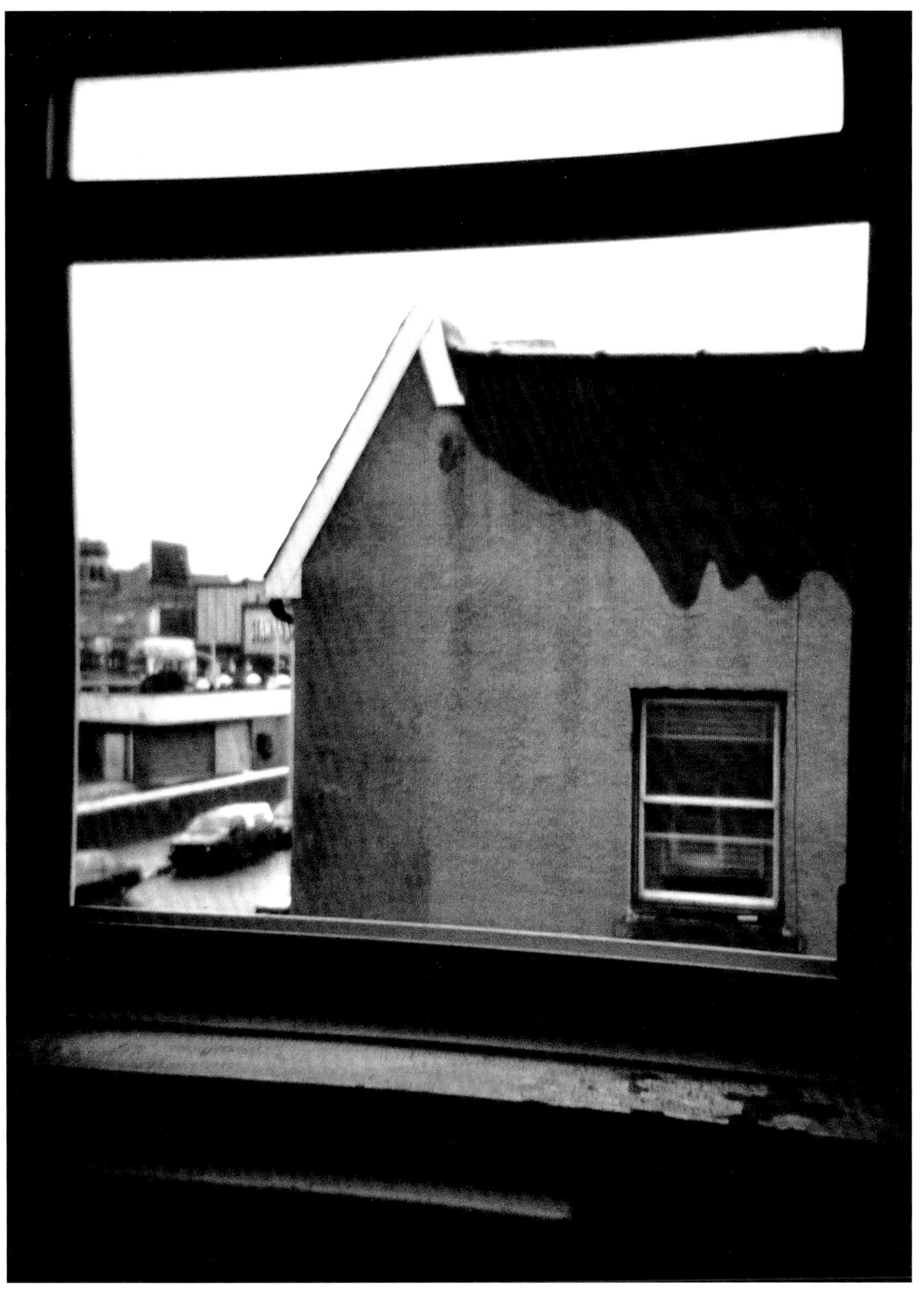

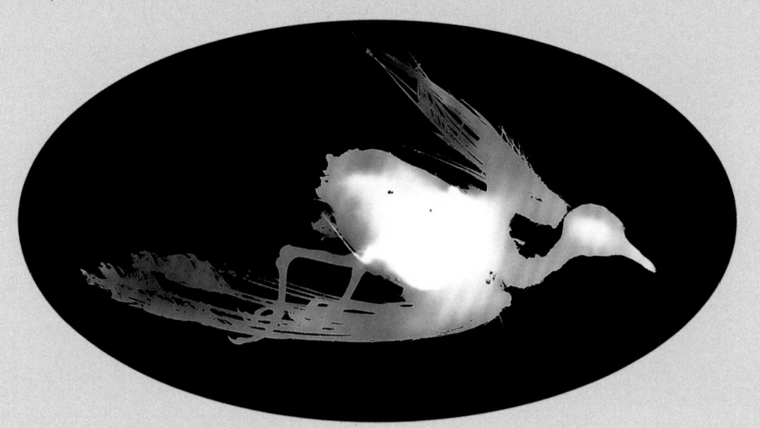

An image of escape into death hangs on my wall adjacent to a photograph of Gabrielle, who is levitating in midair somersault in her mother's nightgown.

Under domed glass, in an oval Victorian frame, held in eternal flight, is a mummified pigeon. I found it on Ellis Island, where it was rumored that construction workers on their lunch break picked off pigeons.

I flew once. As I was chased to the edge of the ocean and almost captured I spread my wings. It was a dream.

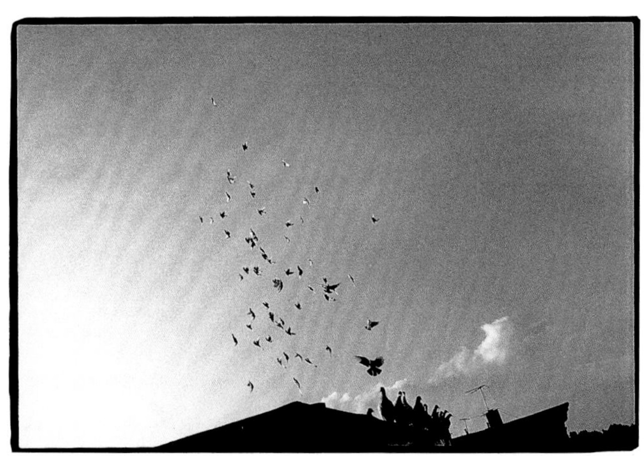

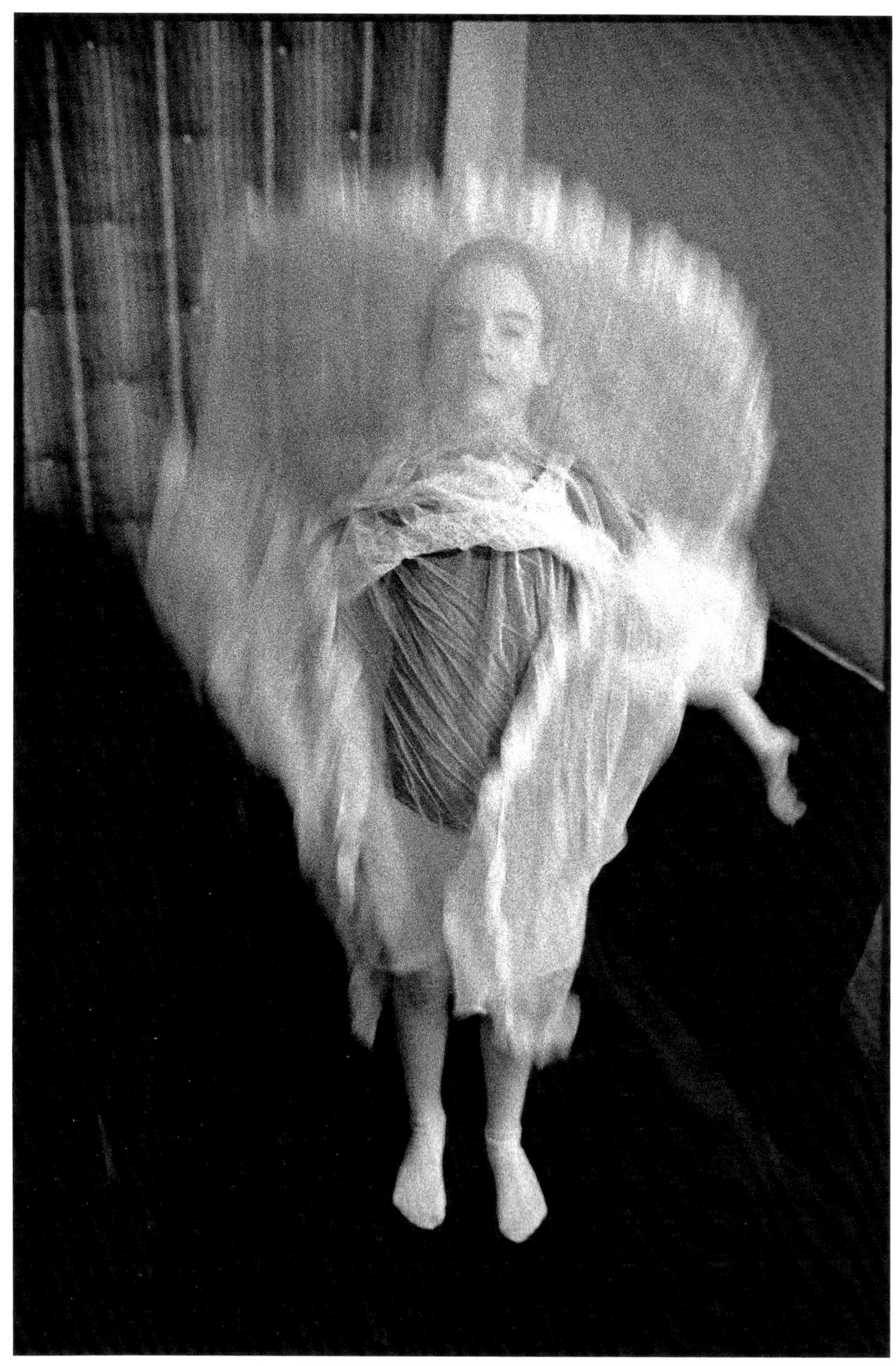

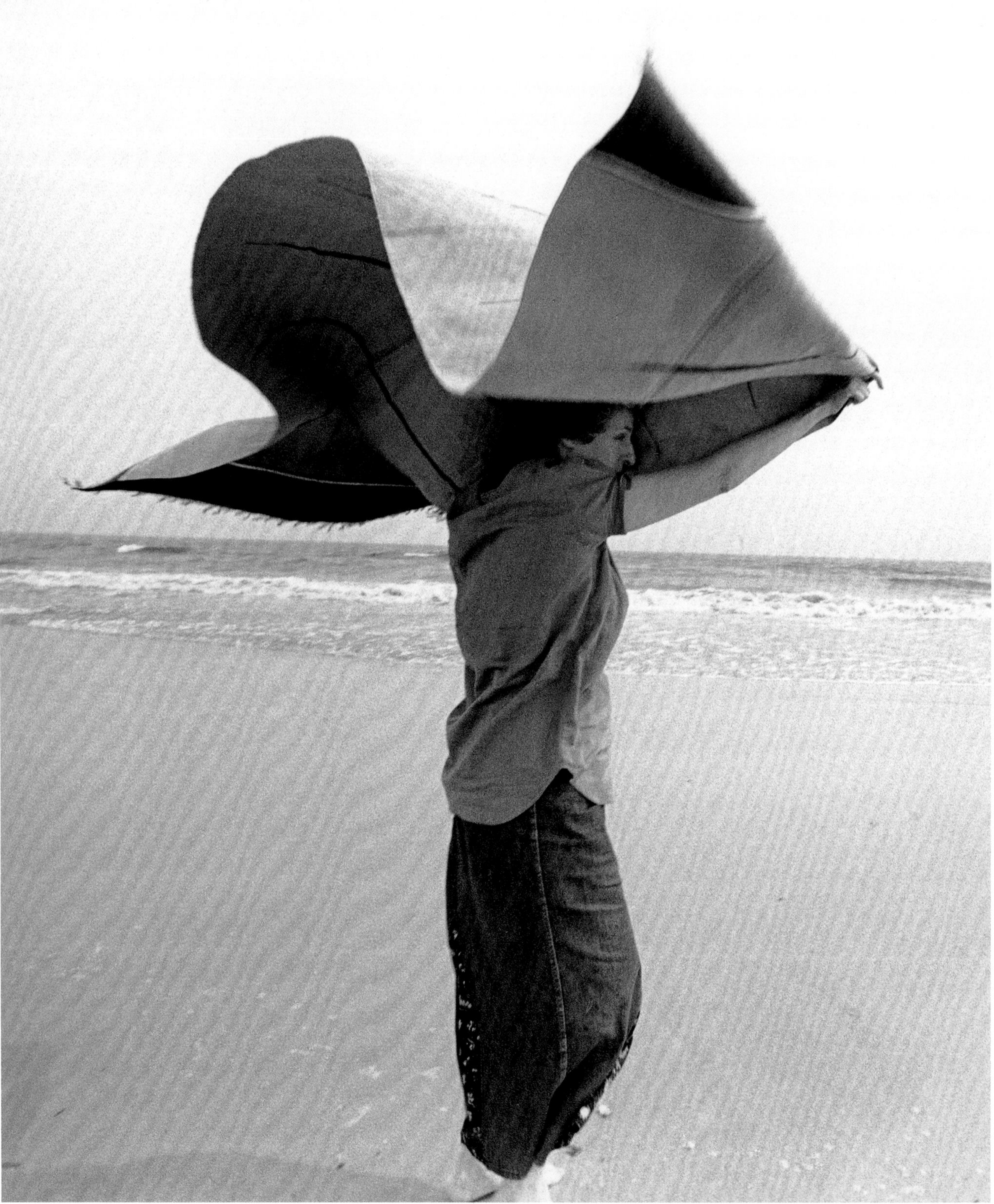

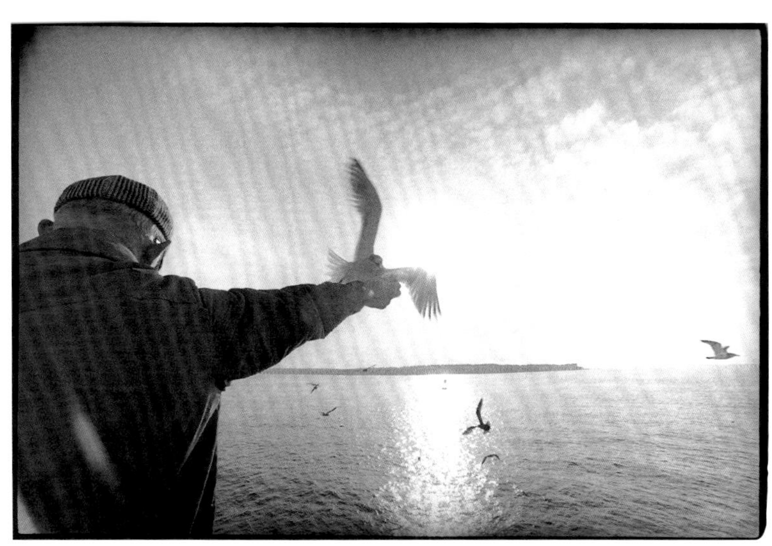

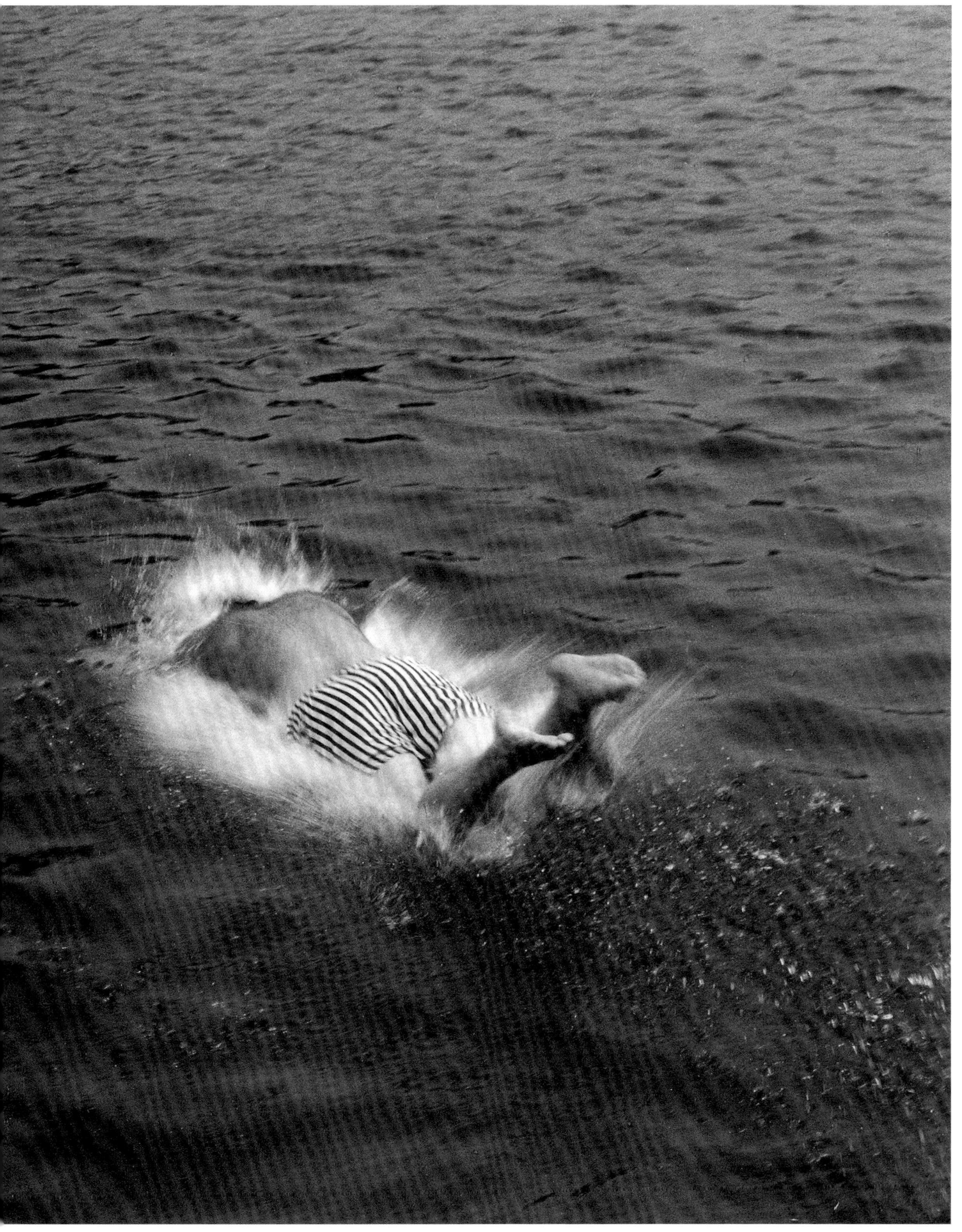

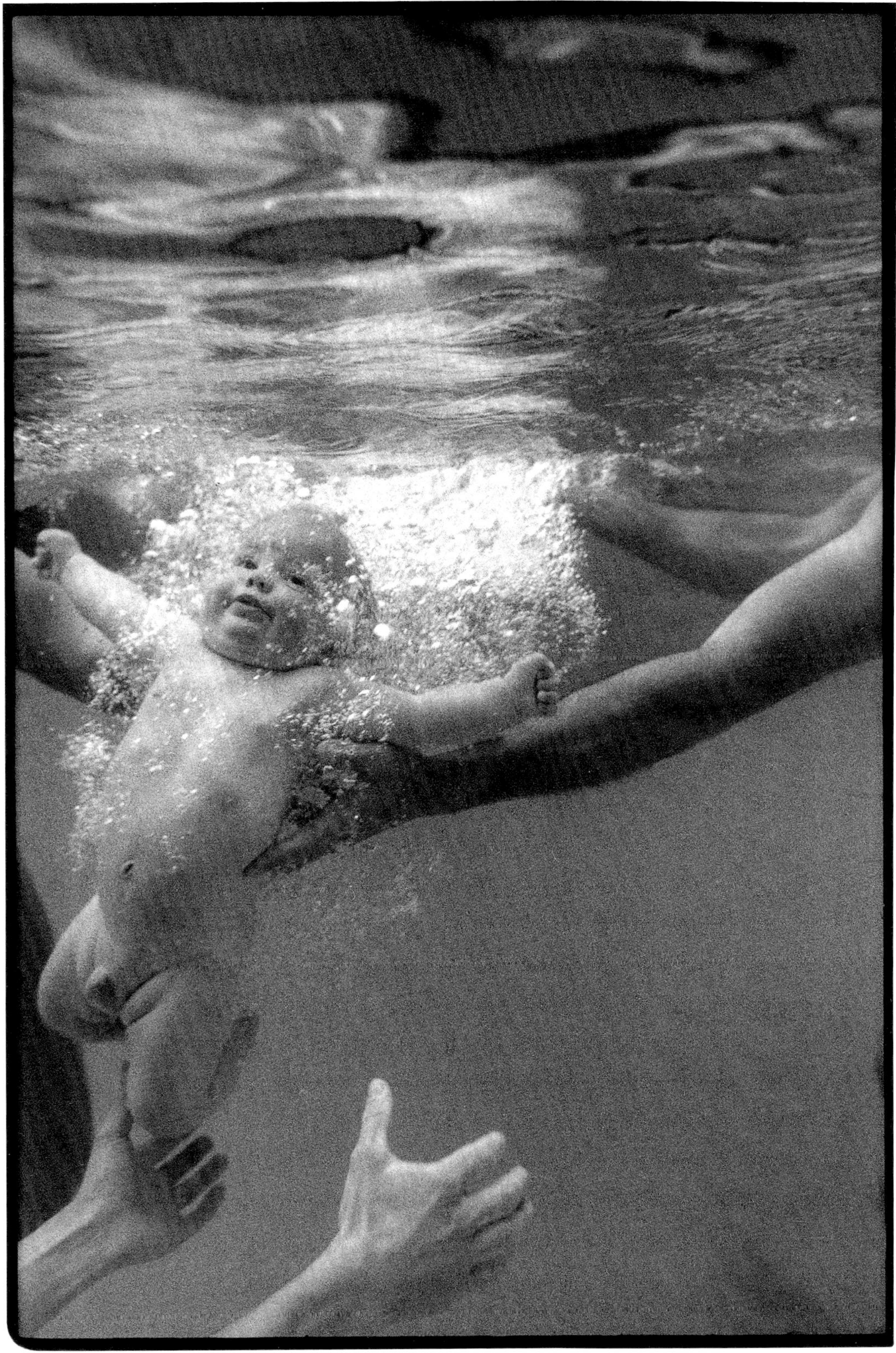

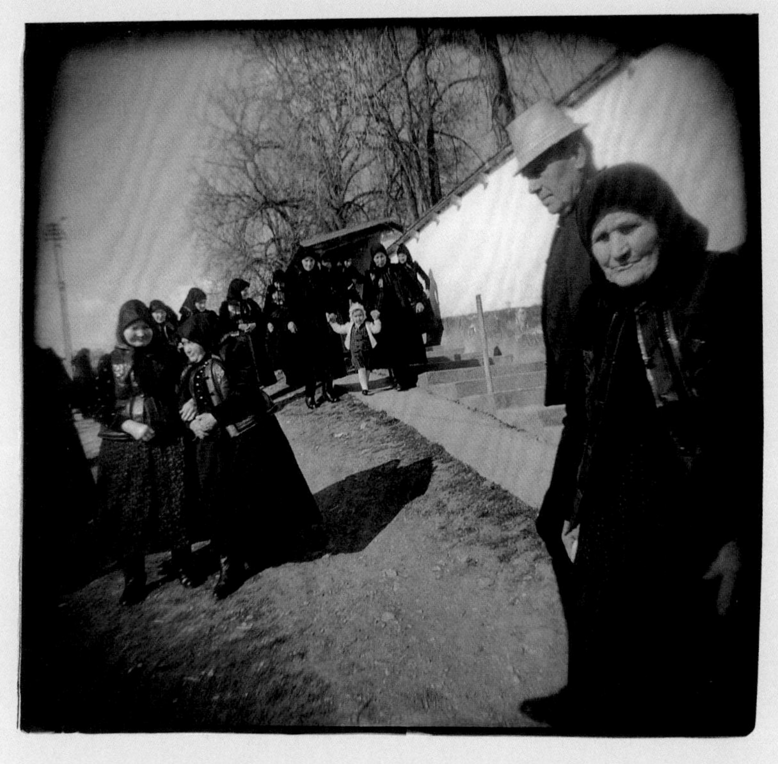

birds of a feather, the gulls of Barcelona gather at the cathedral at dusk. They circle the tower until each finds its perch. And there they sit, motionless until dawn, like elegant white ornaments on a Christmas tree. We, who have no feathers, do alterations, so we too can find our places for a time.

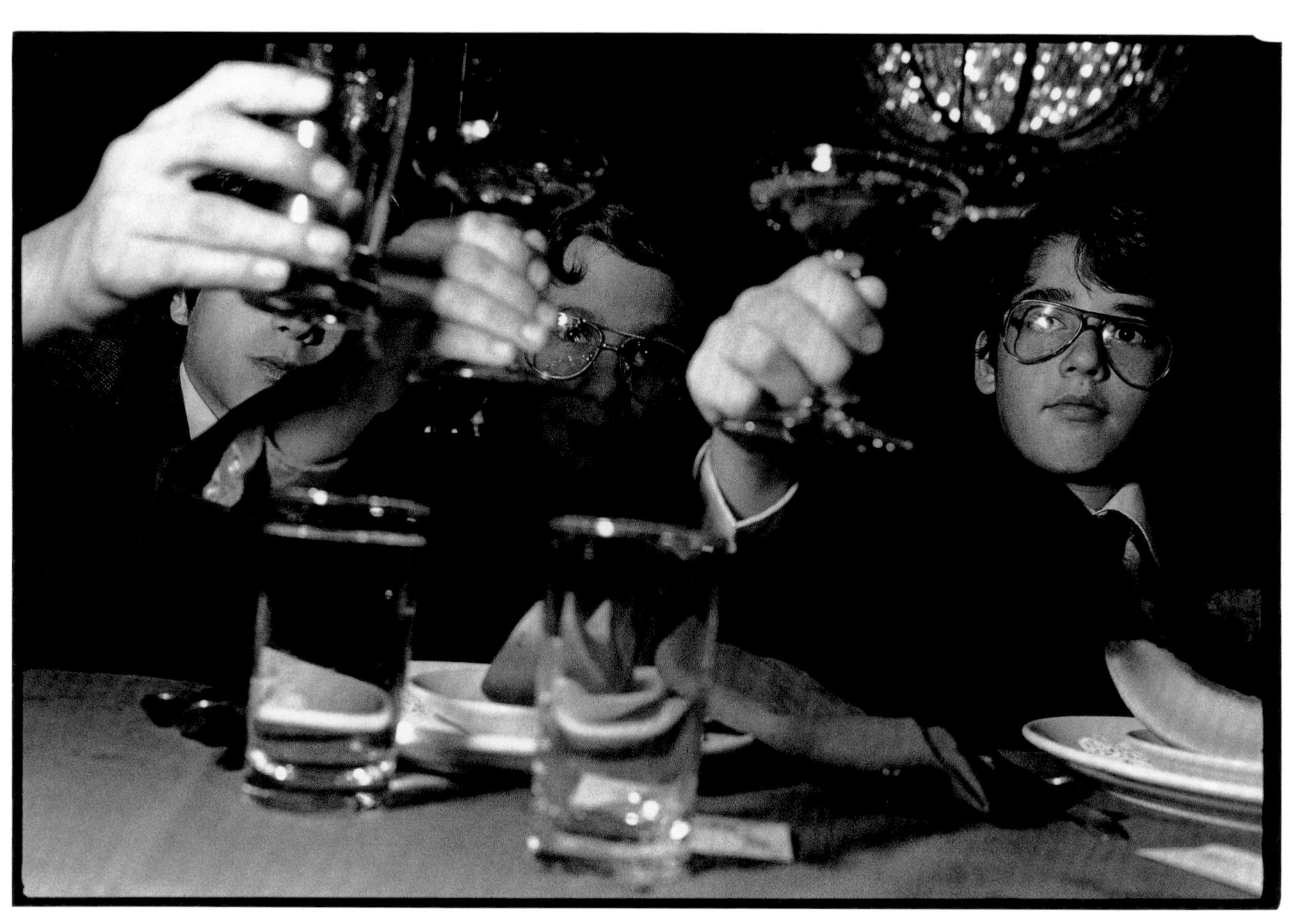

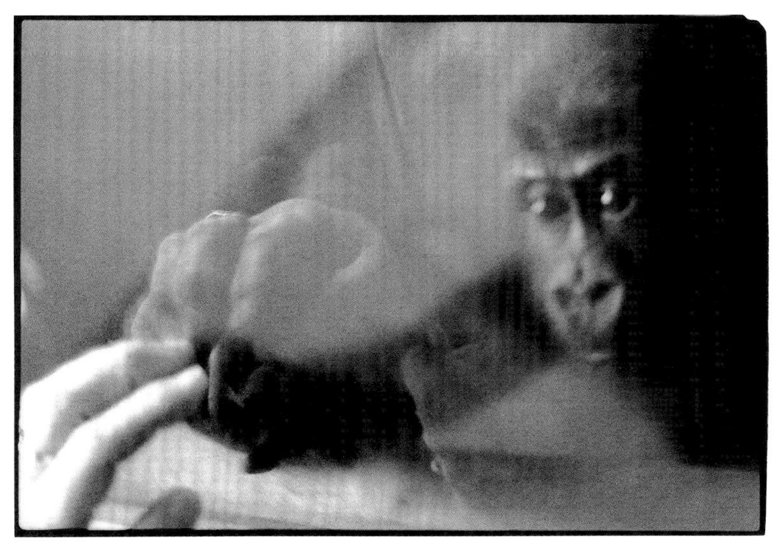

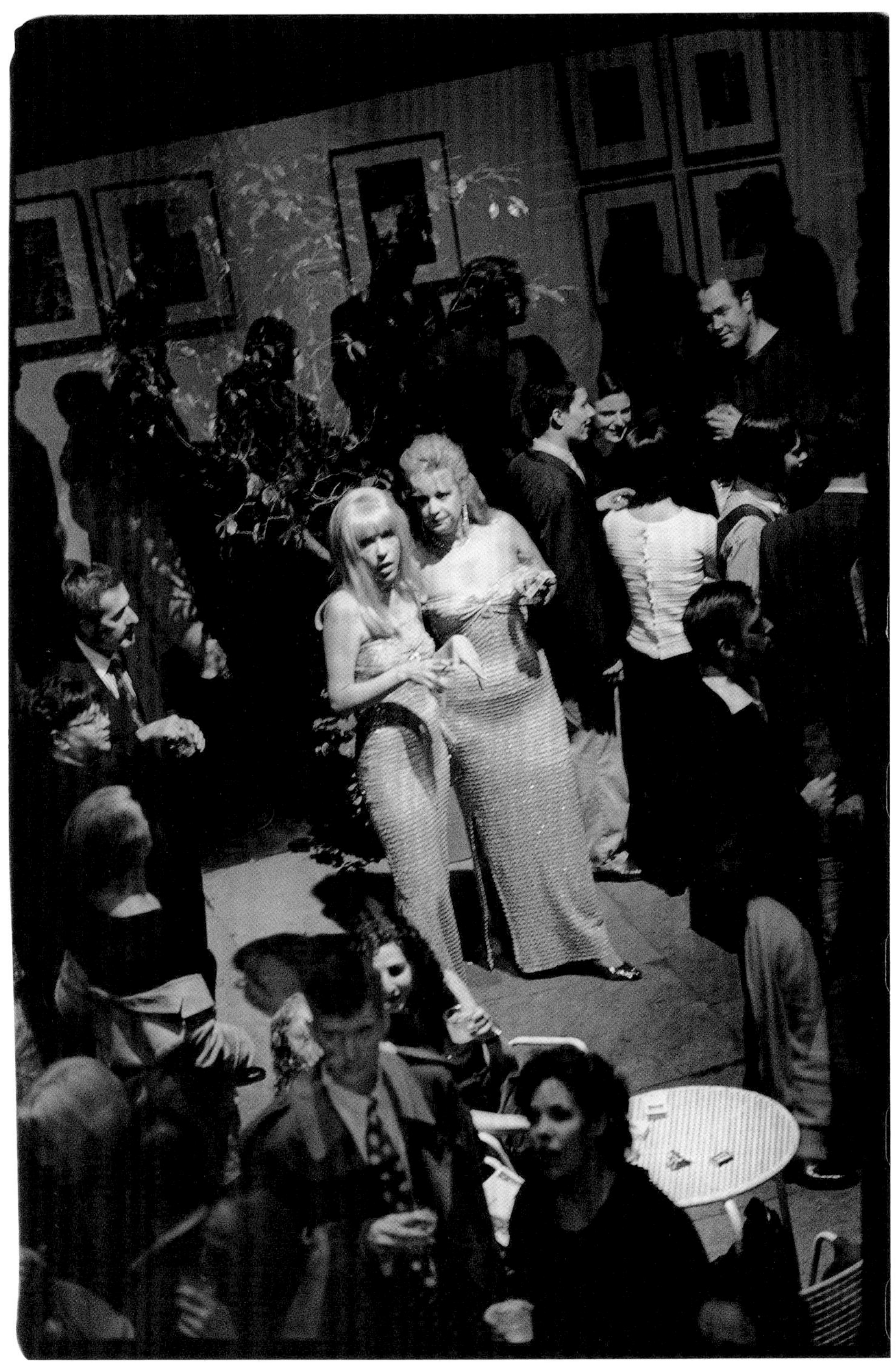

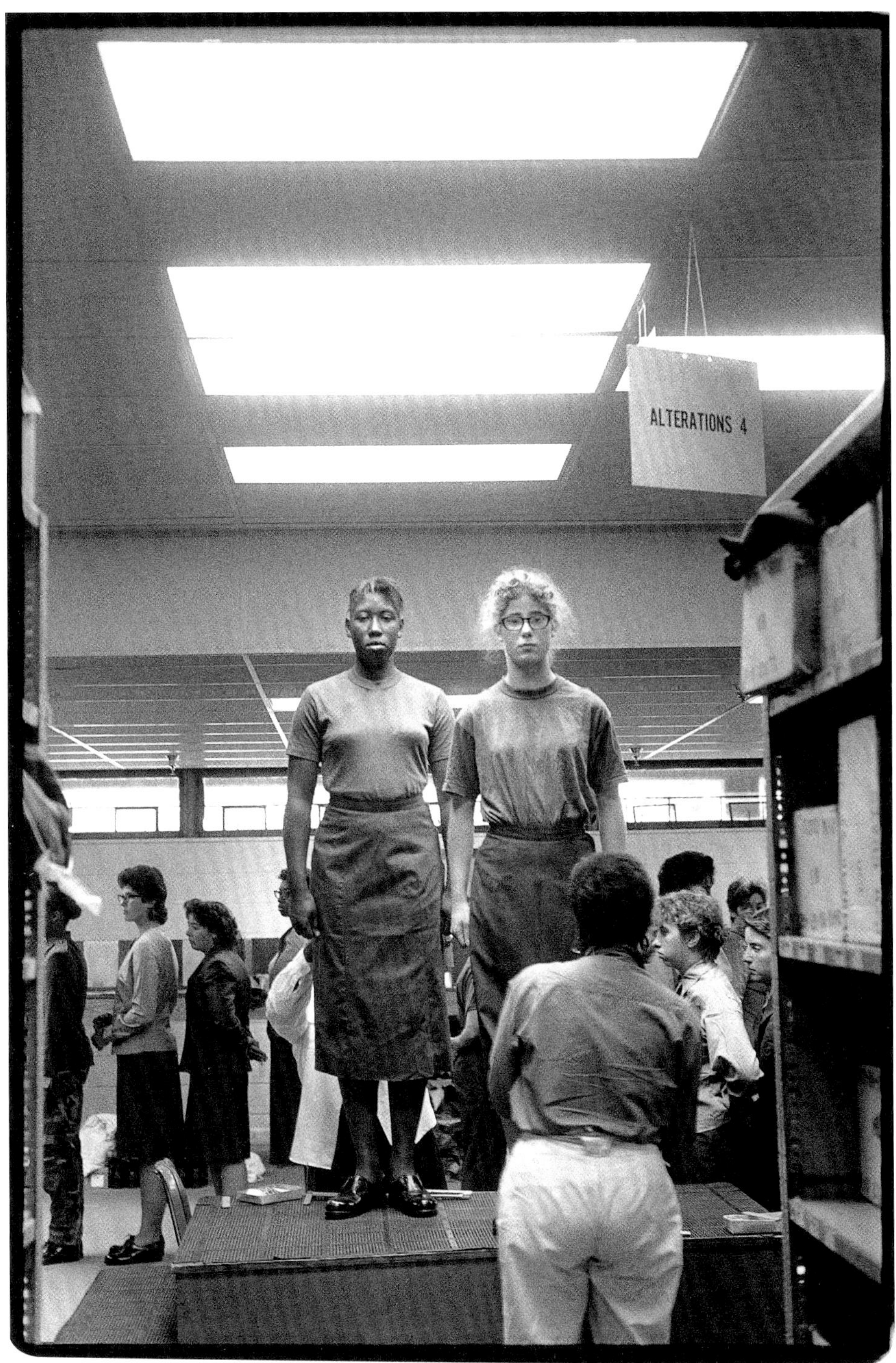
ALTERATIONS 4

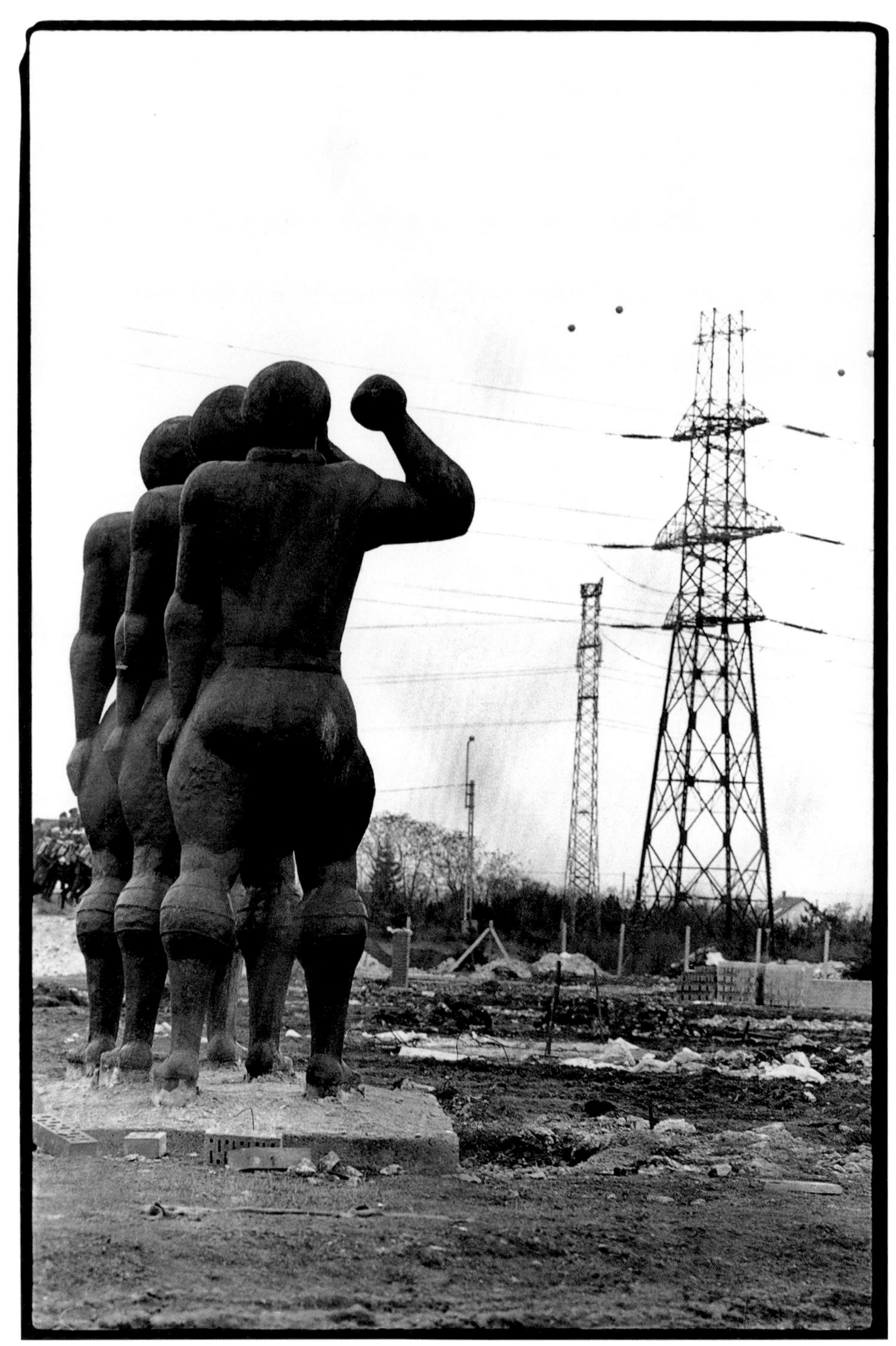

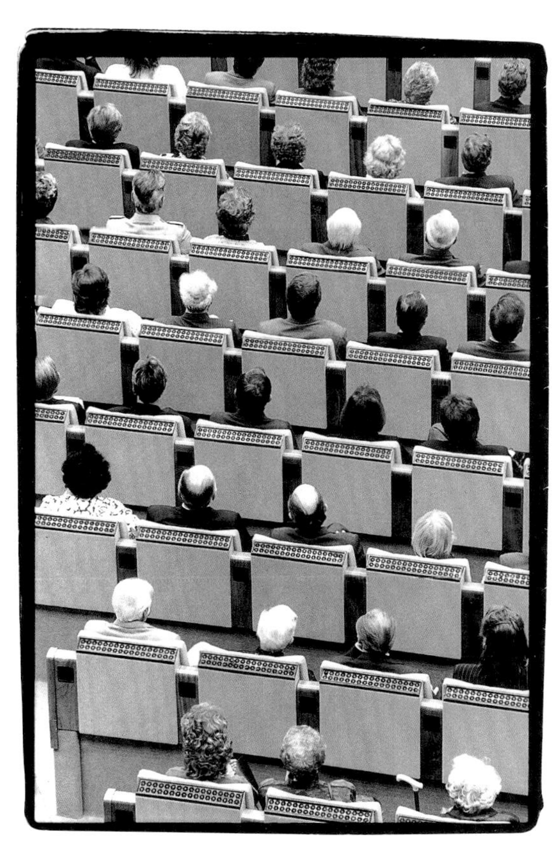

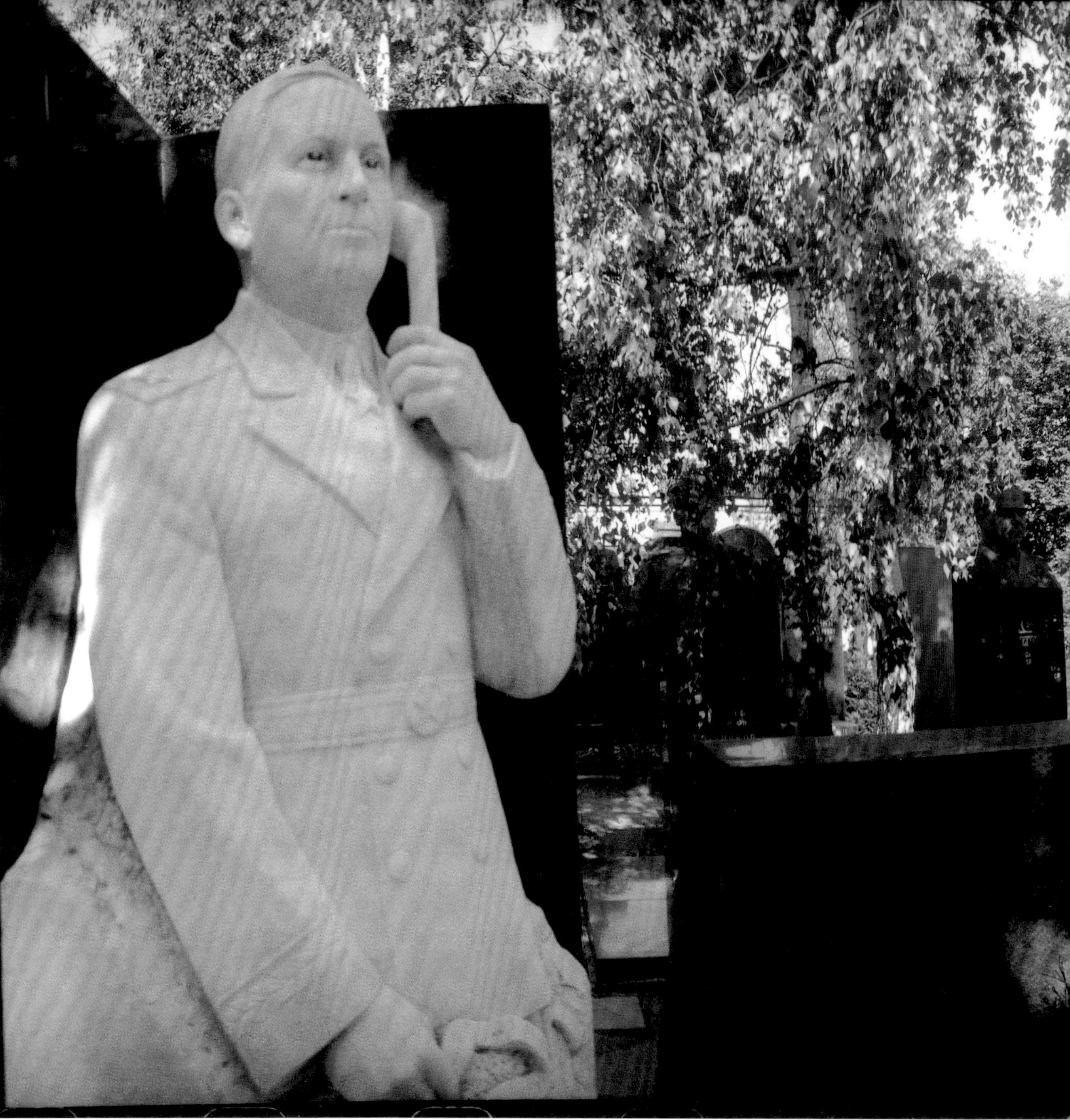

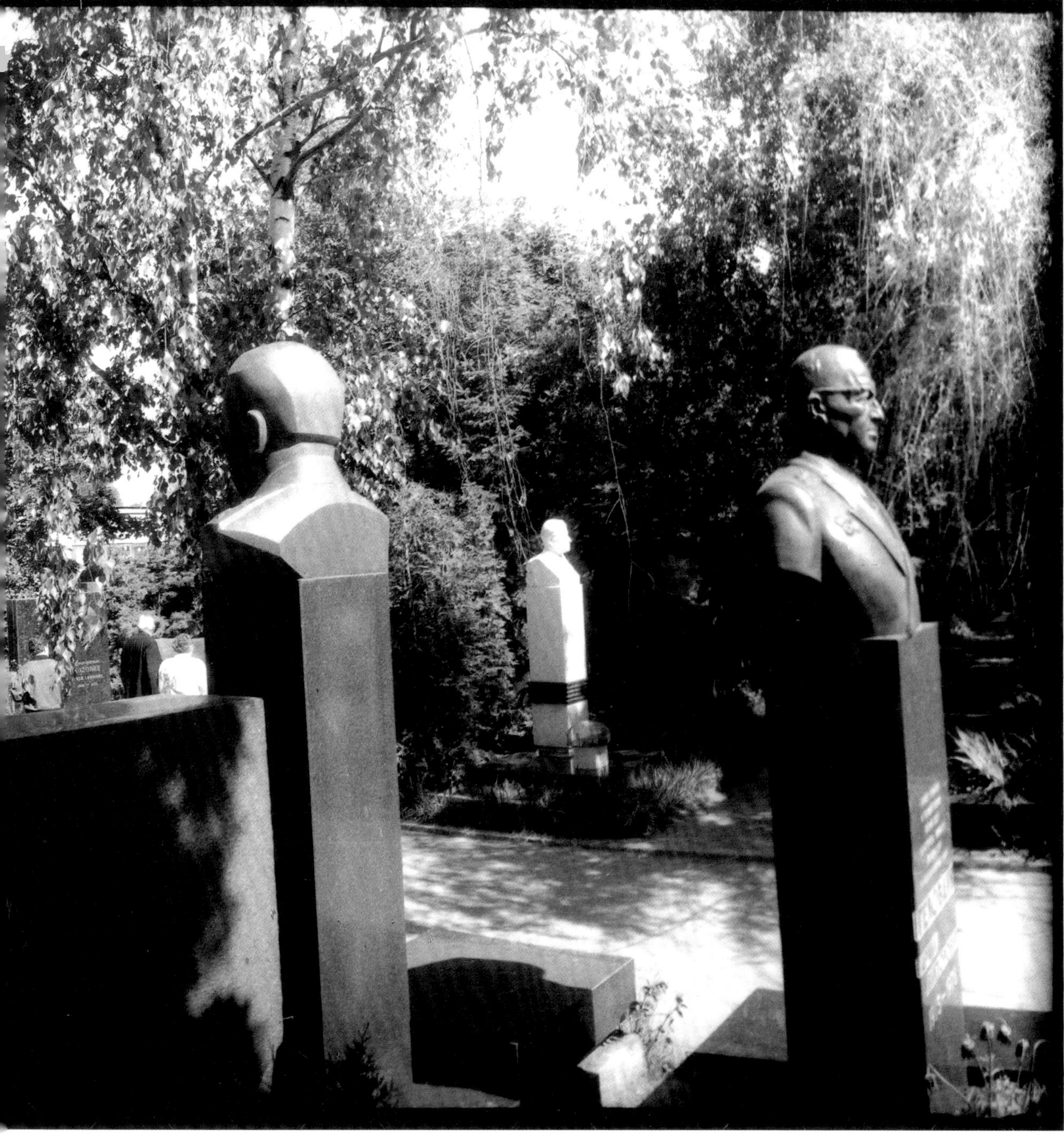

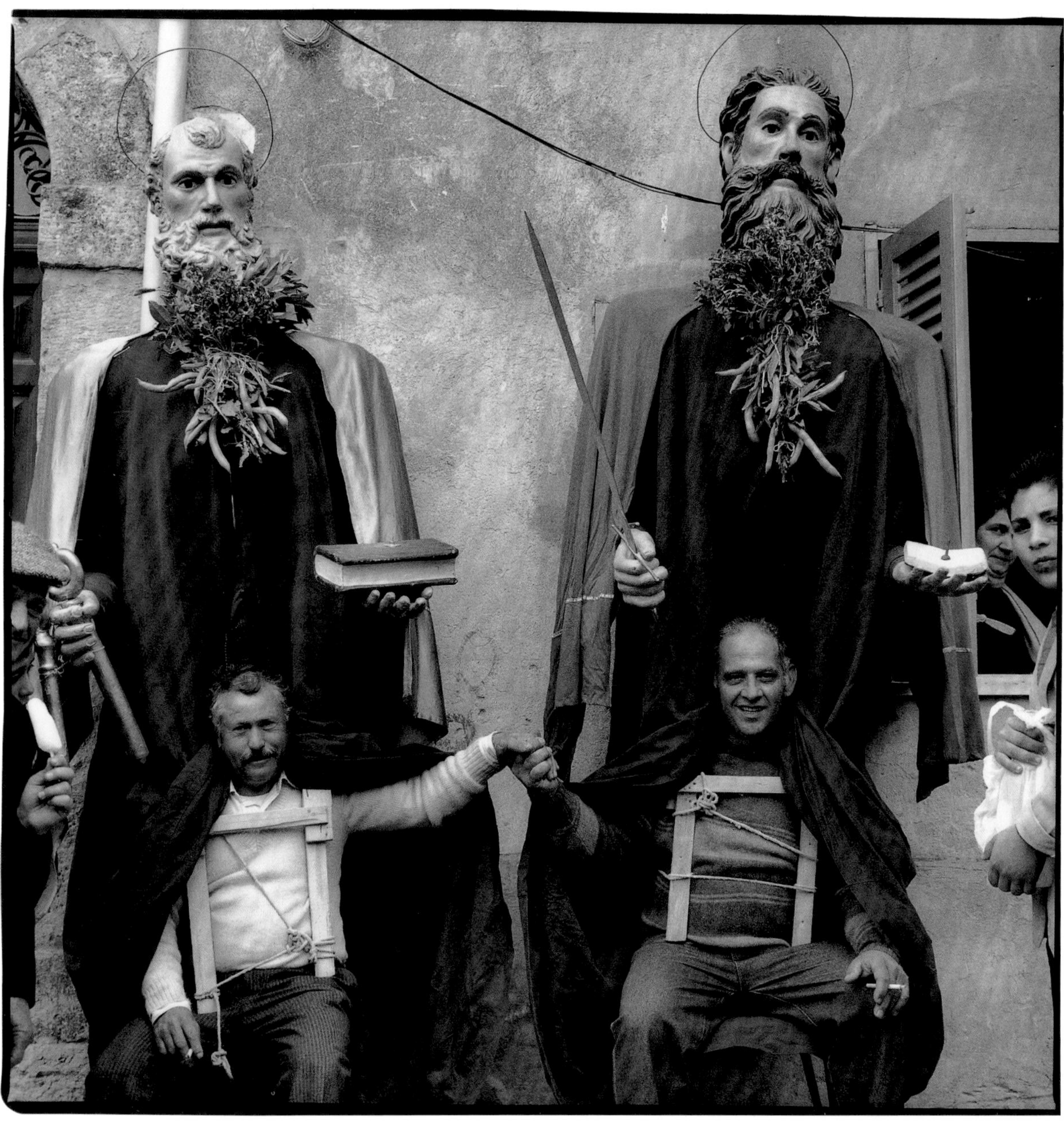

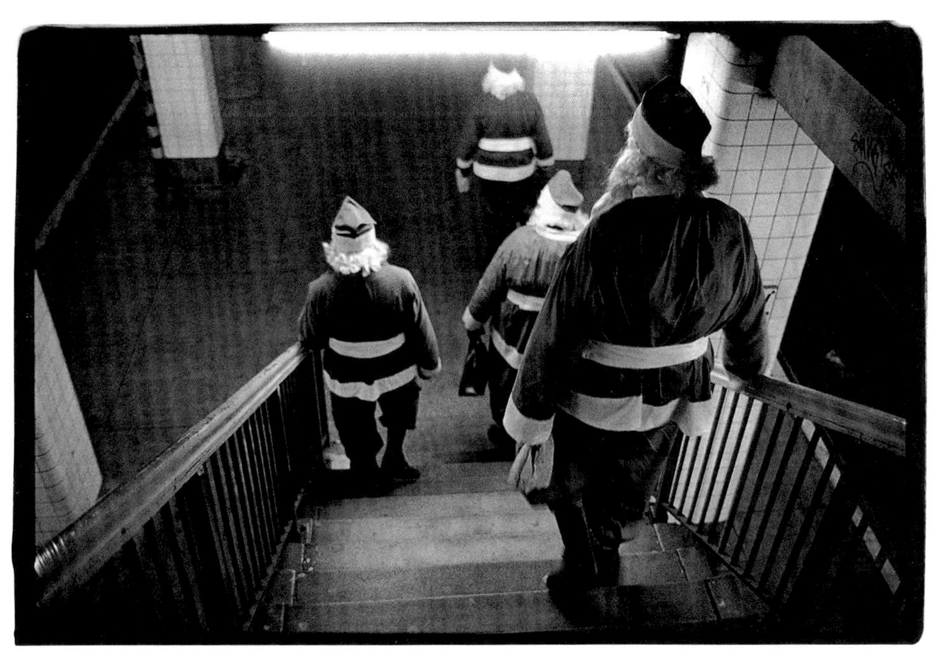

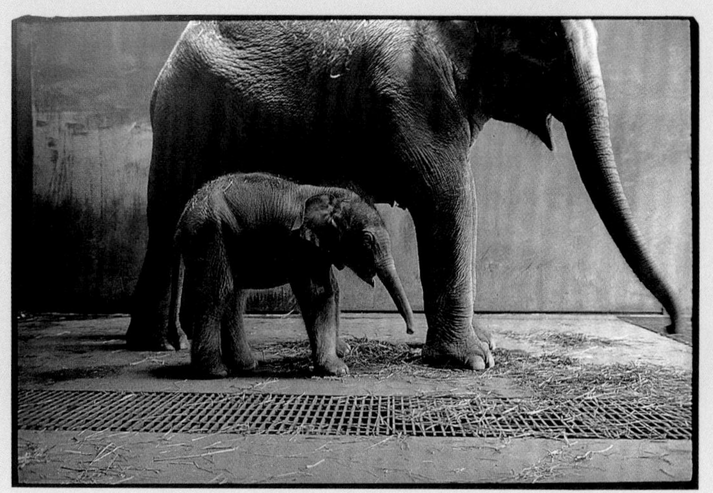

Some people see the Virgin. Some are abducted by aliens. I have déjà vu. Memories burst forth from a shape, just as they might from a sound or a scent. Gestures connect us to our culture and foreshadow the future. As I hold my elbow and one of my arms cradles the other, I think of my aunt and how she held her own paralyzed arm. My pinkie refuses to fall in line with the other fingers when I lift a cup, and I'm reminded of my father and my son, because we've all got that pinkie gene.

Sometimes, unexpectedly, I see a scene that I've seen before in a photograph by Kertész, Lartigue, or Sander. And though I sometimes hesitate, I take that shot to tip my hat to a master.

Our need to belong leads to the celebration of synchronicity, even if its significance is indecipherable—like the deli clerk who said as he weighed my potato salad "Half a pound on the nose. It's my lucky day!"

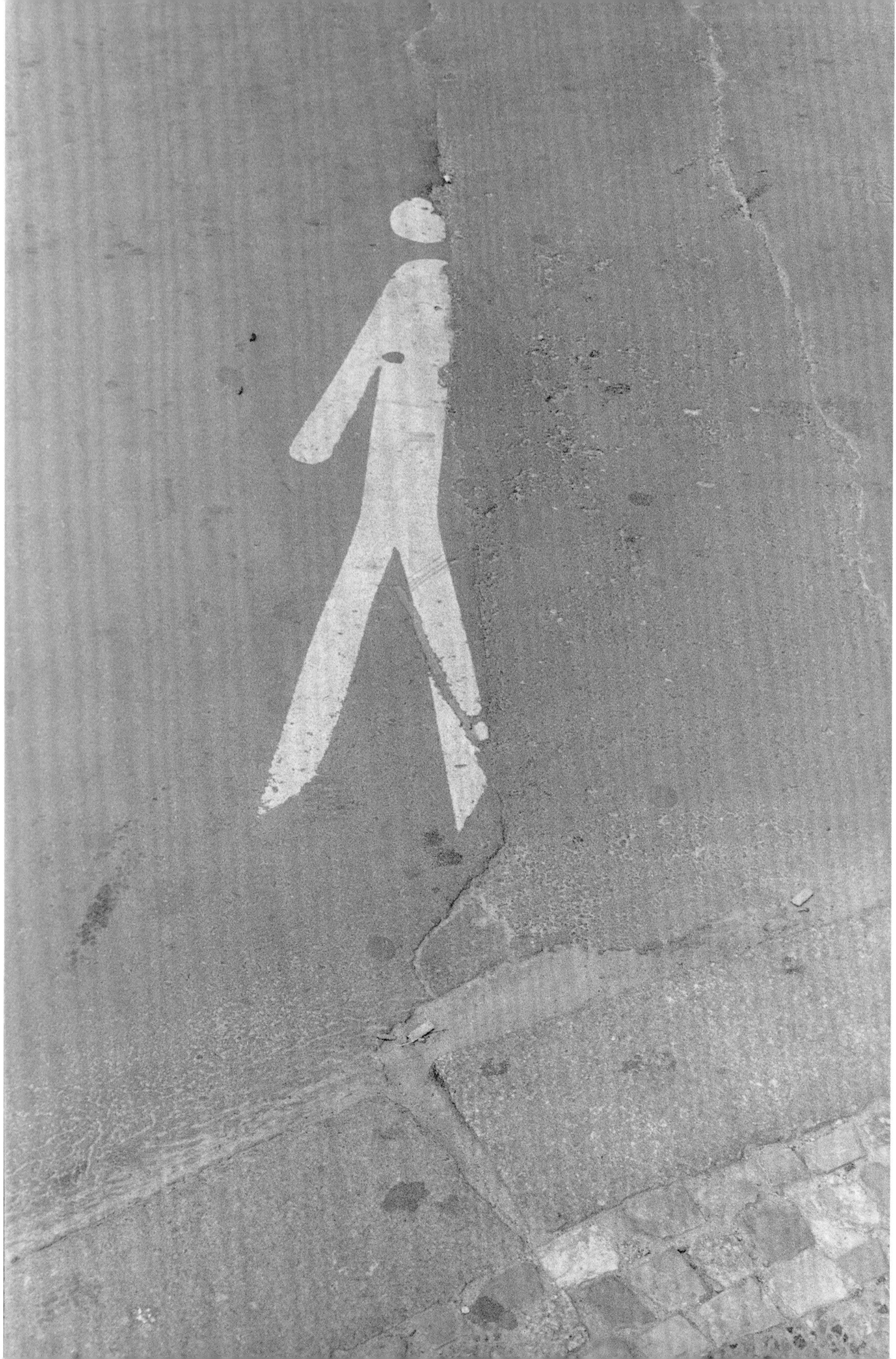

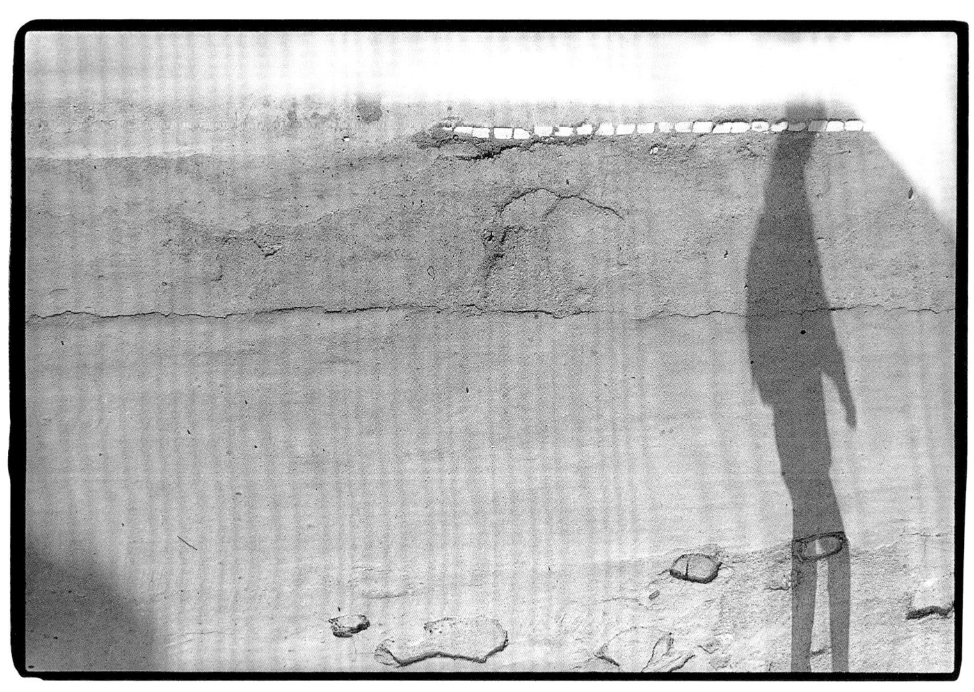

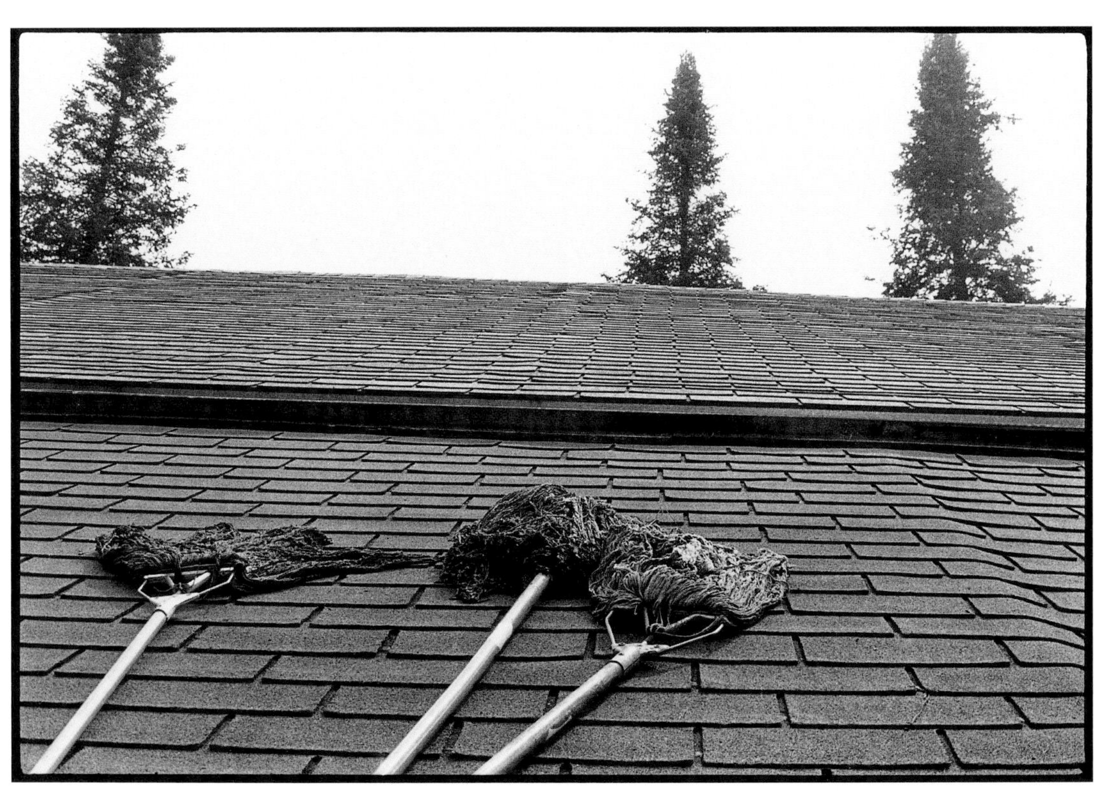

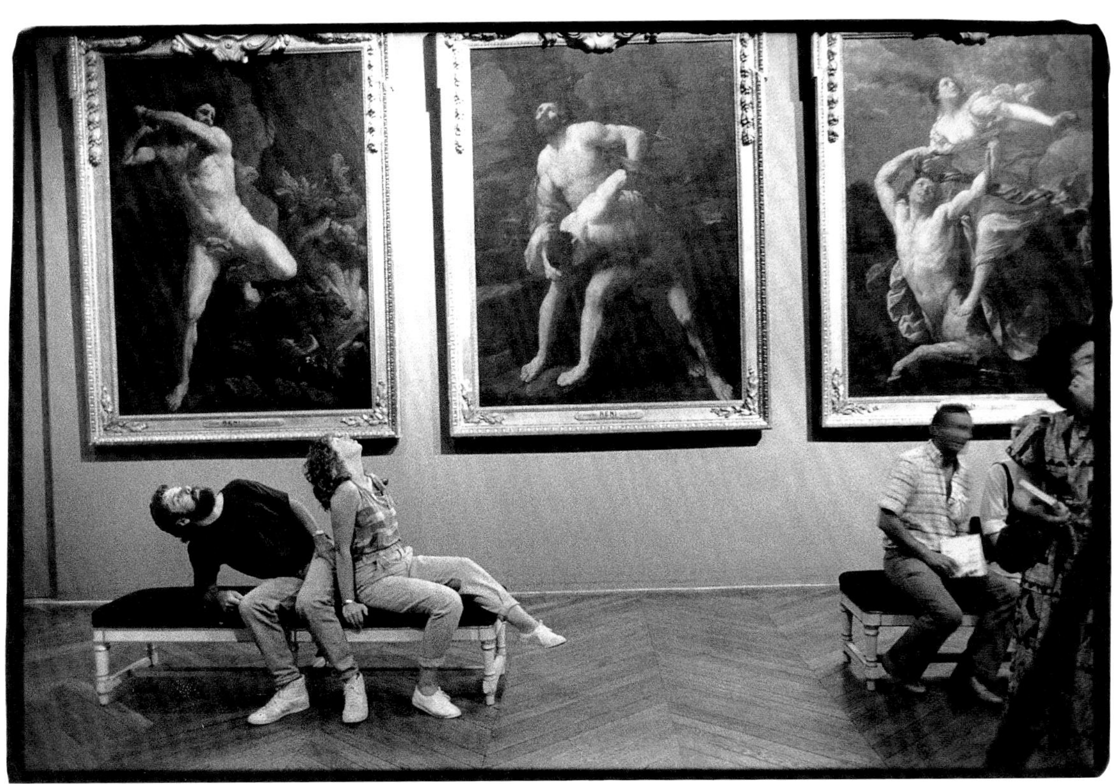

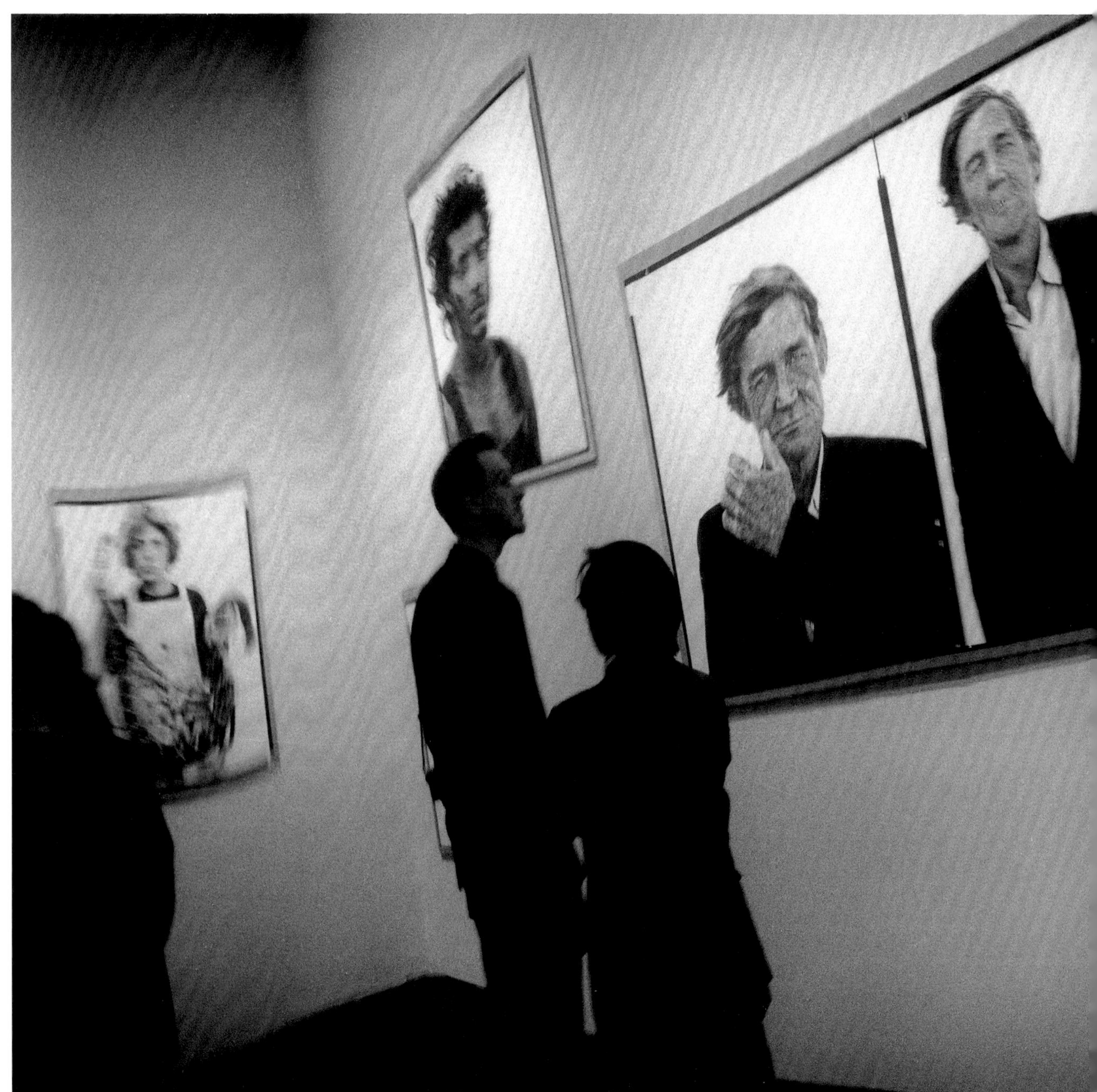

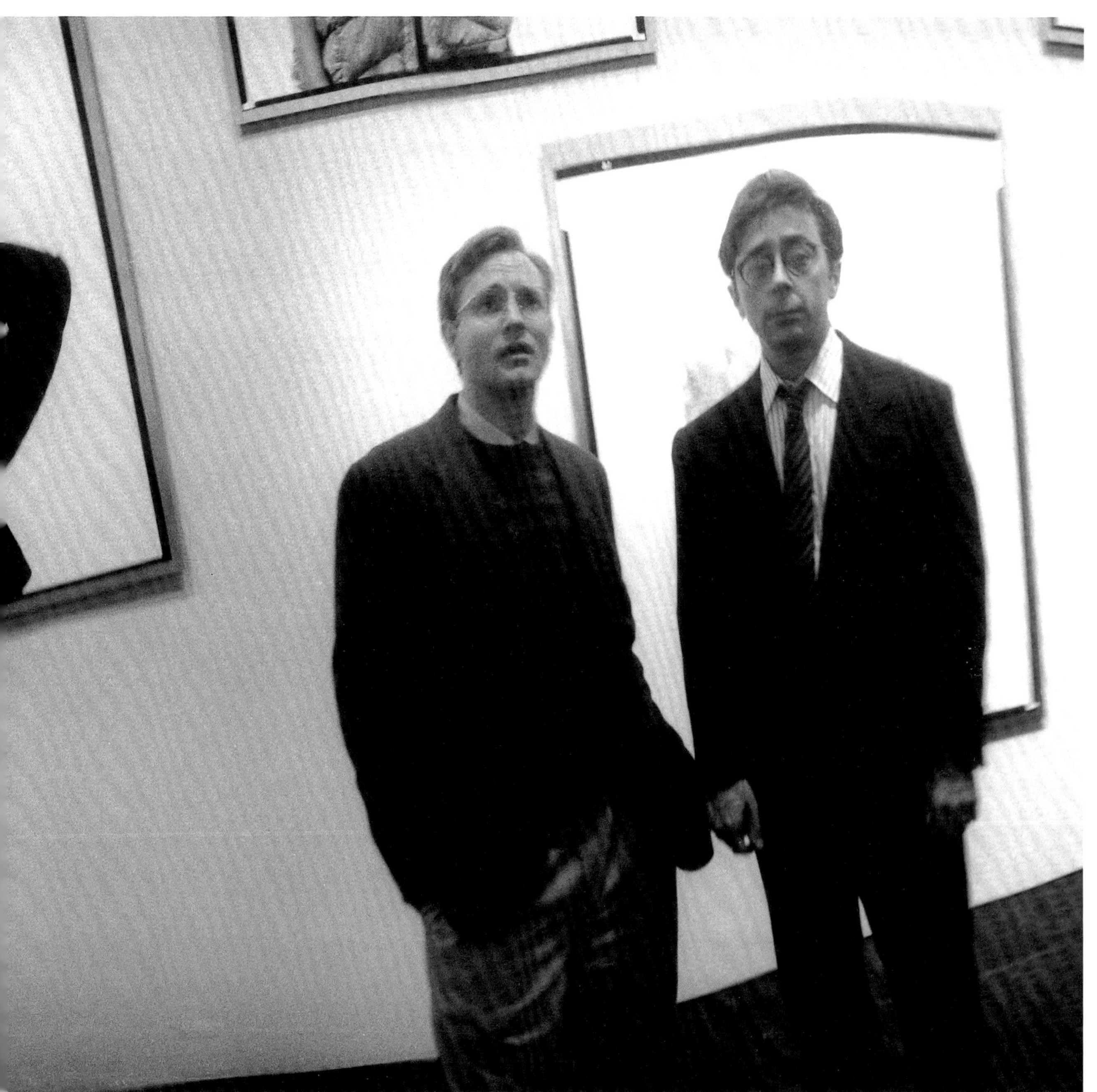

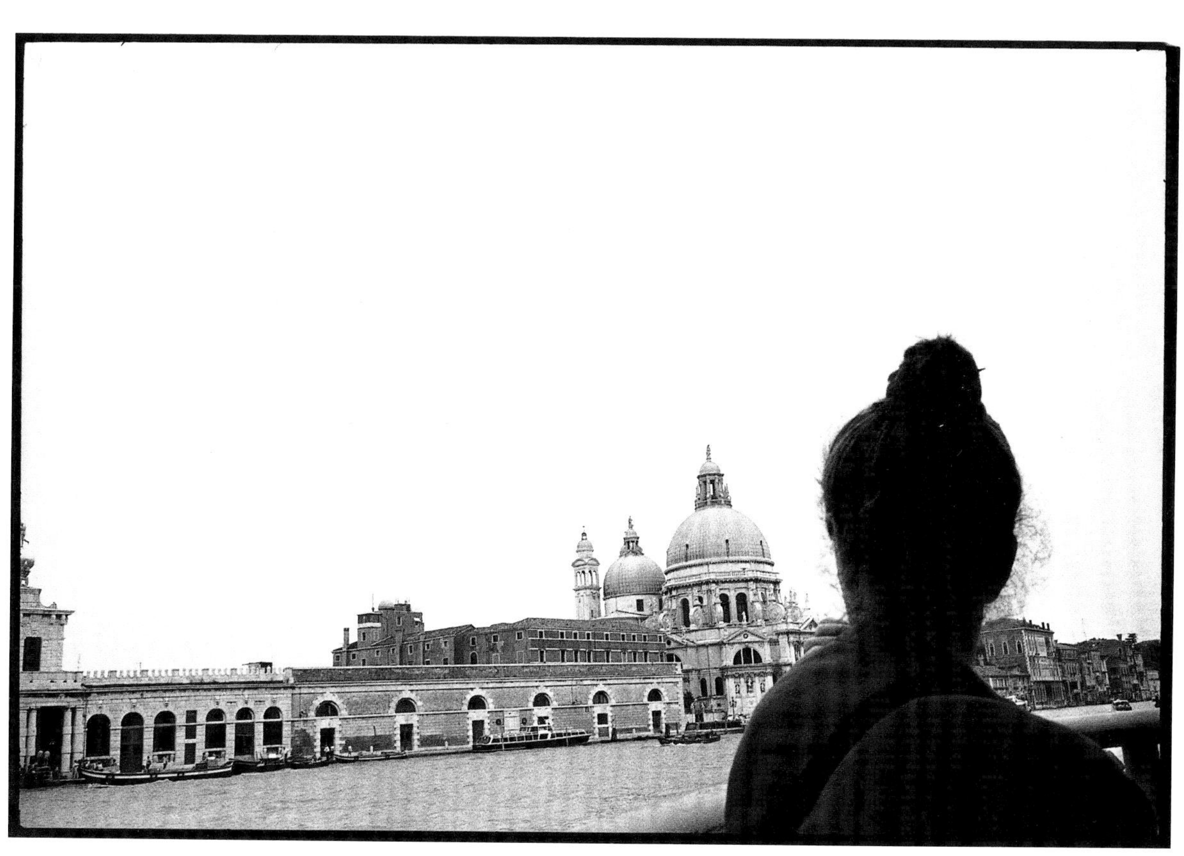

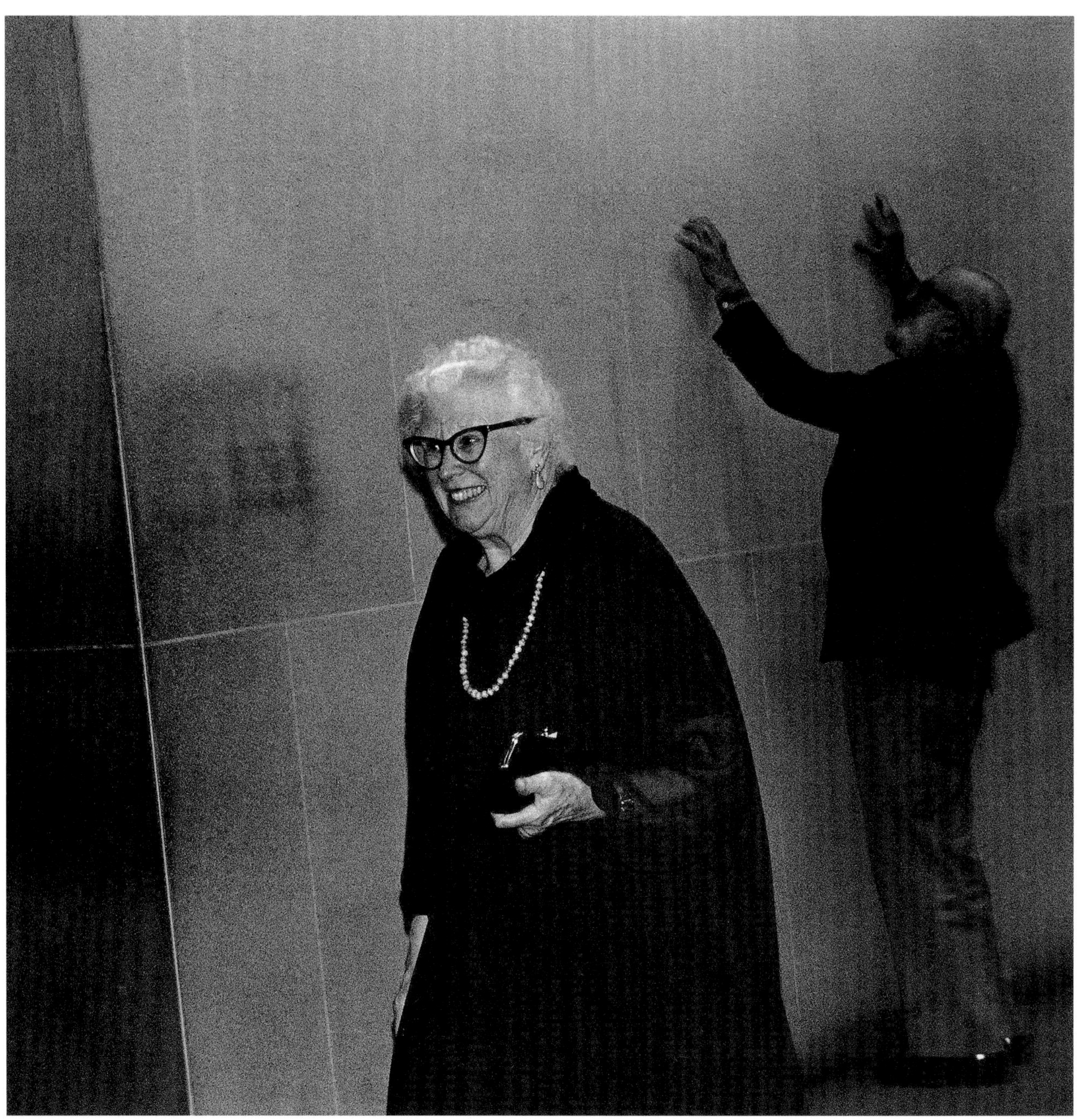

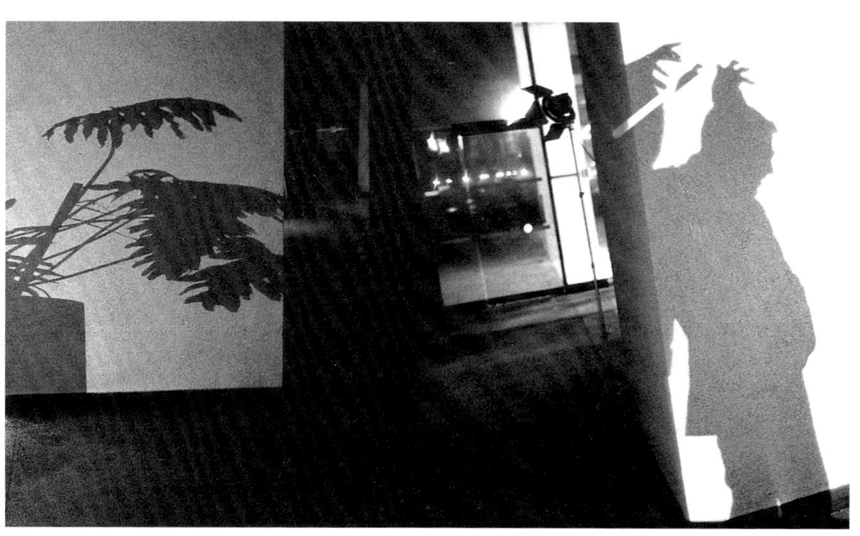

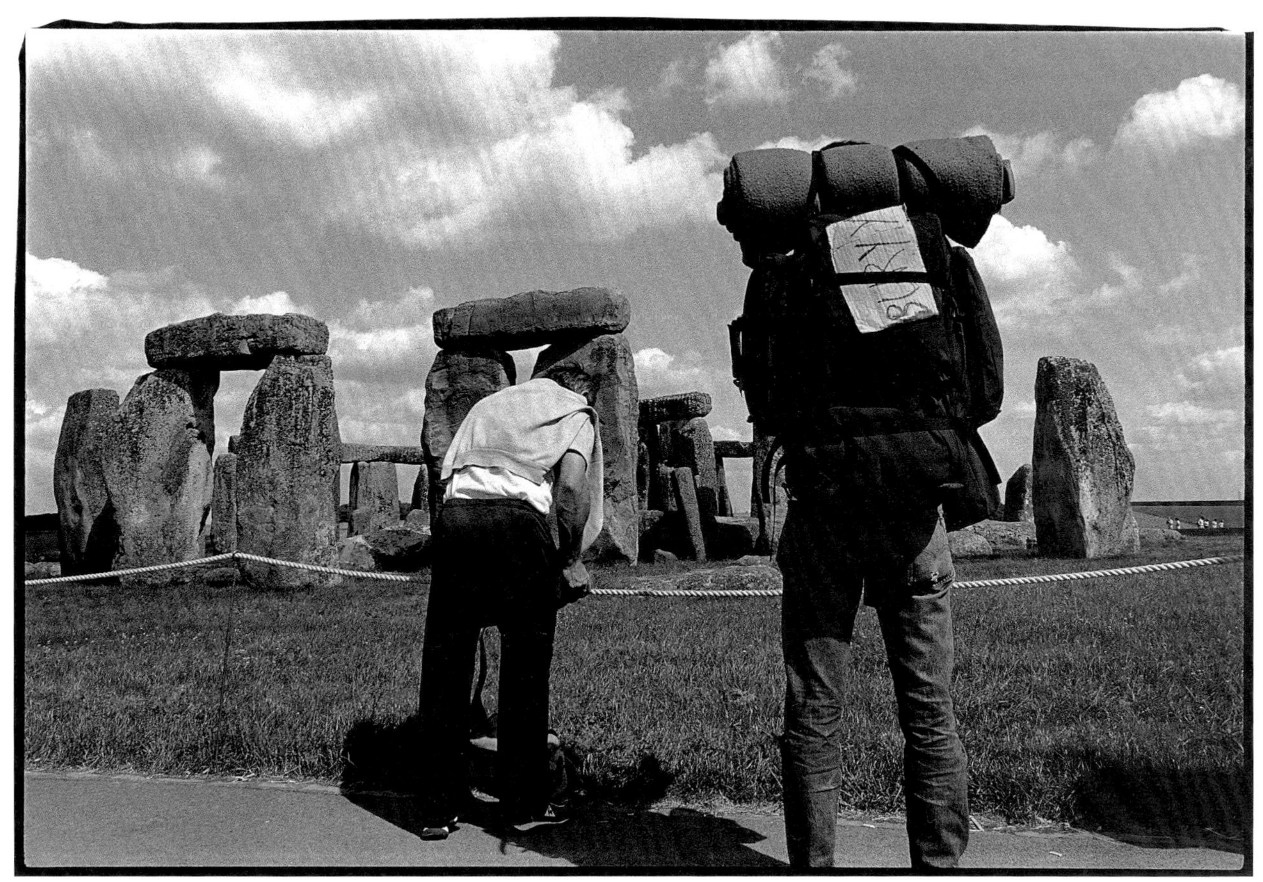

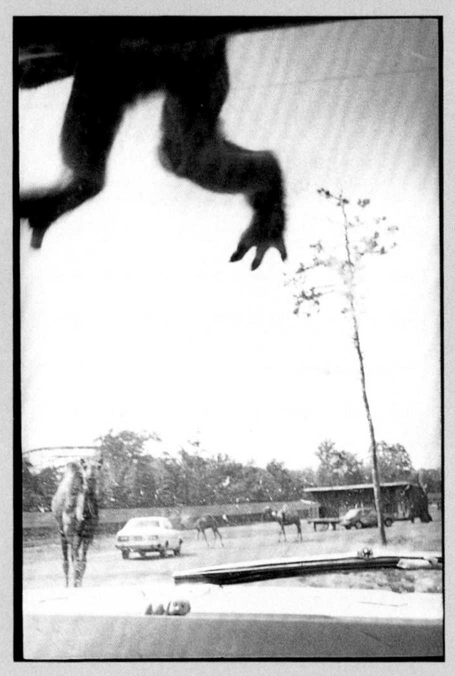

In Budapest in 1950, our second-grade teacher prepared a treat for us. In the hushed silence, two older girls showed us their experiment. On a slab of wood was a horror version of Gulliver: with its chest open and held down by pins, with its tiny heart still beating, lay a frog.

Ever since that day the smell of ether disturbs me and I question the methods of science.

Years later, on a trip in the south of France, I saw a similar spread-eagle image, a tableau in the Museum of Horror, where lovingly carved miniature humans were torturing each other.

A man on a rack, a woman raped, a gutted deer hanging under a distant sky in the Rockies echo my early lesson in school.

In fairy tales a **frog** could also be a prince.

Once, driving along Prince Street, I saw a frog, or was it a hopping piece of paper? It turned out to be a toad. I carried its cool outstretched body to a party for two-year-old twins, who were delighted, and later freed him near a pond. He lived happily ever after . . . I hope.

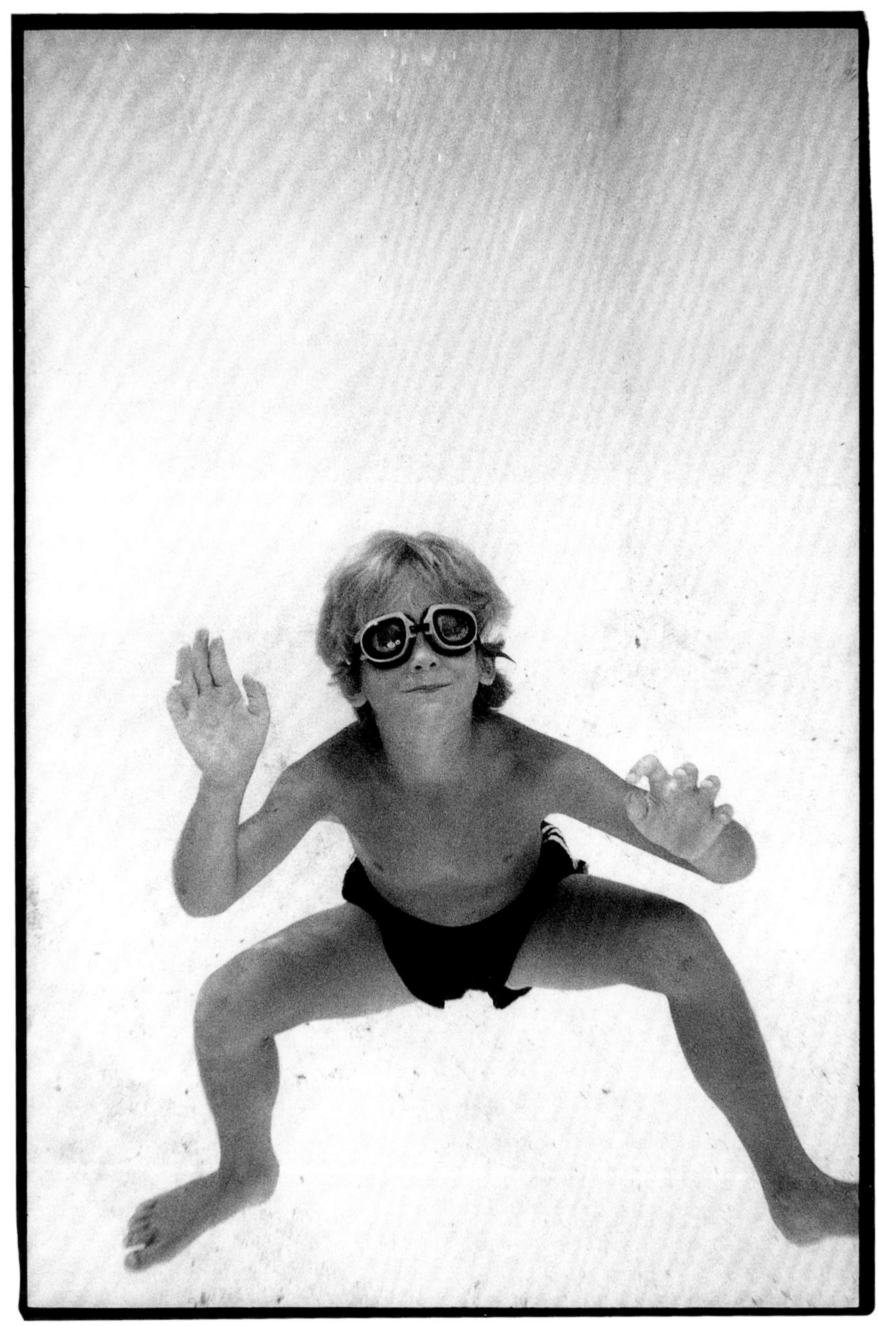

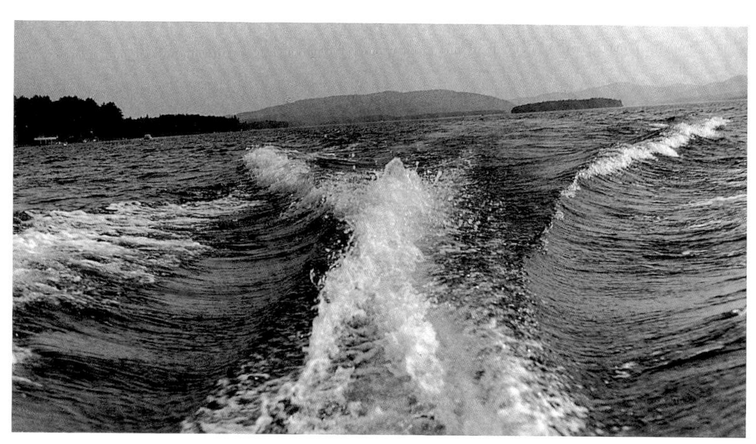

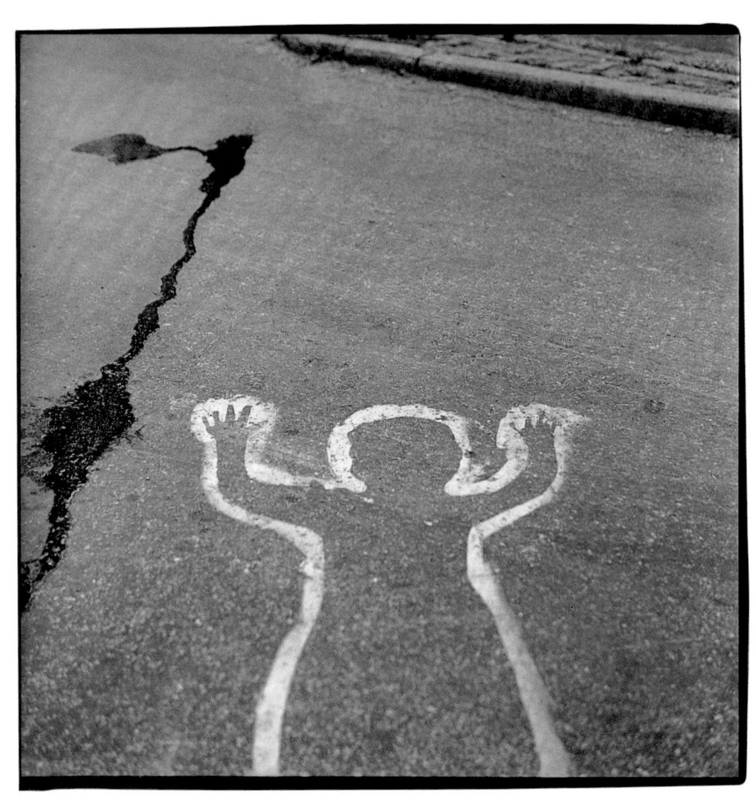

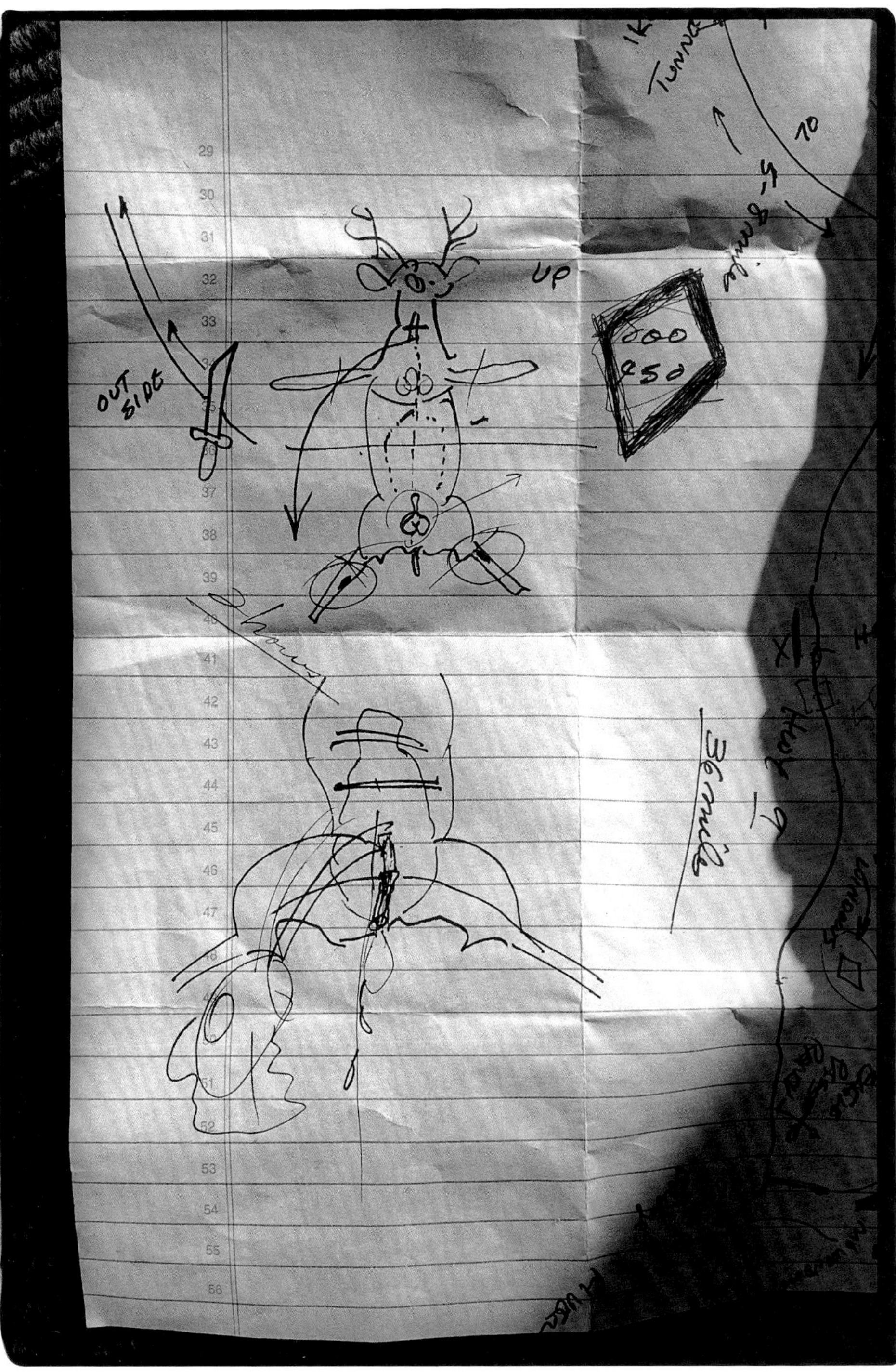
OUT SIDE
UP

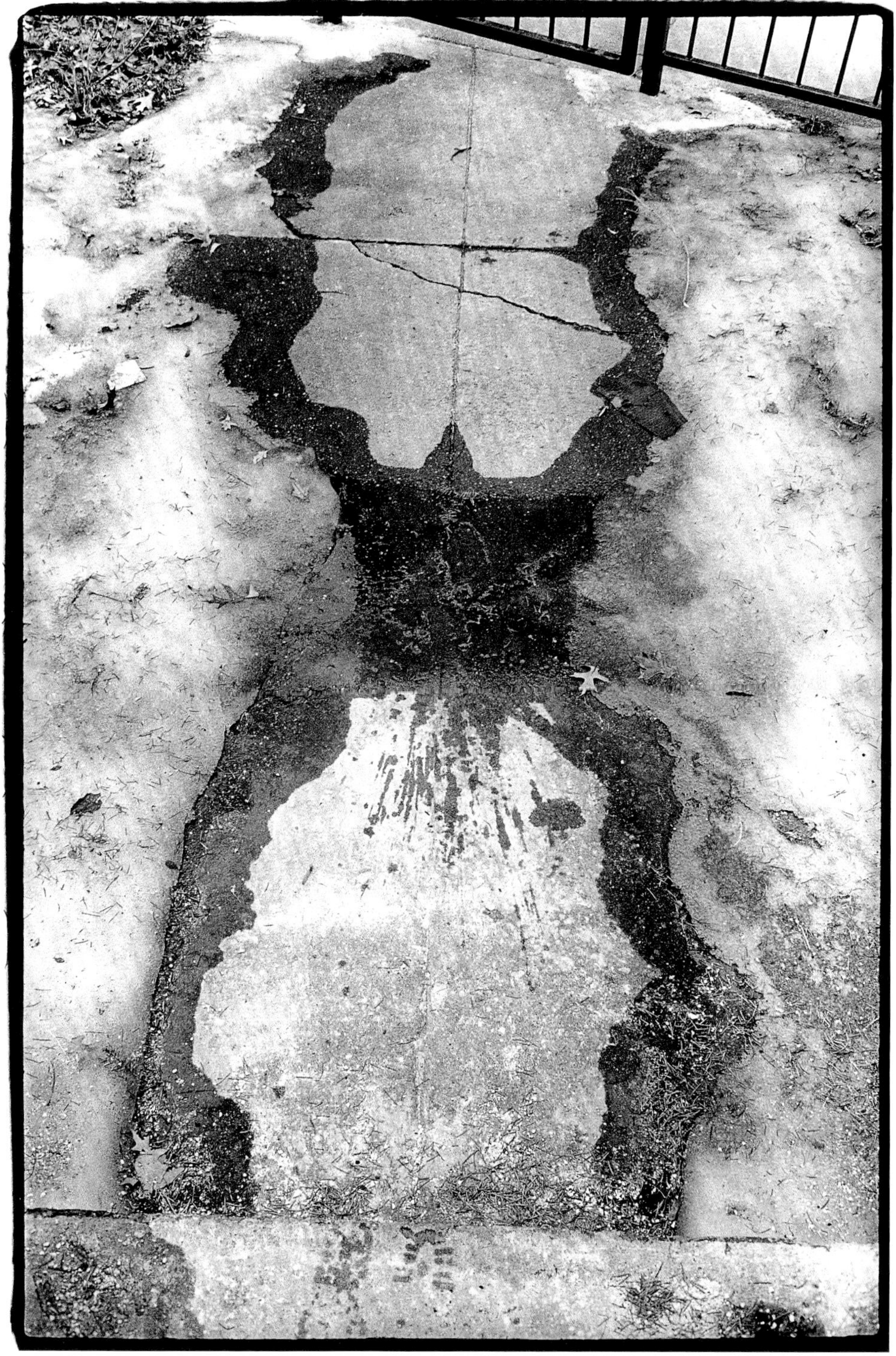

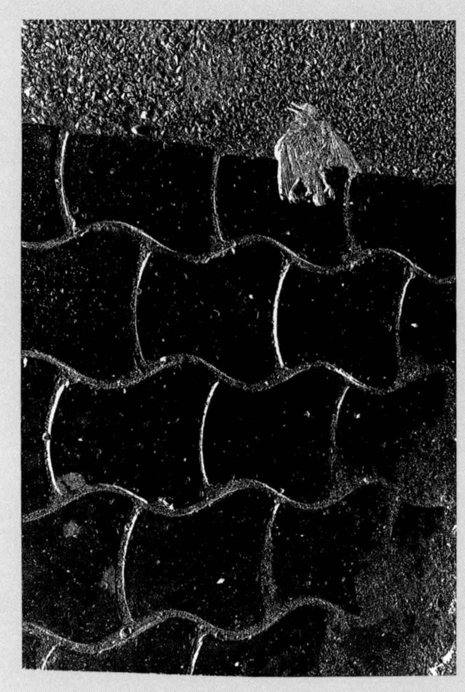

In the city, nature means human nature. As for the rest of the animal kingdom, only the hardiest of squirrels, pigeons, sparrows, and strays survive. Wild animals are in the zoo and we keep pets if they behave.

As quiet solace in a concrete world, pictorial representations of animals abound. They are the most manageable sort—except if they happen to be rats. Once in Soho, Xeroxed life-size images of rats were pasted at ground level to walls of buildings. Within a week someone removed them.

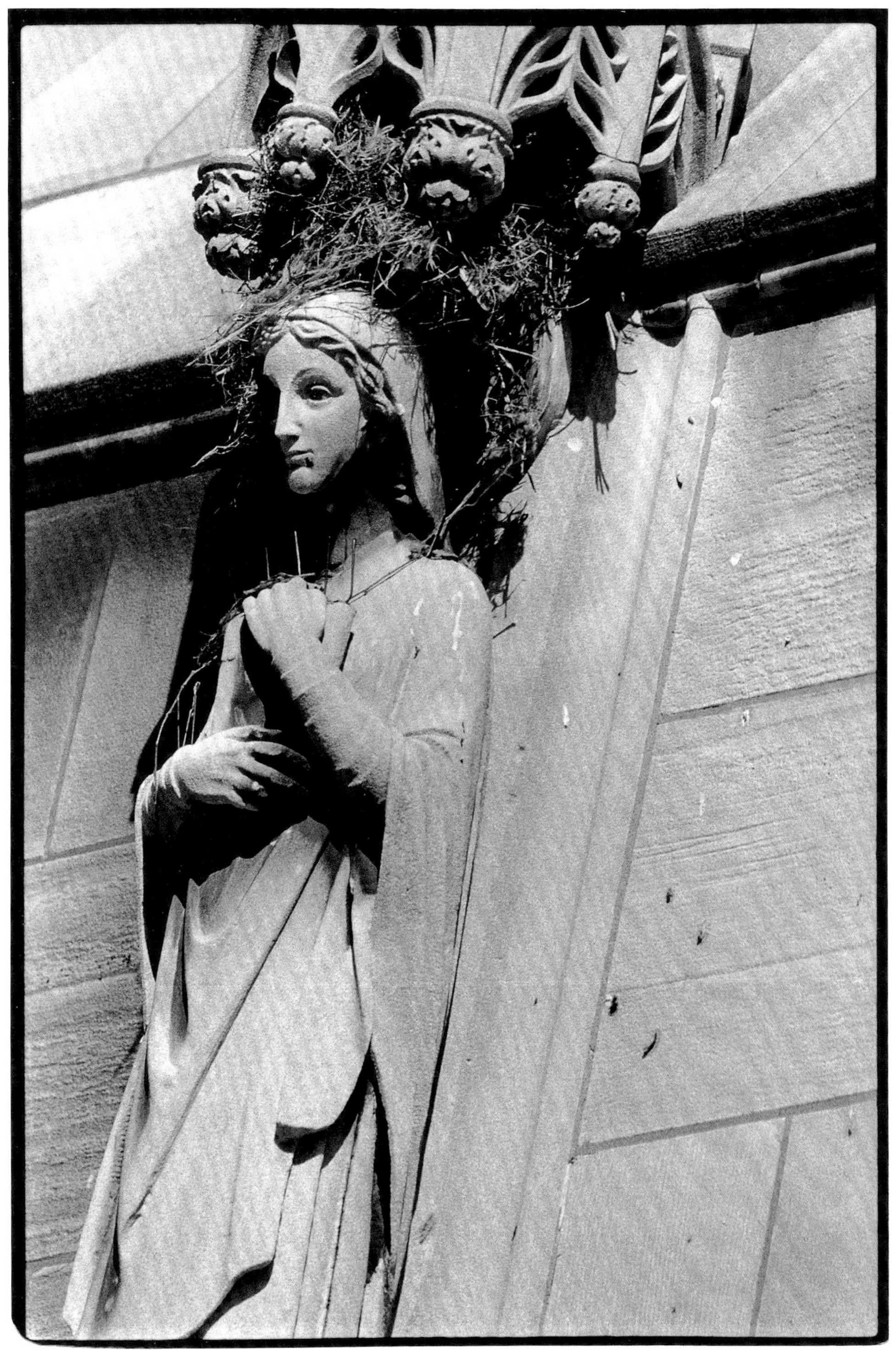

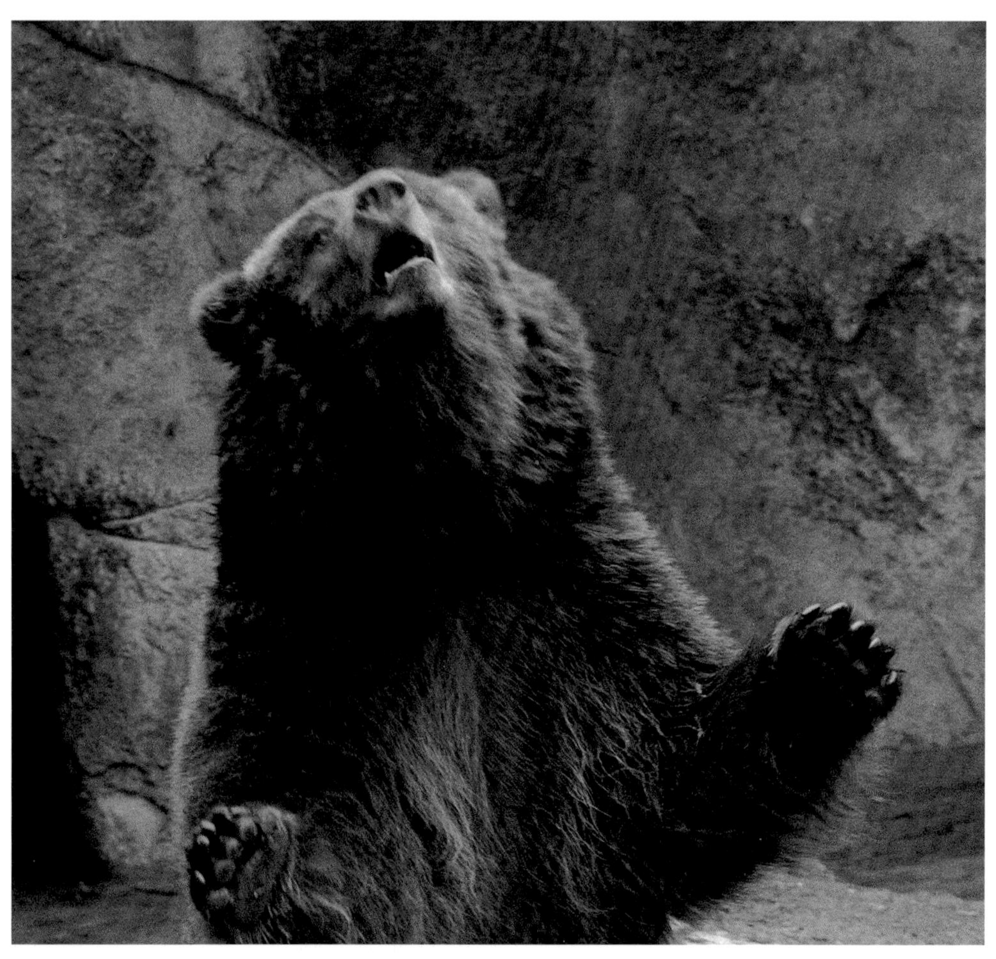

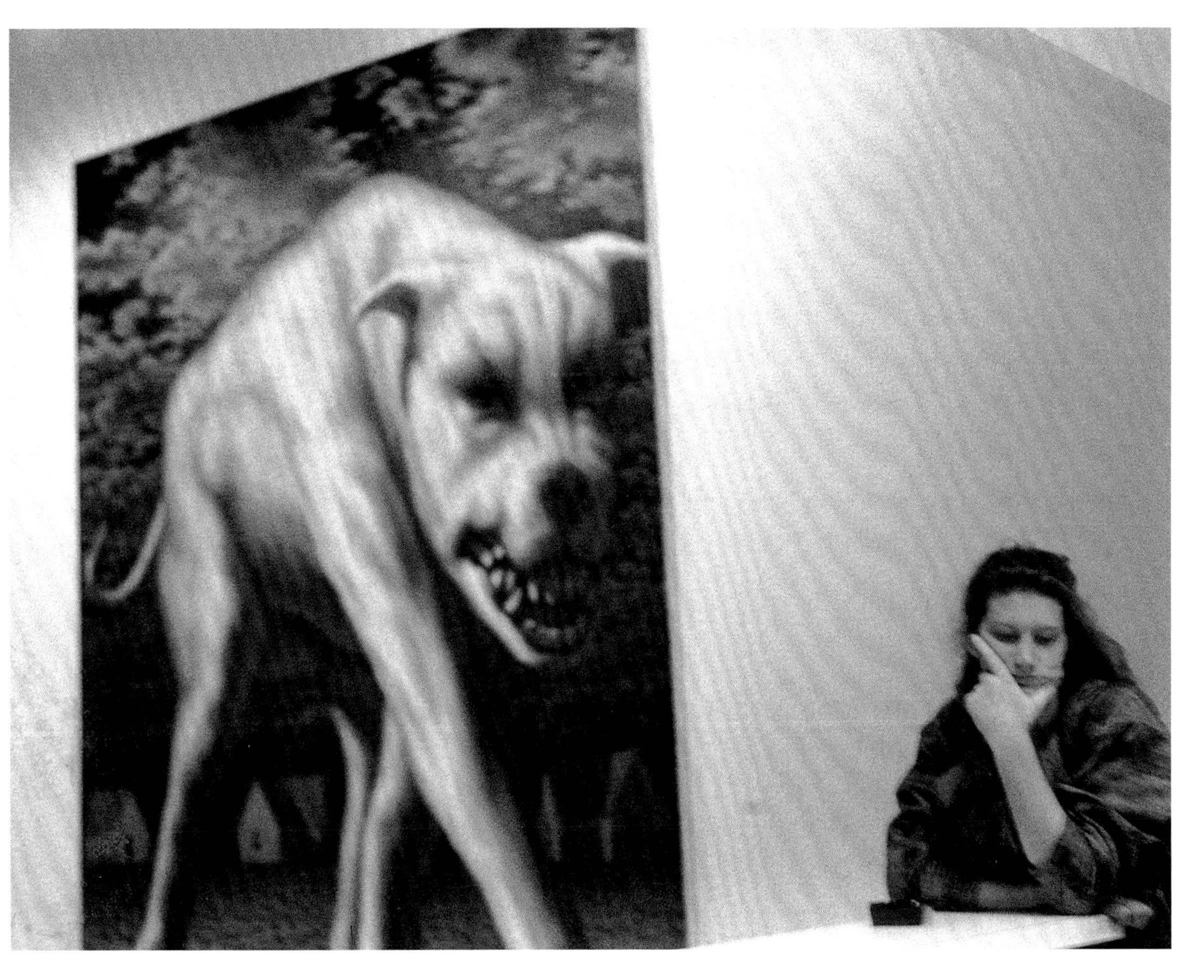

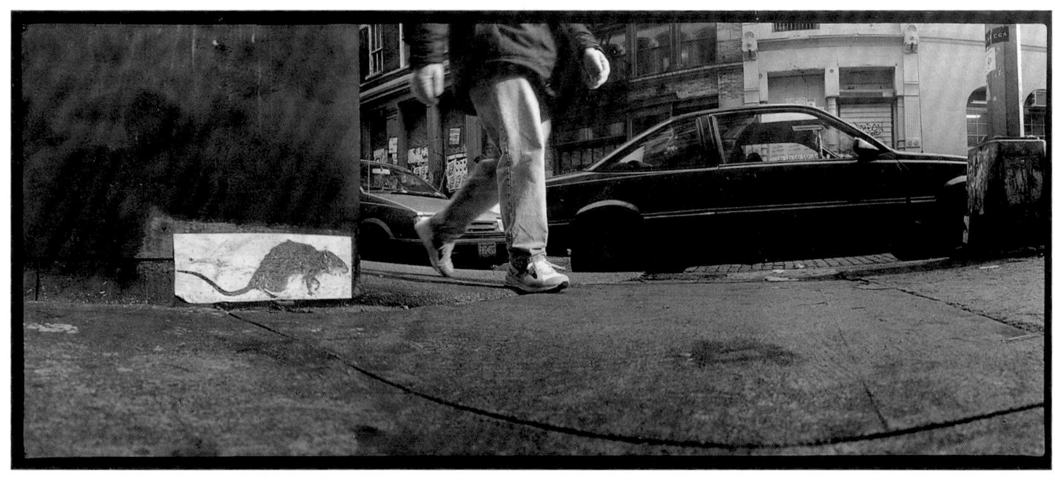

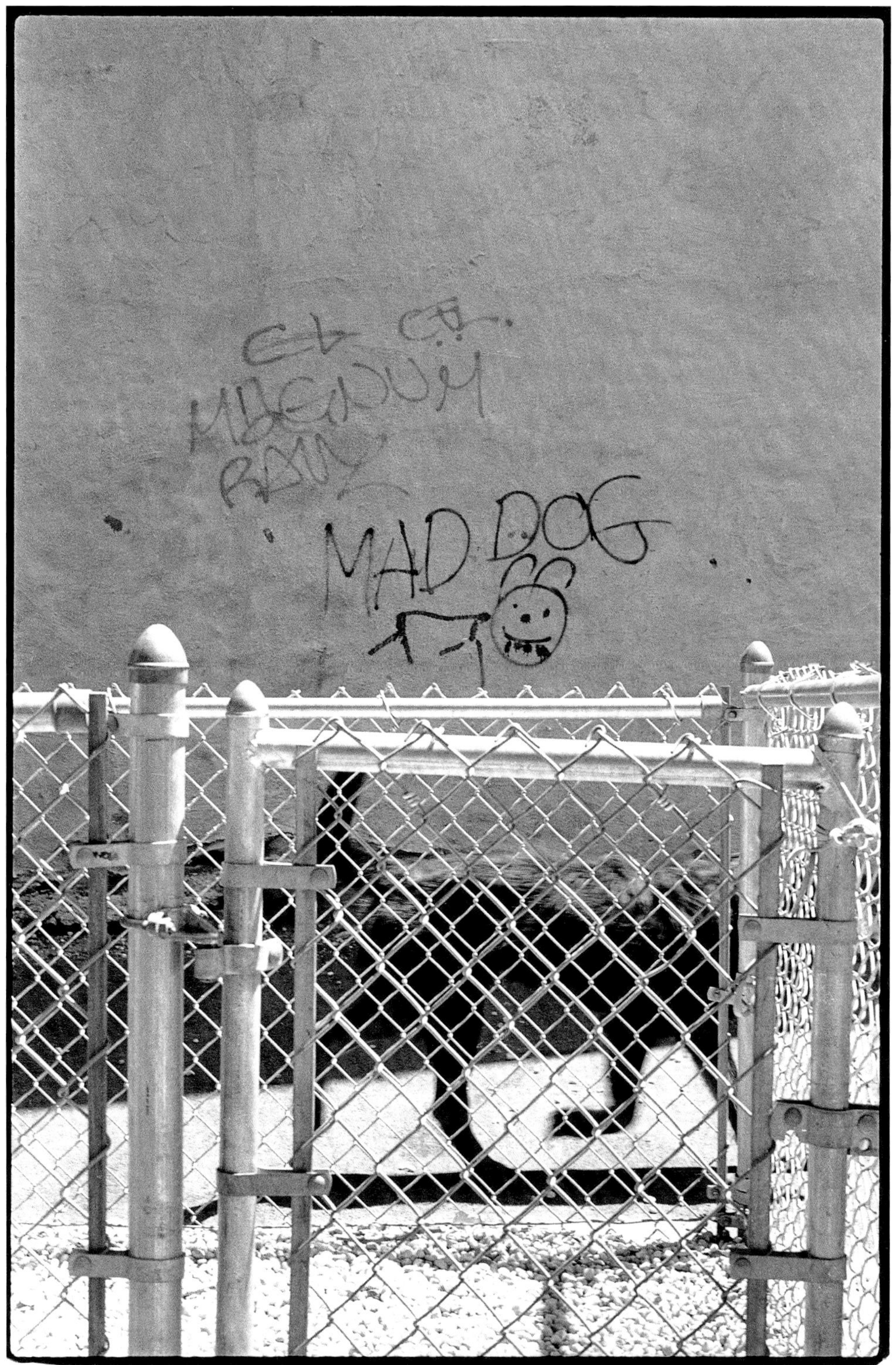
MAD DOG

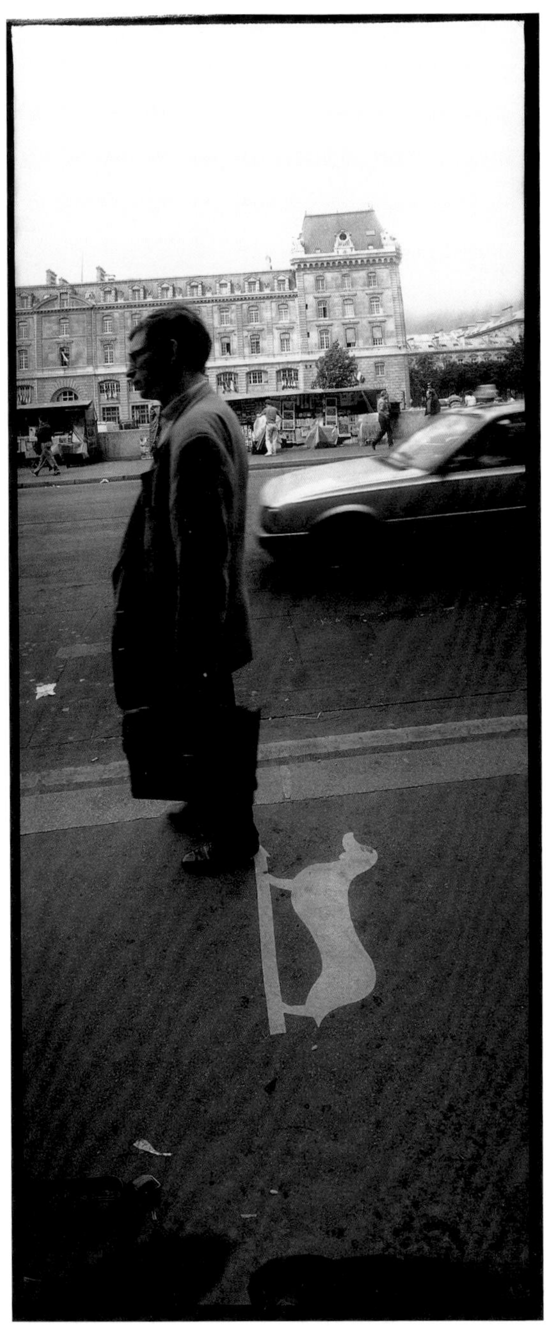

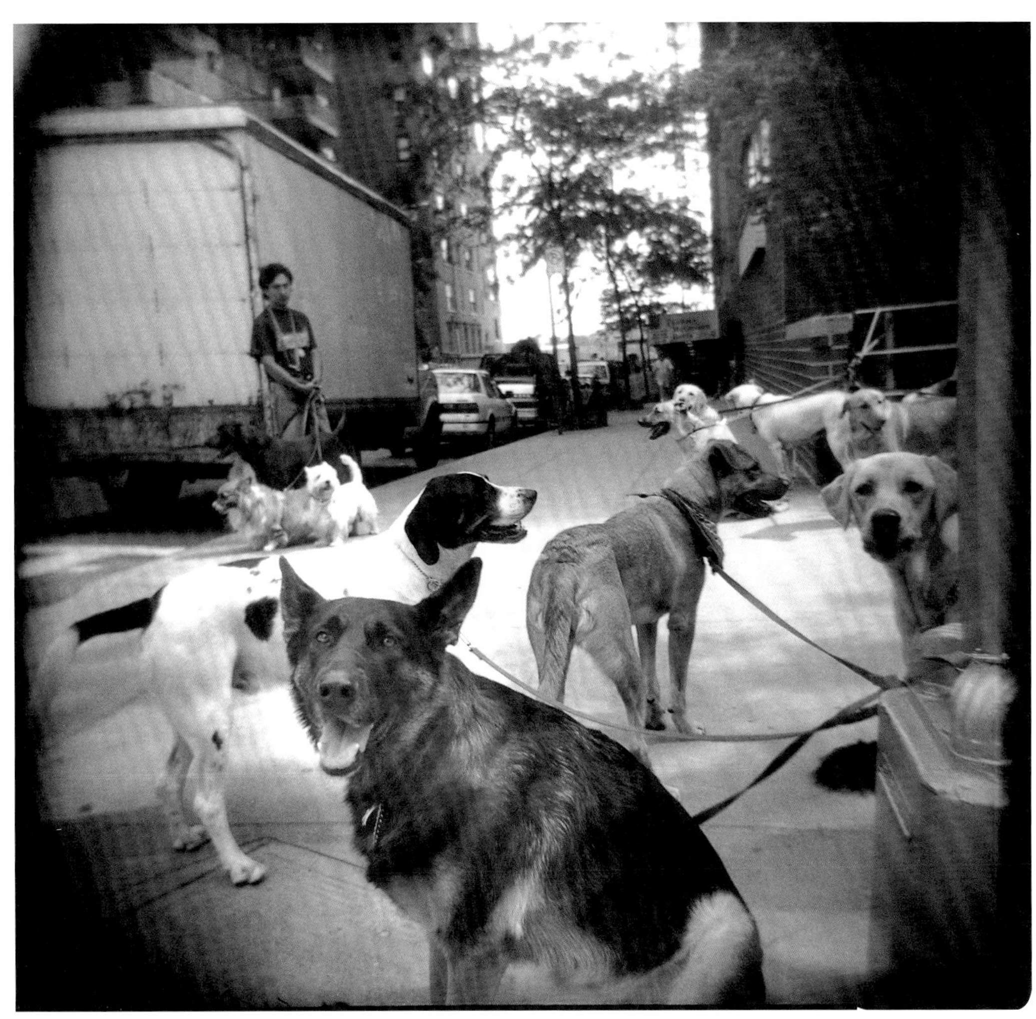

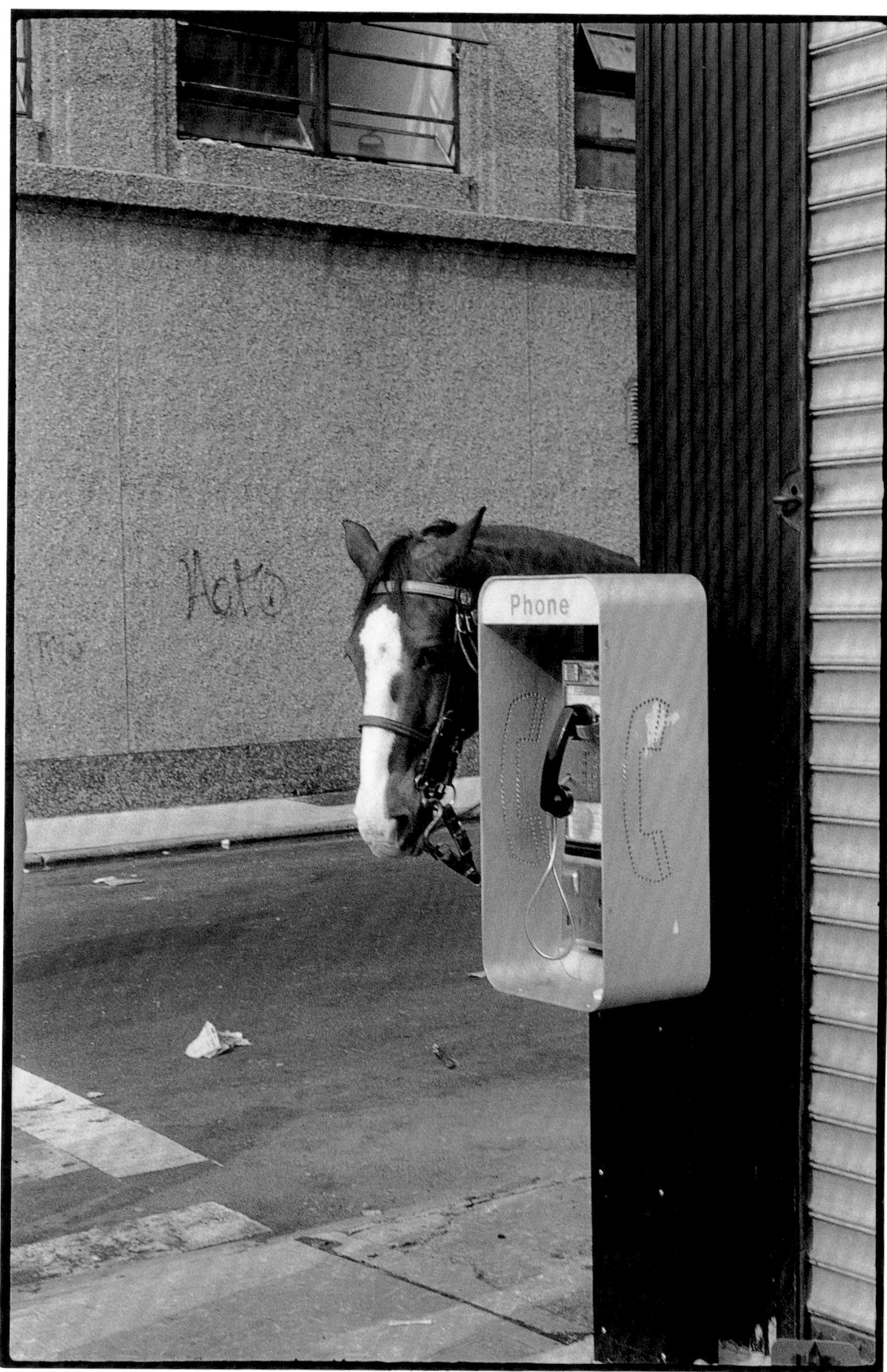
Phone

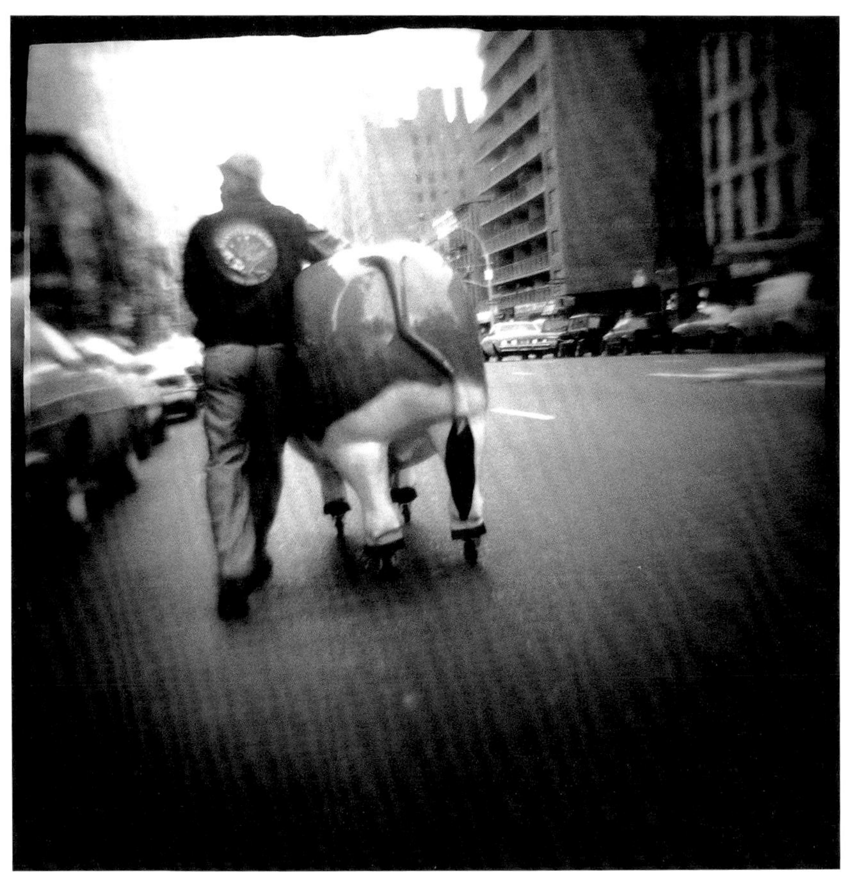

ange the plates Brin

s-nds dh' pletsz brin

y attention, you have spi

he cloth. How do you find

l klath hau du ju fajnd

After Romania's bloody revolution in 1990, in the city of Timişoara, the longest lines were not for bread but for newspapers.

Two stories above her boisterous Irish clan, in the dusty quiet of the attic, Mary Jane read *Thus Spake Zarathustra* aloud to me. We were two high-school girls hungry for poetry in Jersey City.

As children in Budapest, Lulu and I used to sit in a garden reading forbidden books and eating fruit under a mulberry tree. I craved frivolous "little girl" books about tea parties and frilly clothes, not the required reading about heroic partisans and Father Stalin. Amazingly, in one story, Csöpike the heroine burned a chocolate cake and didn't get punished.

On a page, ideas like crumbs are carried by a procession of black ants. Whether they lie or speak the truth, instruct or take us on trips, they lead us to our own thoughts—under certain conditions, the study of advanced algebra can end in a kiss.

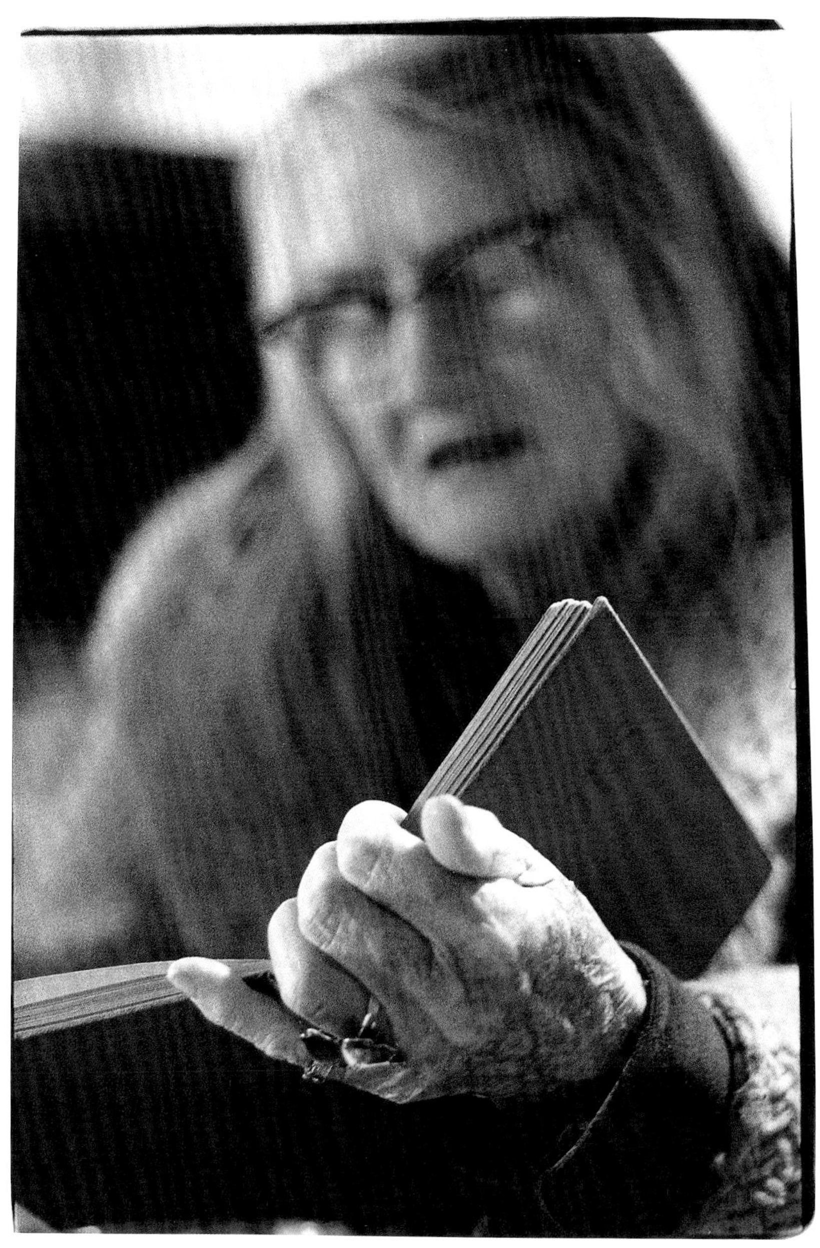

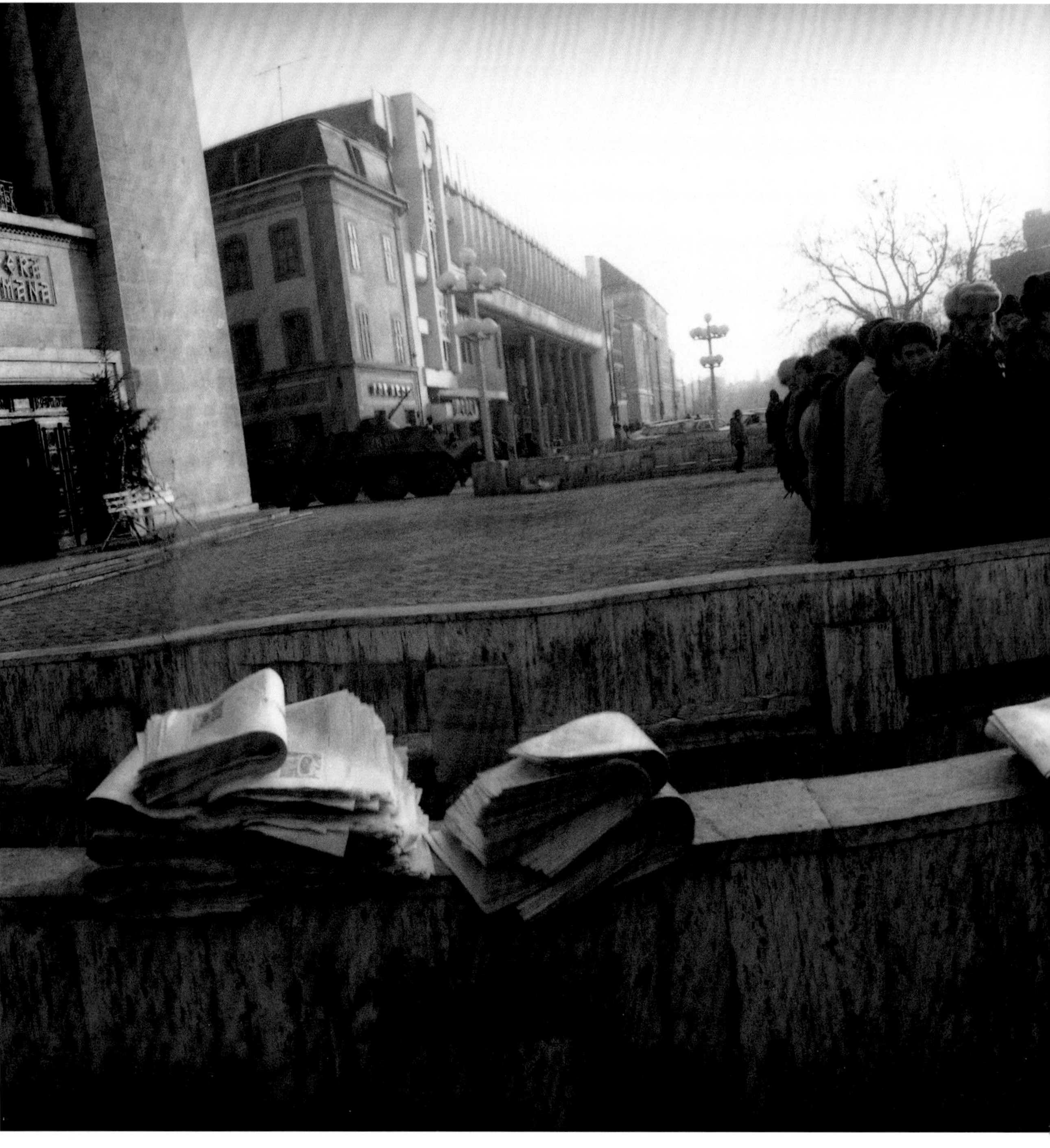

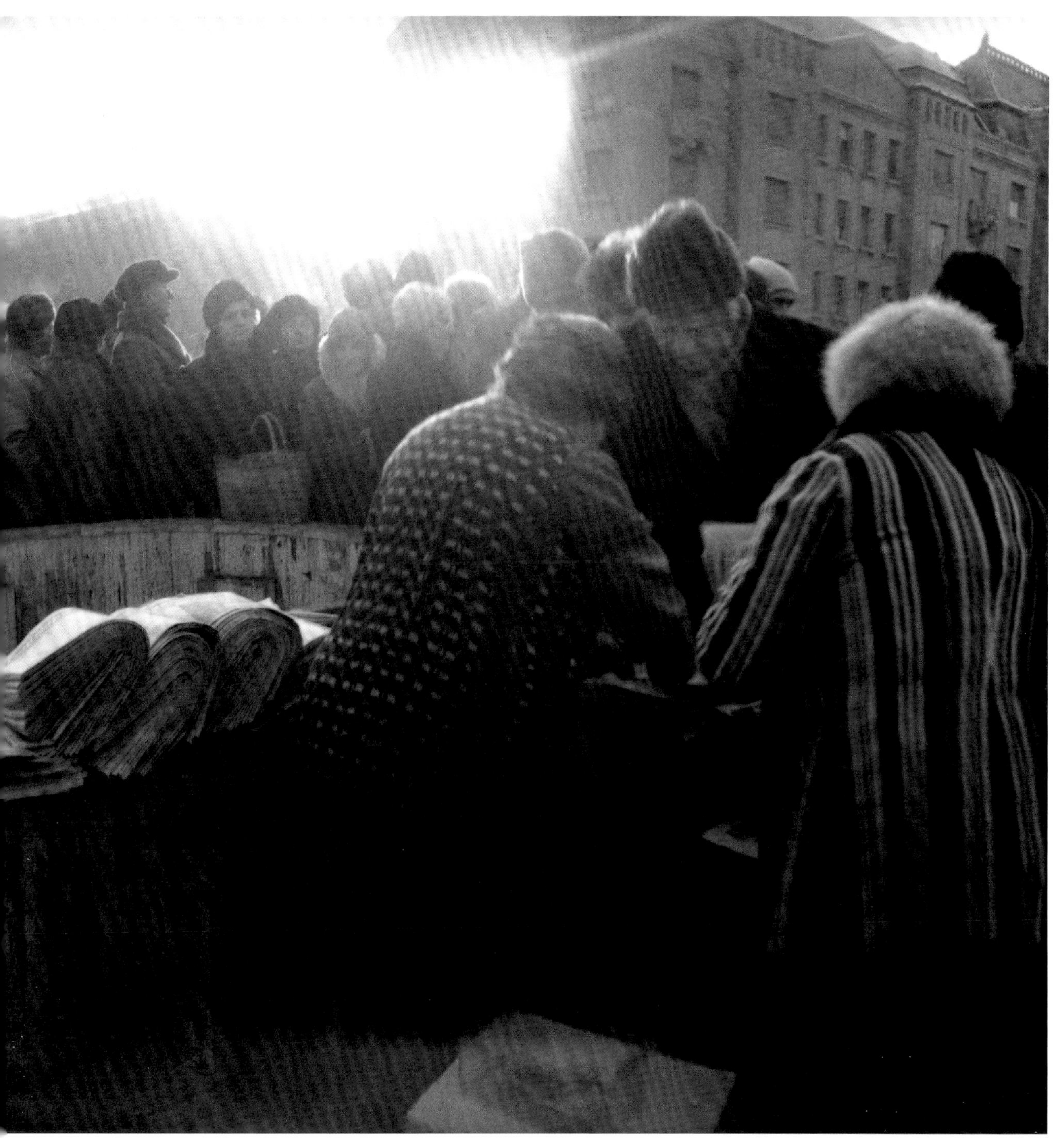

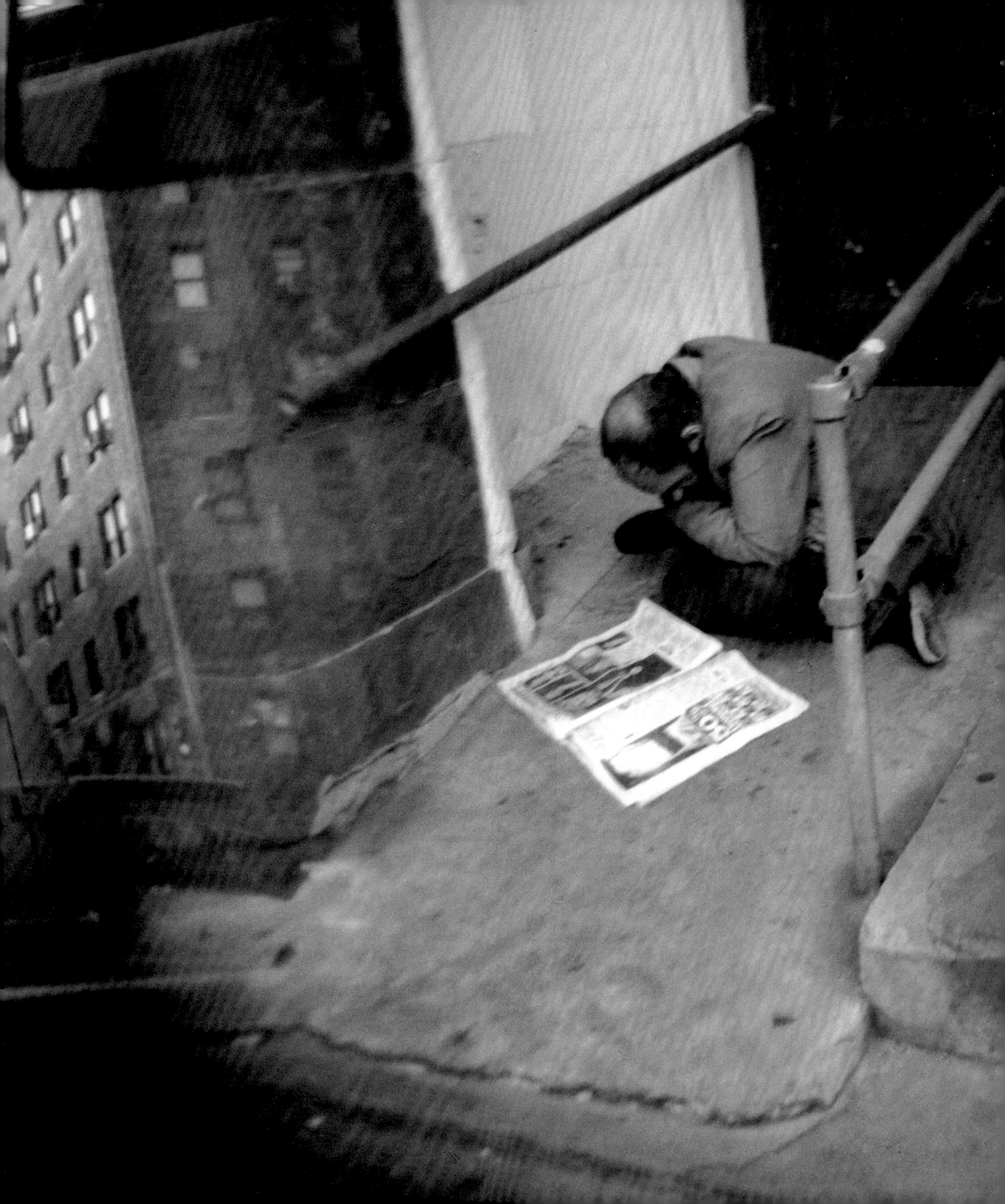

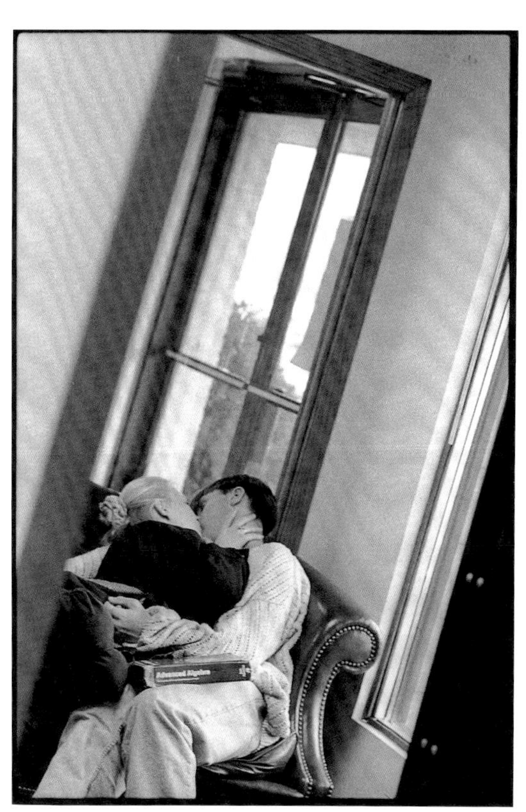

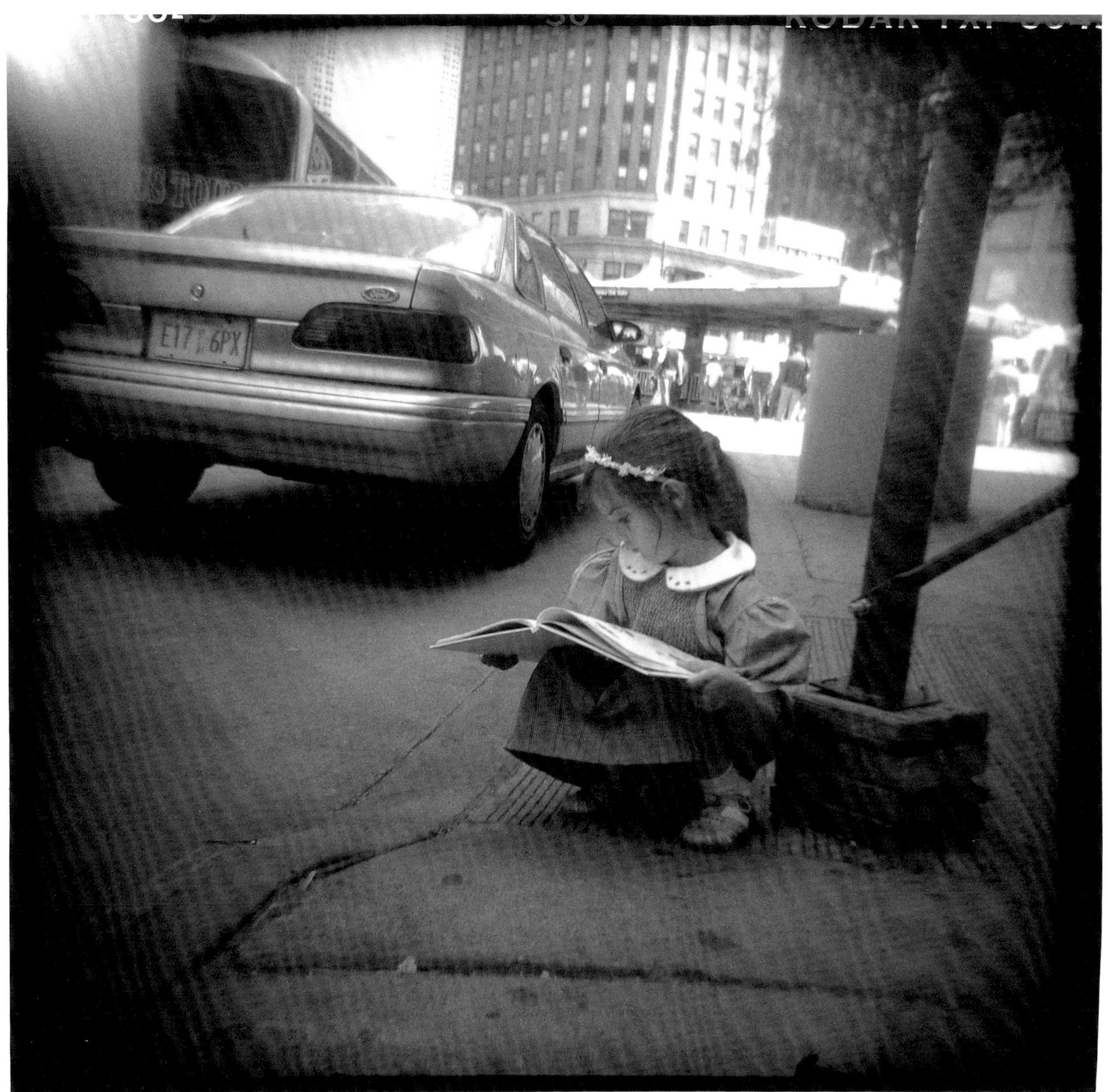

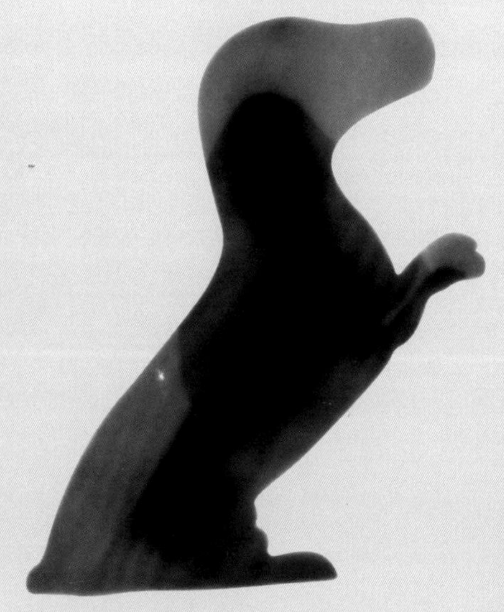

"sit," we say to a dog to calm him. We sit to collect ourselves. "It's better to sit than to stand" goes an old Chinese proverb.

Monsieur Merceron, je voudrais acheter la chaise! Mr. Merceron, I would like to buy the chair! A finger in Paris once traced these words on the dusty windowpane of an empty shop. Facing out, in the center of the store, was a wooden chair. Someone responded to its paint-chipped, rickety presence but realized the futility of the request and left no number.

Rebecca Moore sat for her portrait next to a chair. She is a performer. Since her father died, she leaves a chair empty at each of her shows. The sign reads "Reserved for Peter Moore."

At a sitting we offer up our best image for perpetuity. In Hungarian, the verb for taking a picture is *megörökiteni,* which means "to make it last forever."

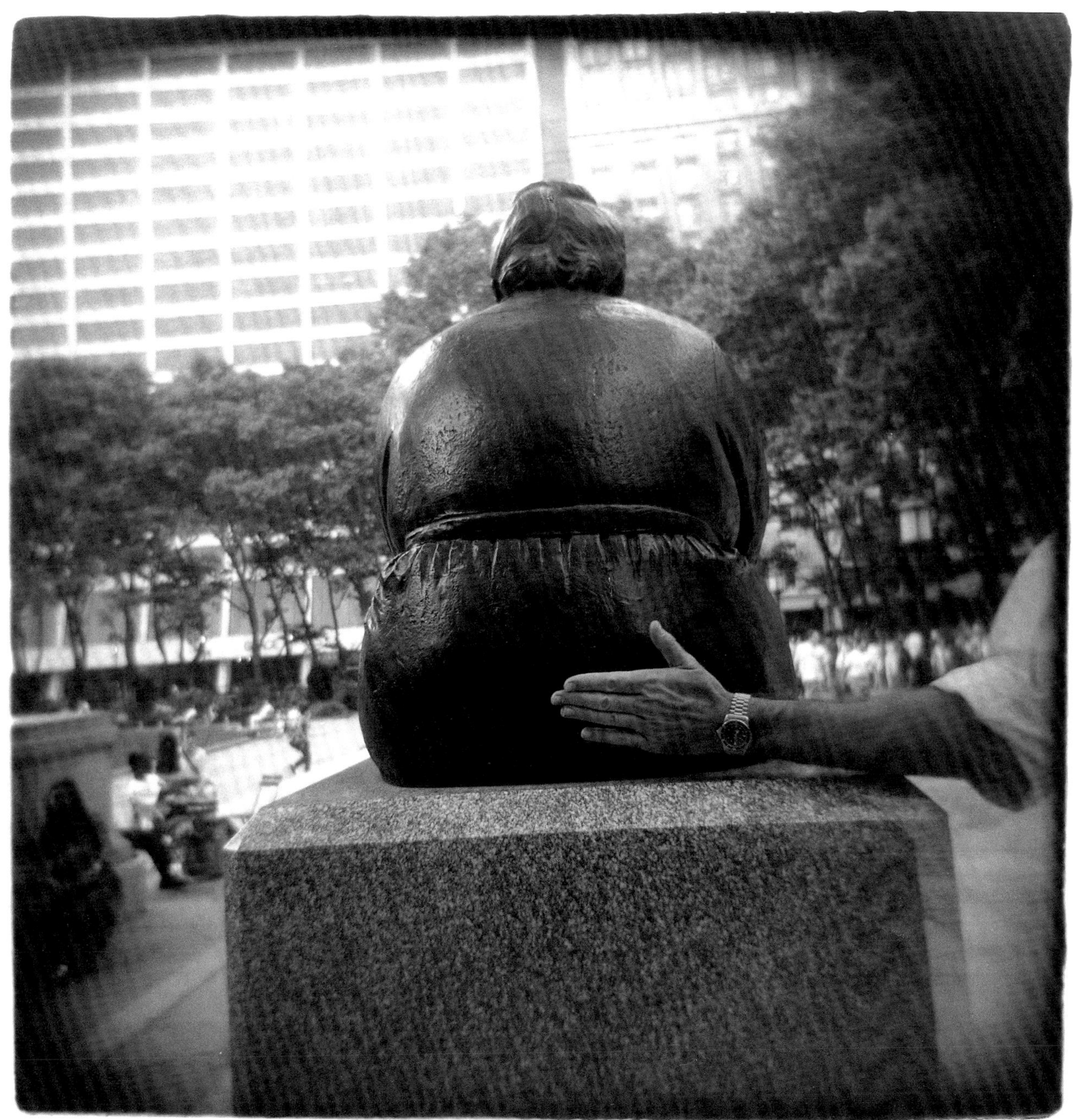

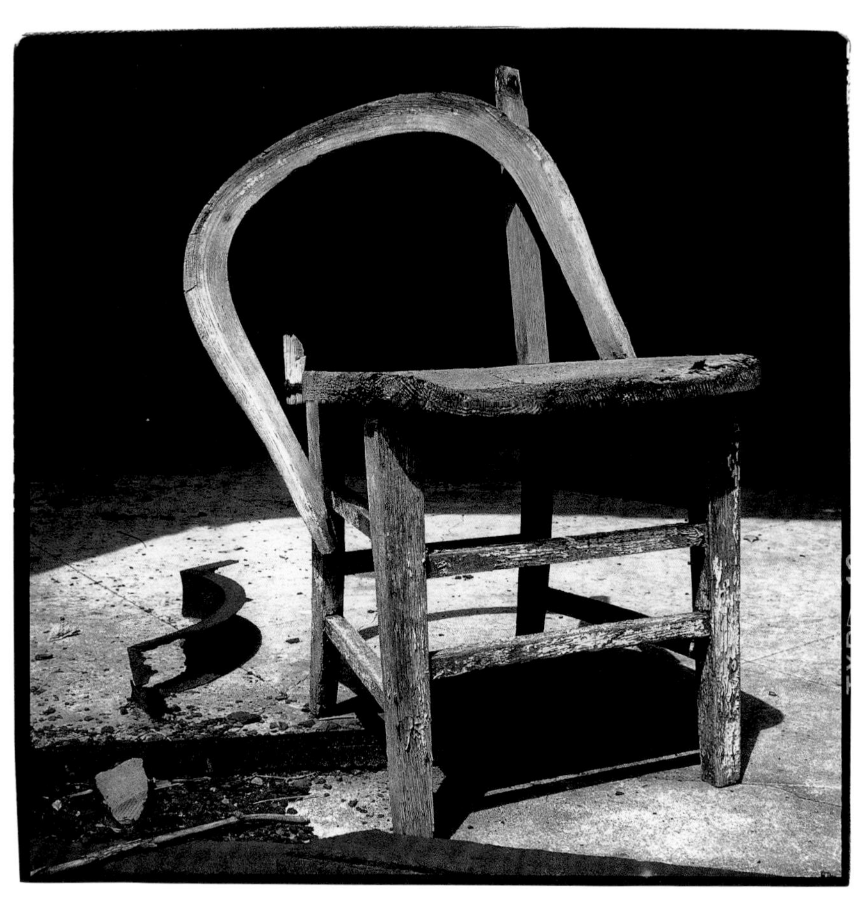

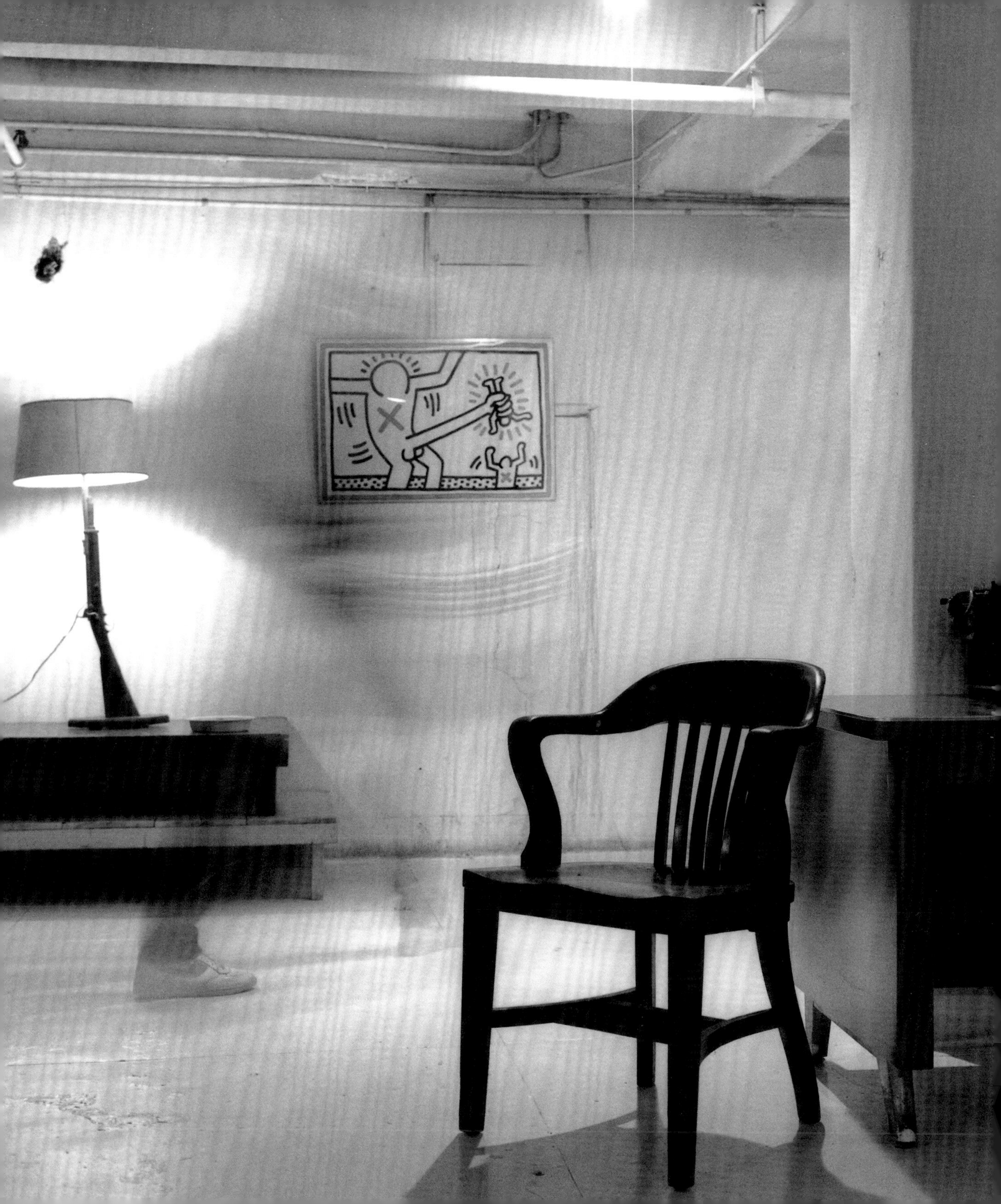

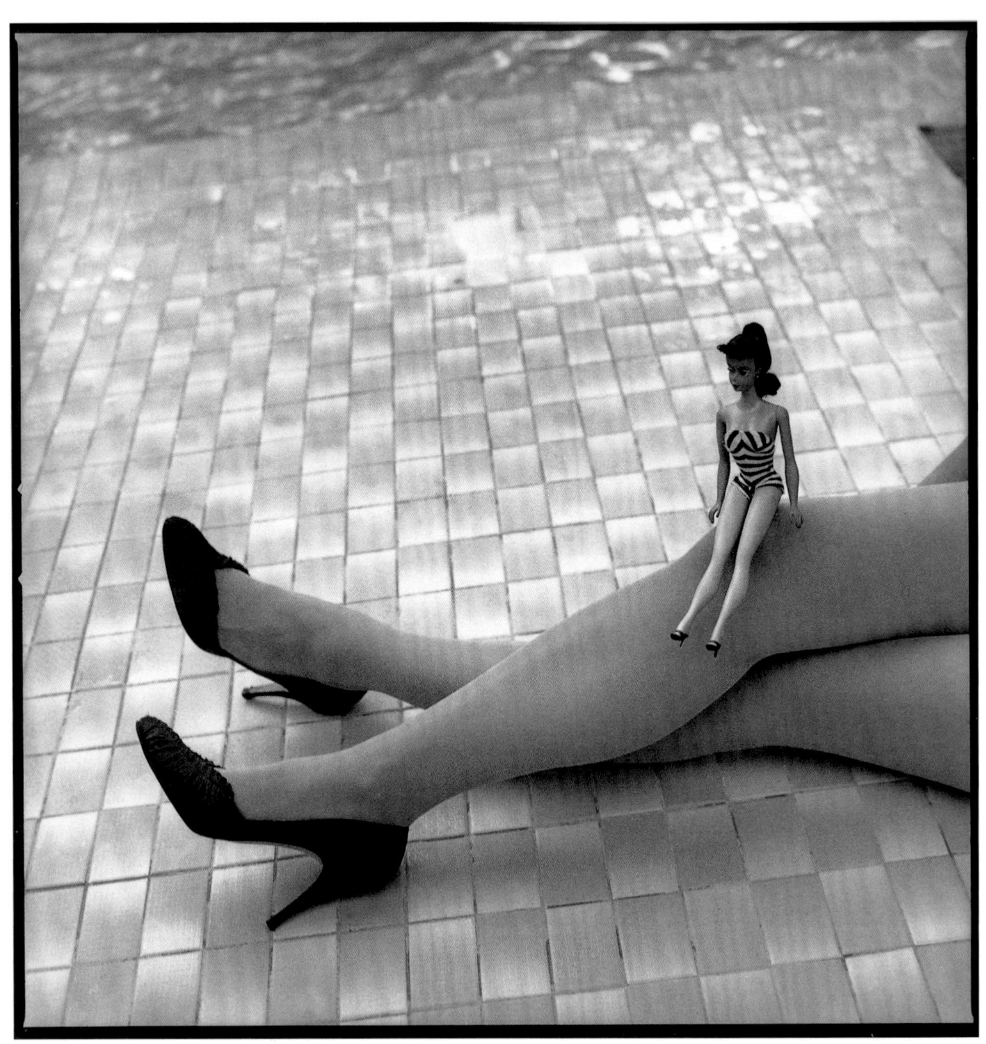

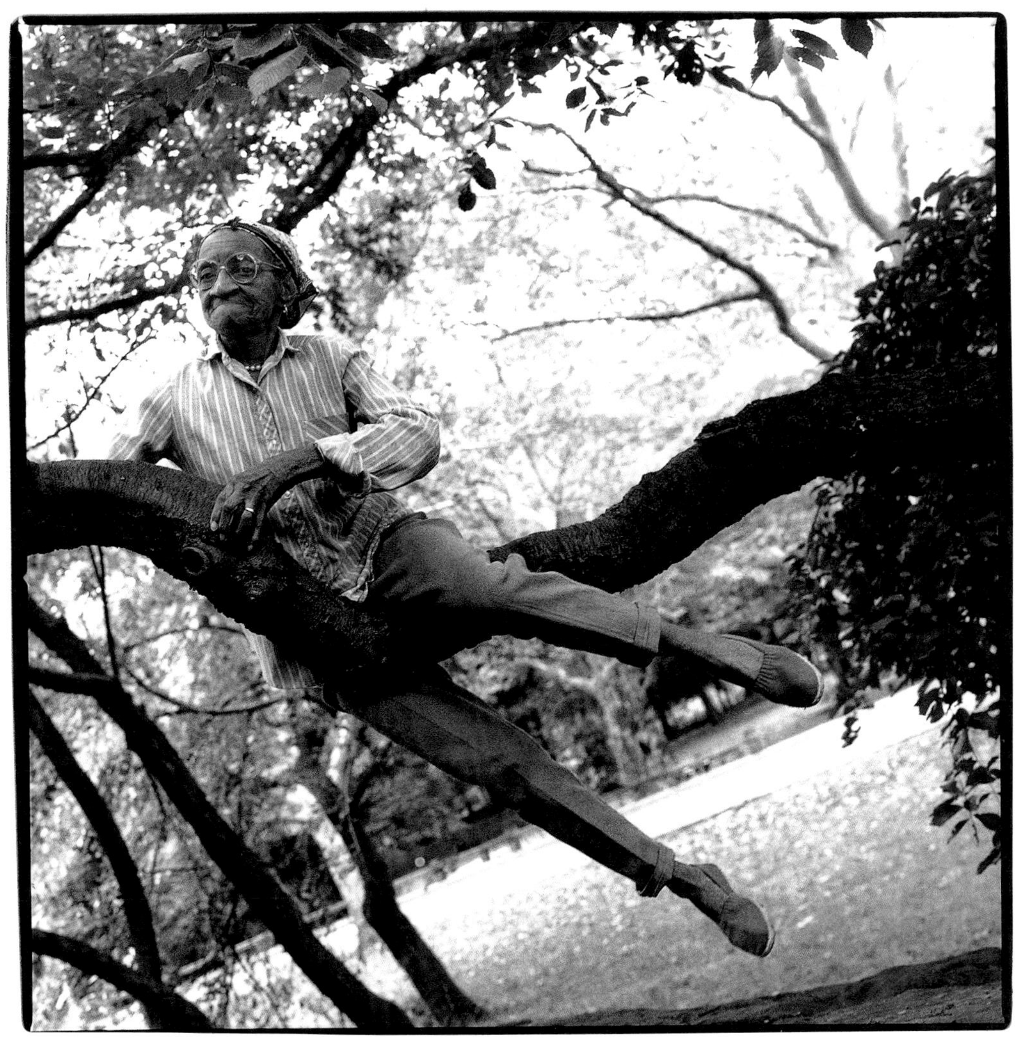

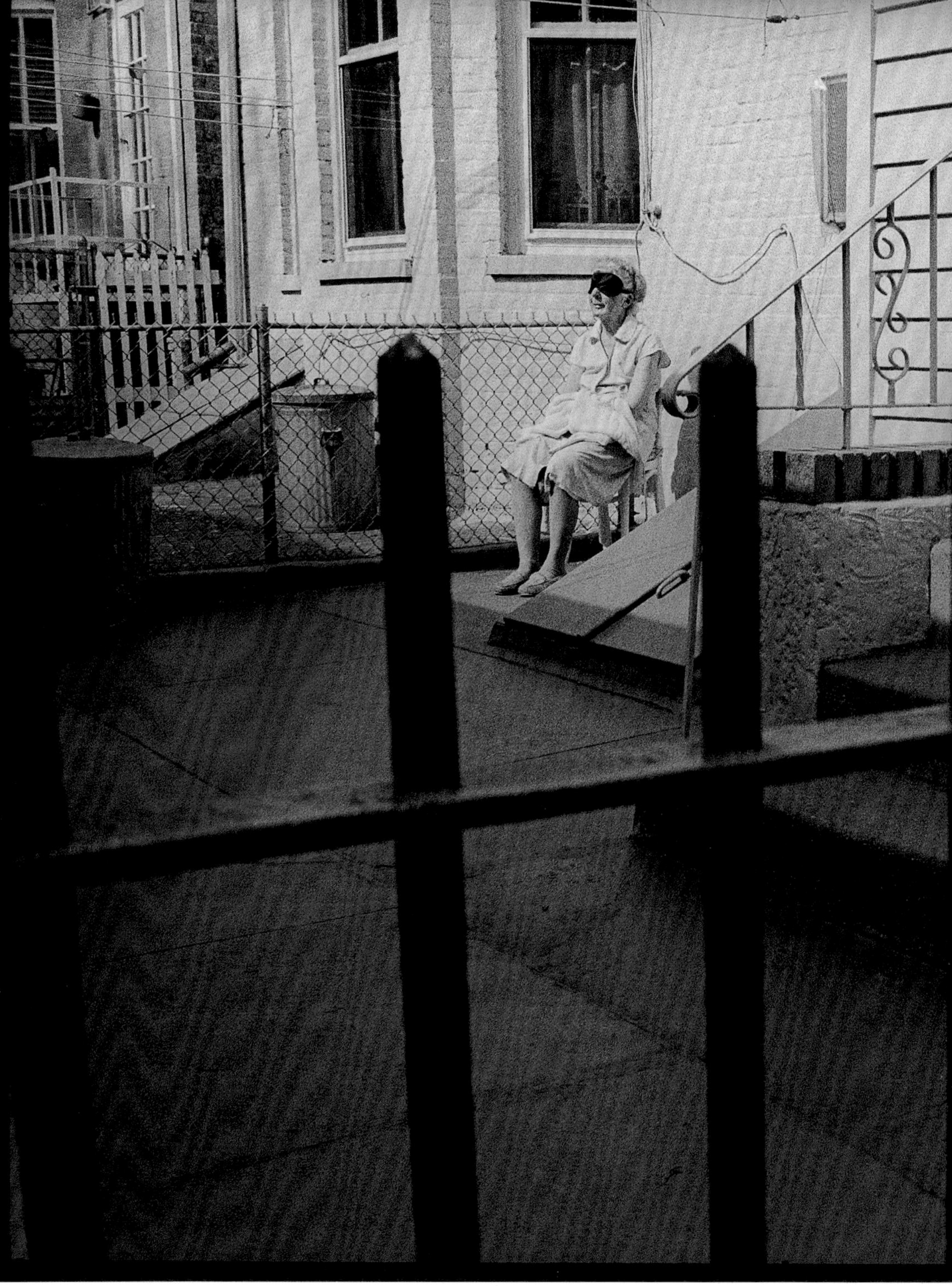

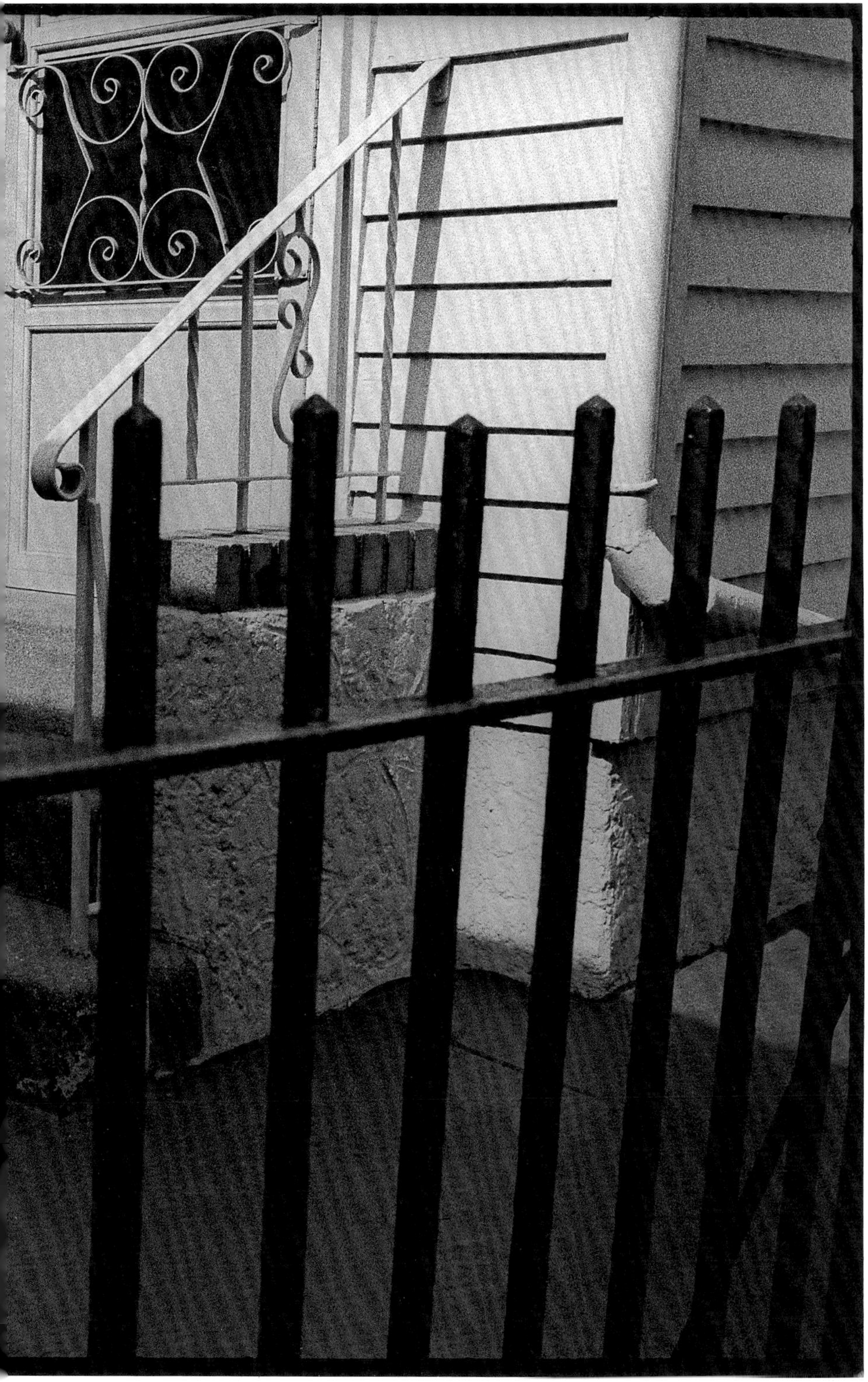

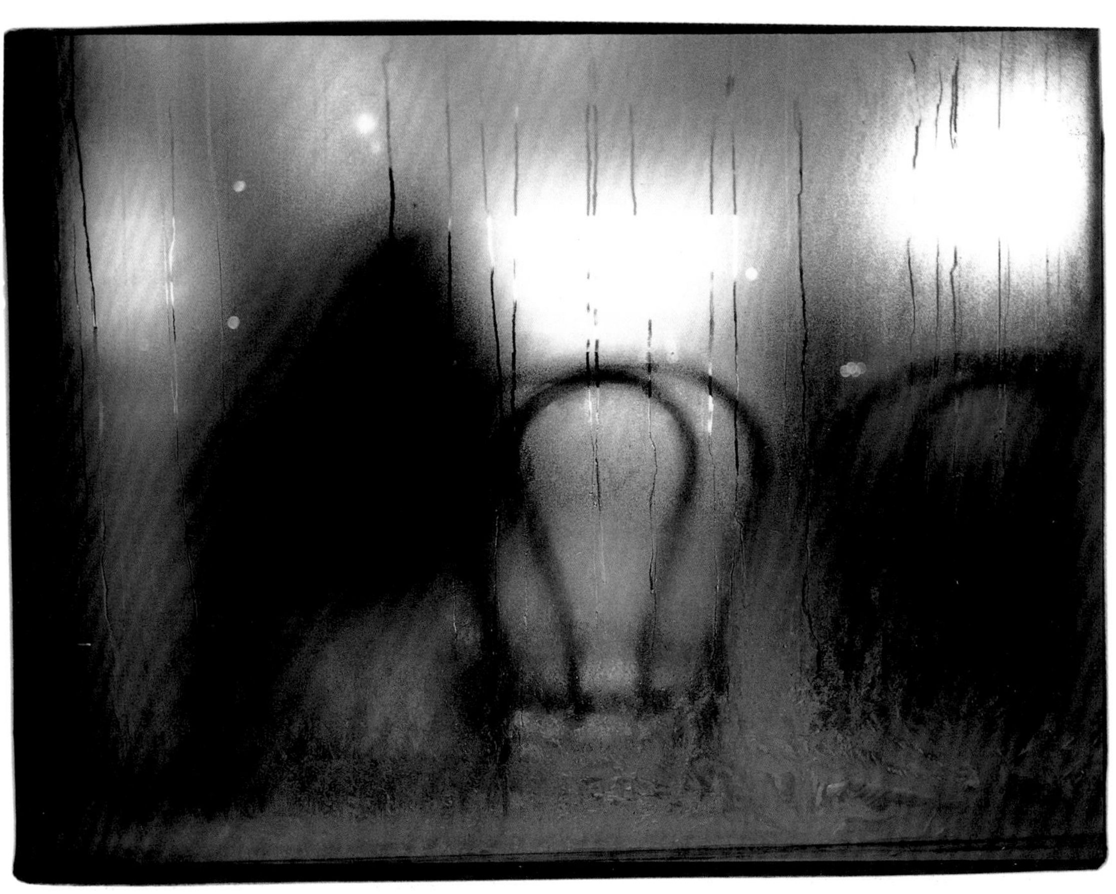

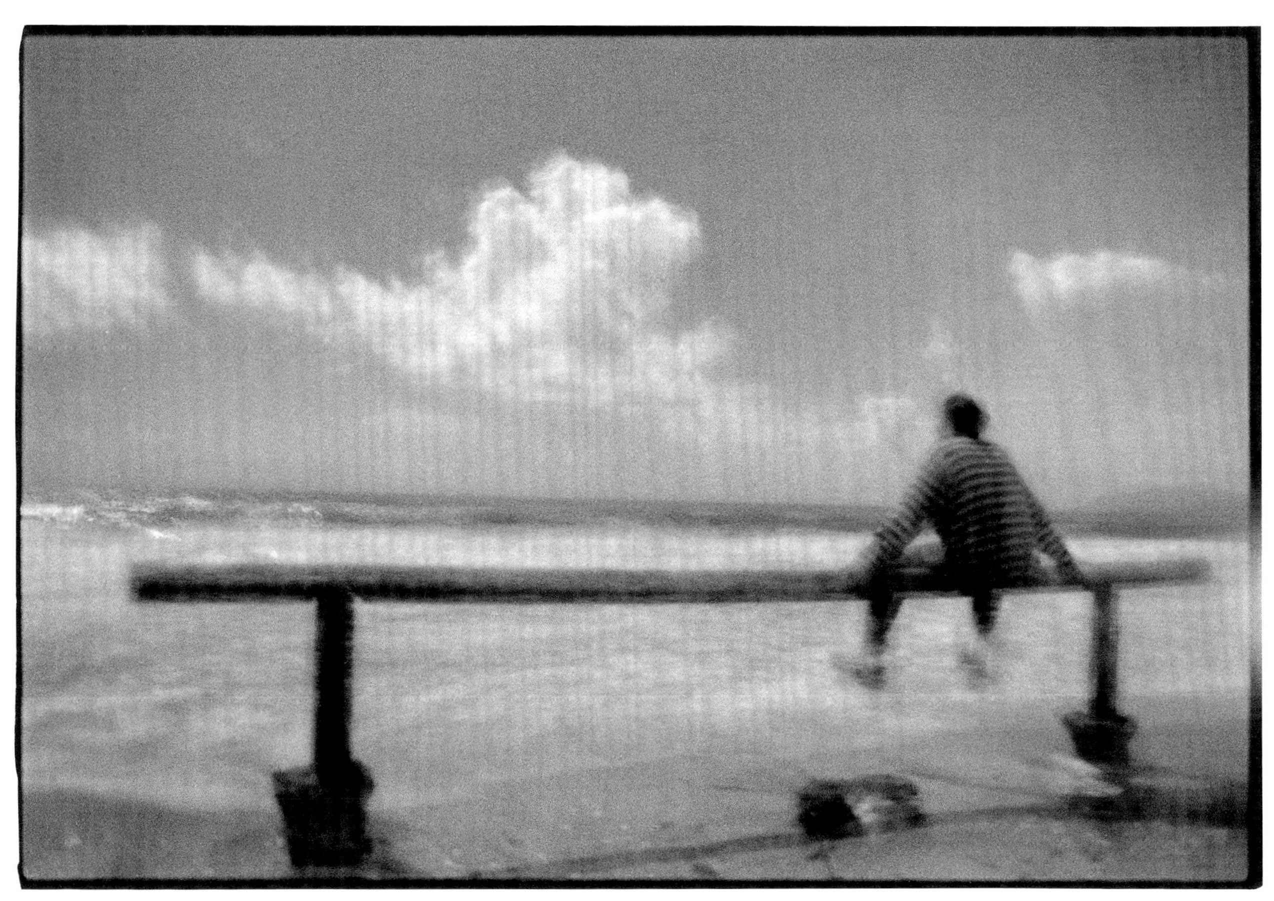

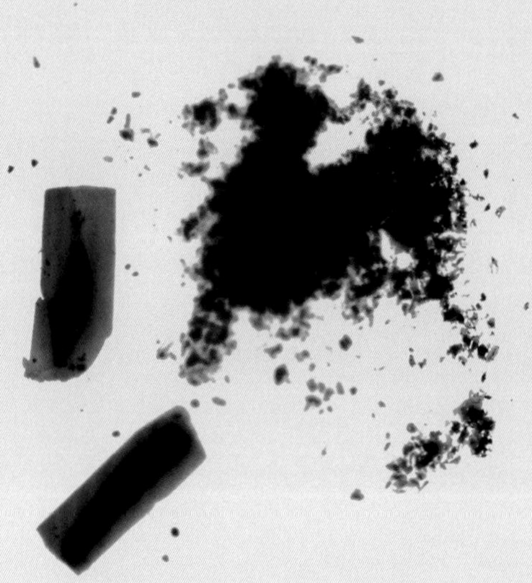

When I was sixteen and just back from my first job in a summer camp, I lit a cigarette in the kitchen, flung the match into the trash, and made my grand entrance. My parents jumped up in shock, not because I was smoking but because the kitchen was in flames.

For twenty years I smoked. Sometimes it choked me; mostly it comforted me. Finally I gave it up in order to set a good example for my son.

A portrait with cigarette recalls the elegance of the forties. smoke softens the edges; the center is a whirl, a private space to hide in. It's beautiful, it's mysterious, it's deceitful.

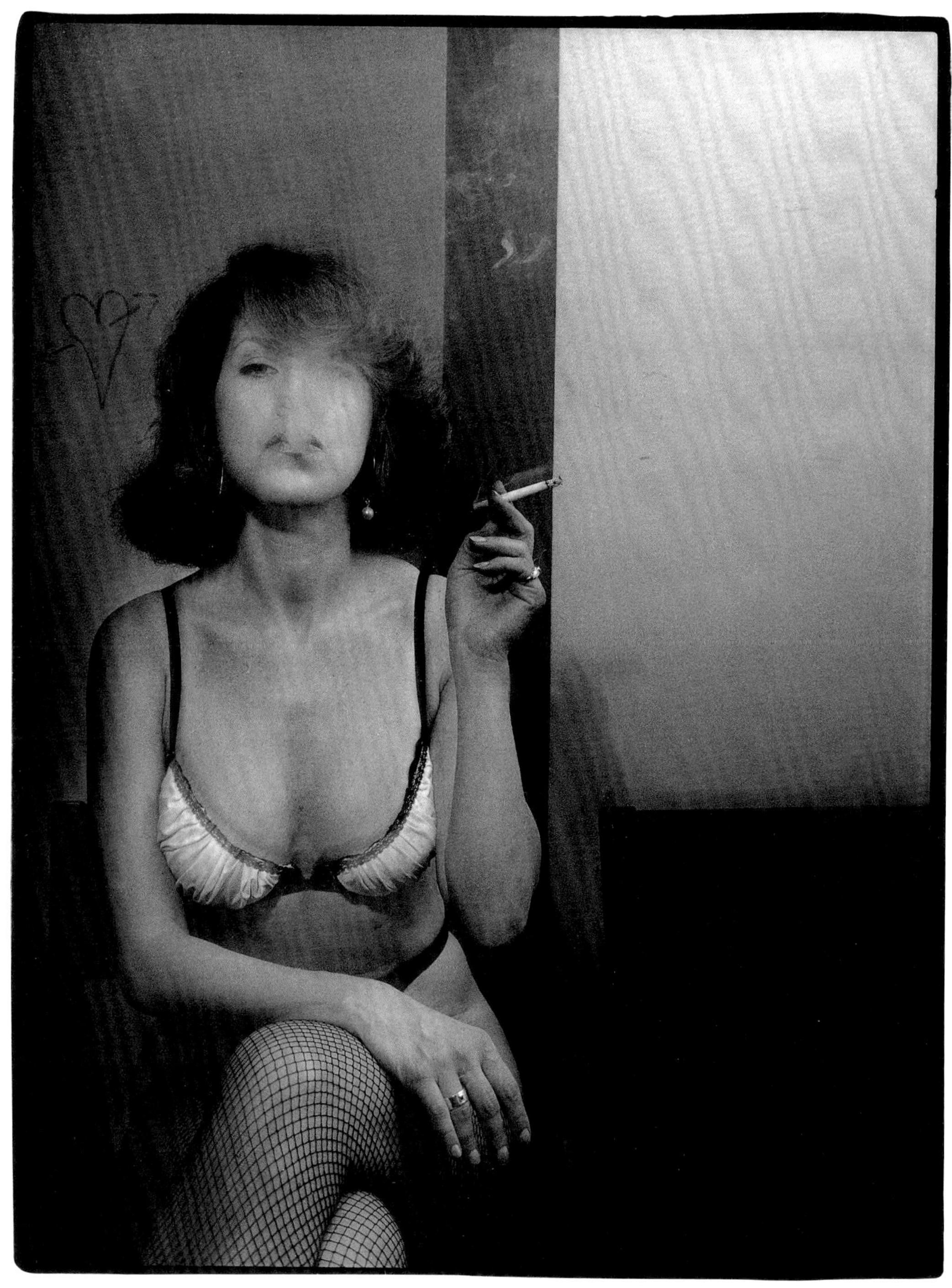

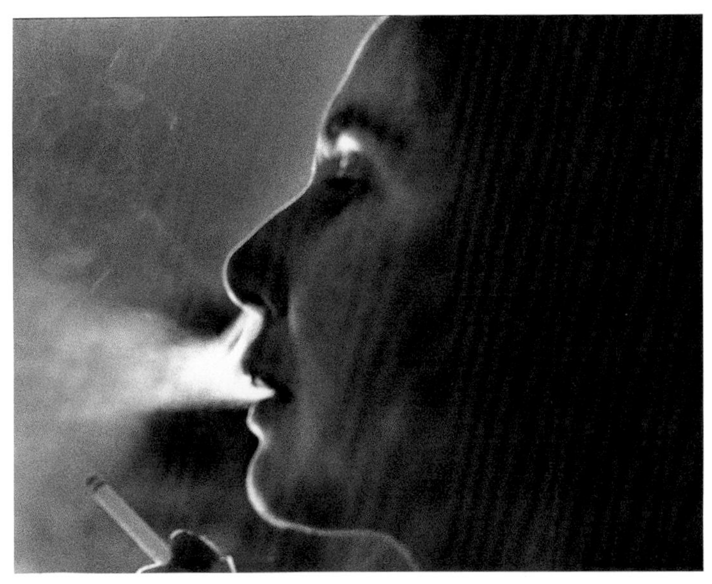

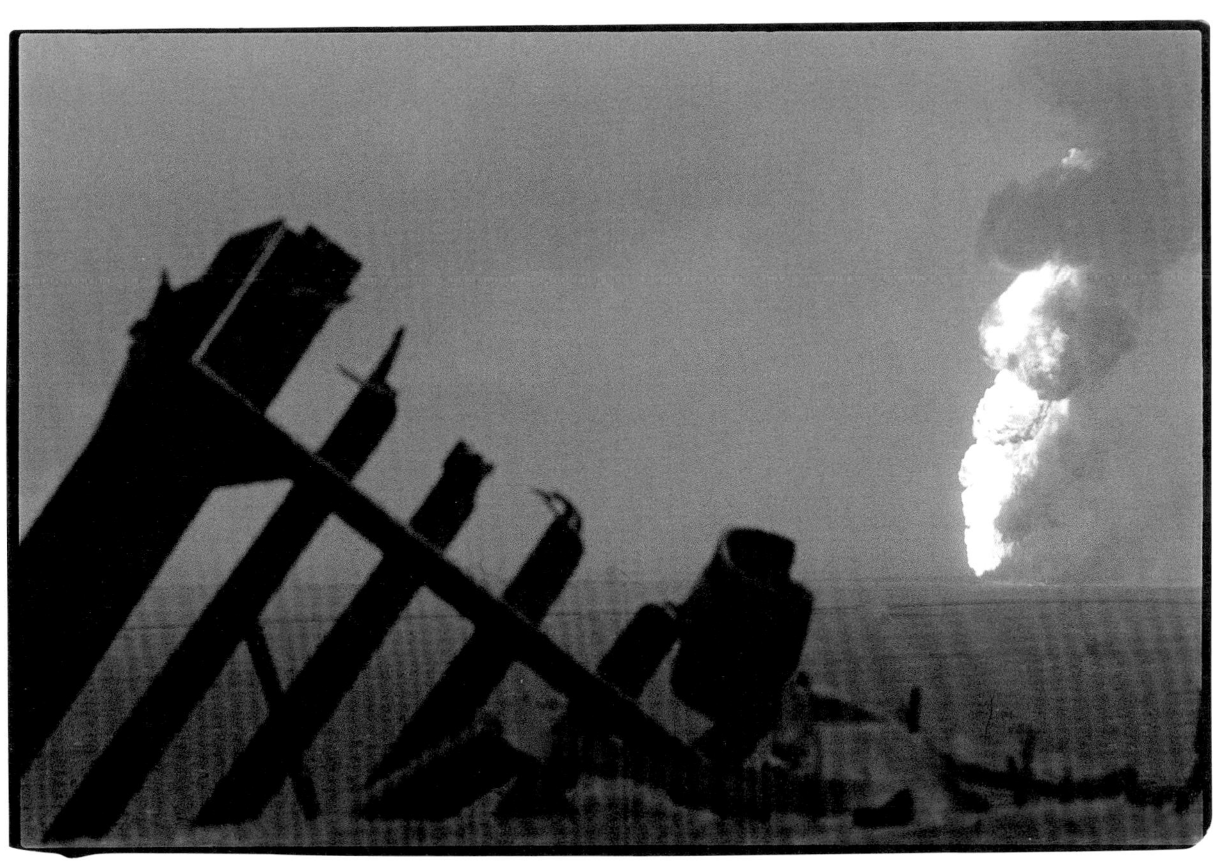

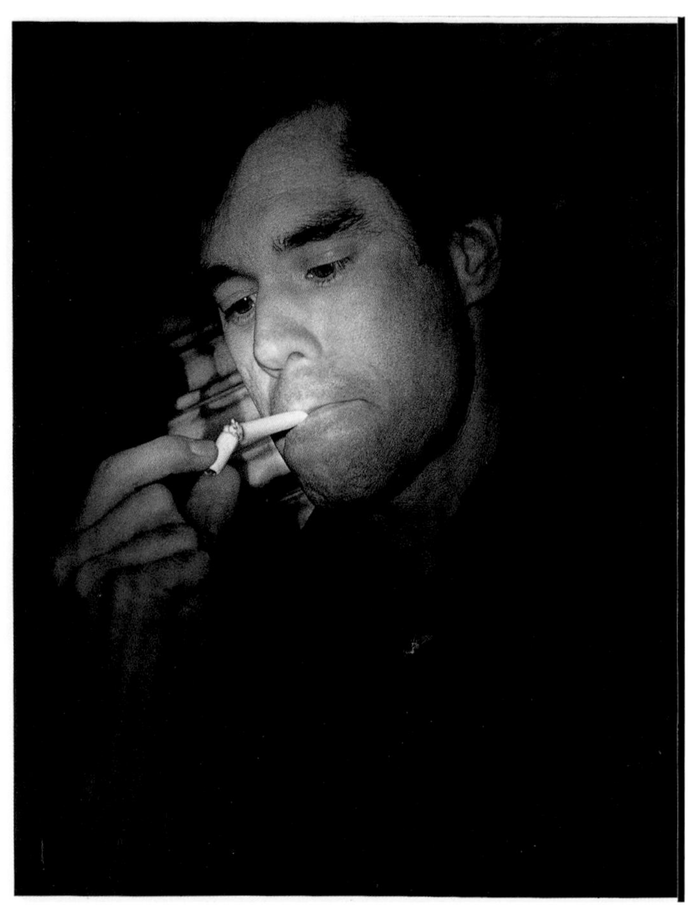

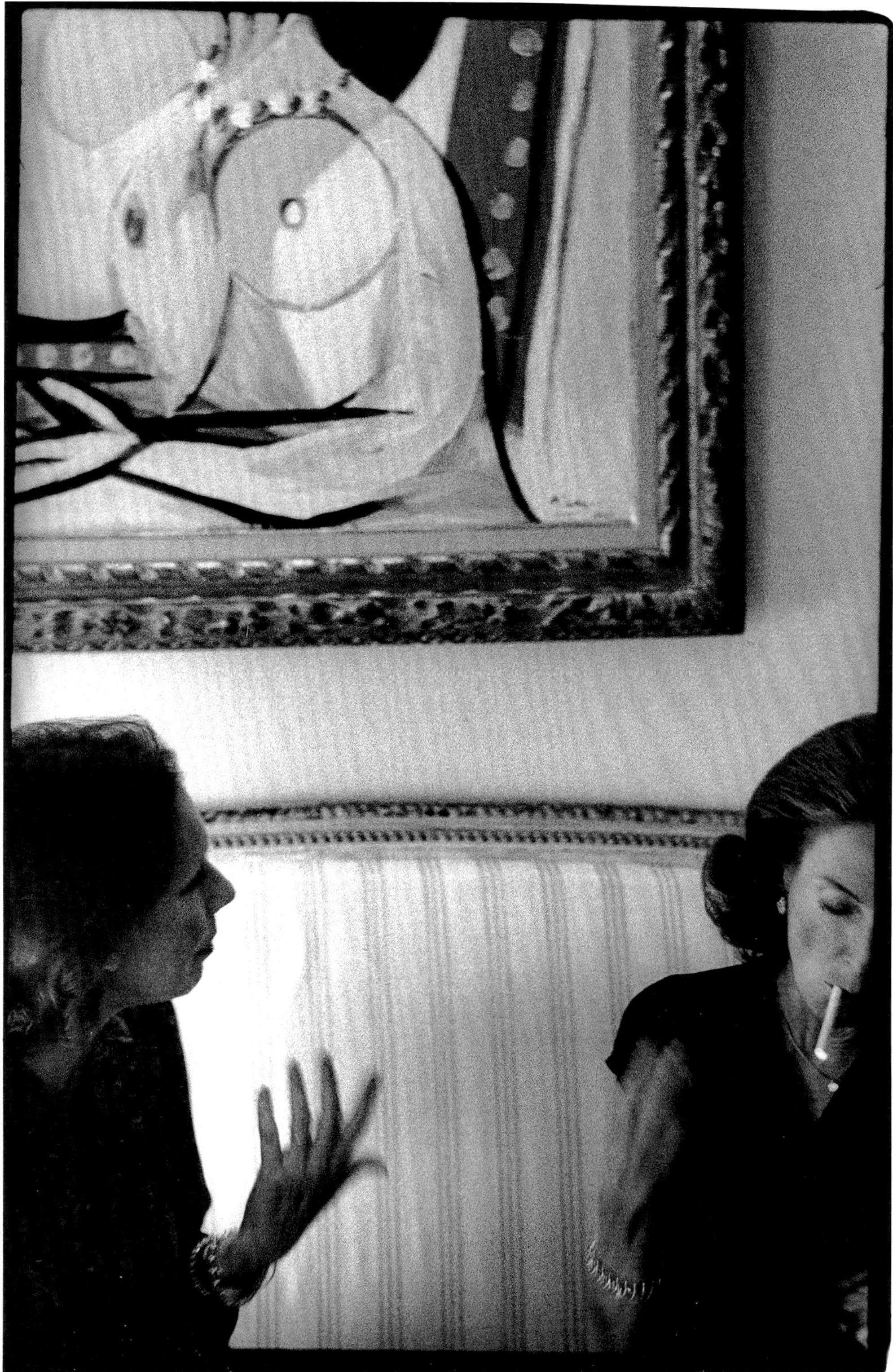

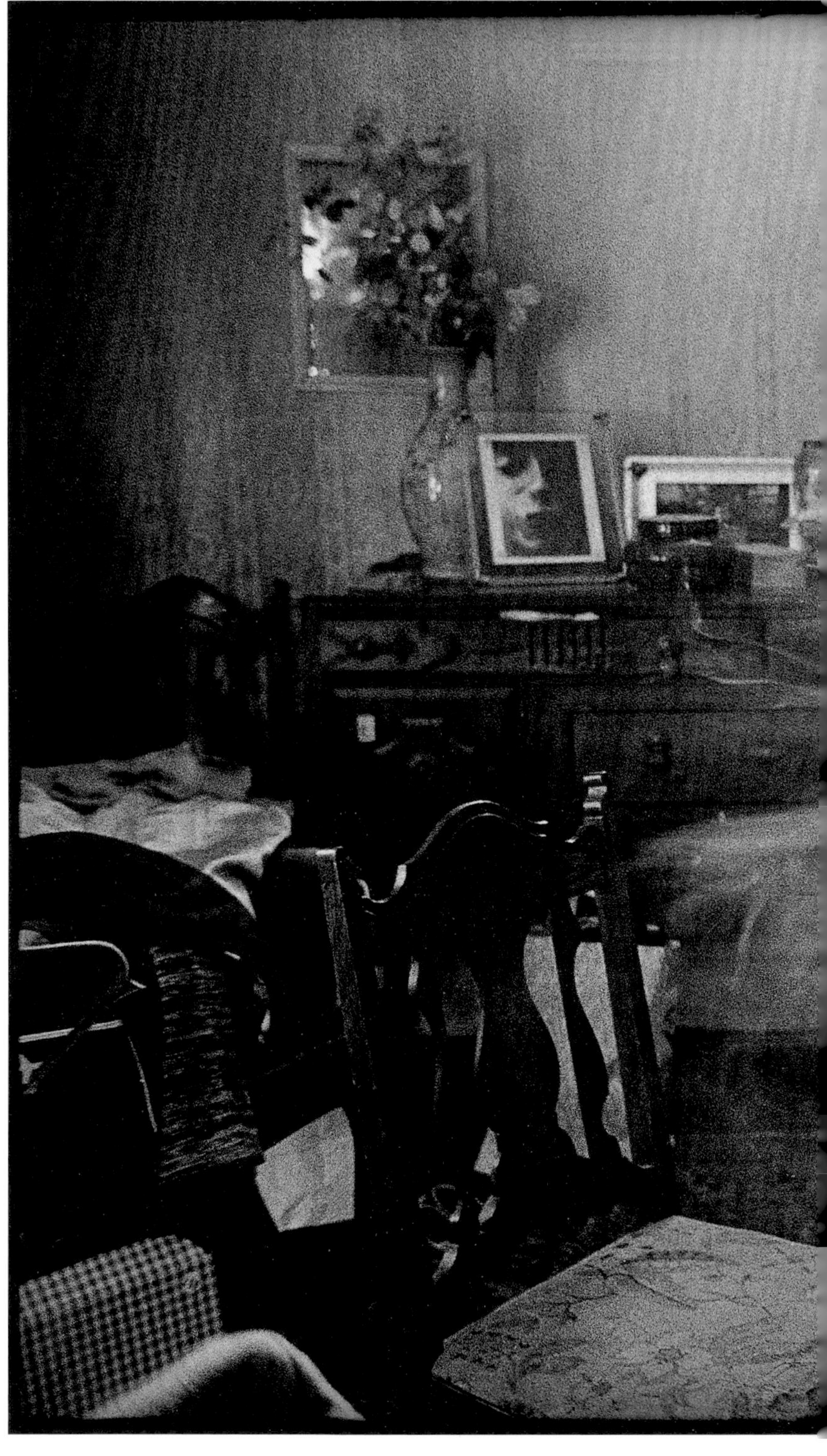

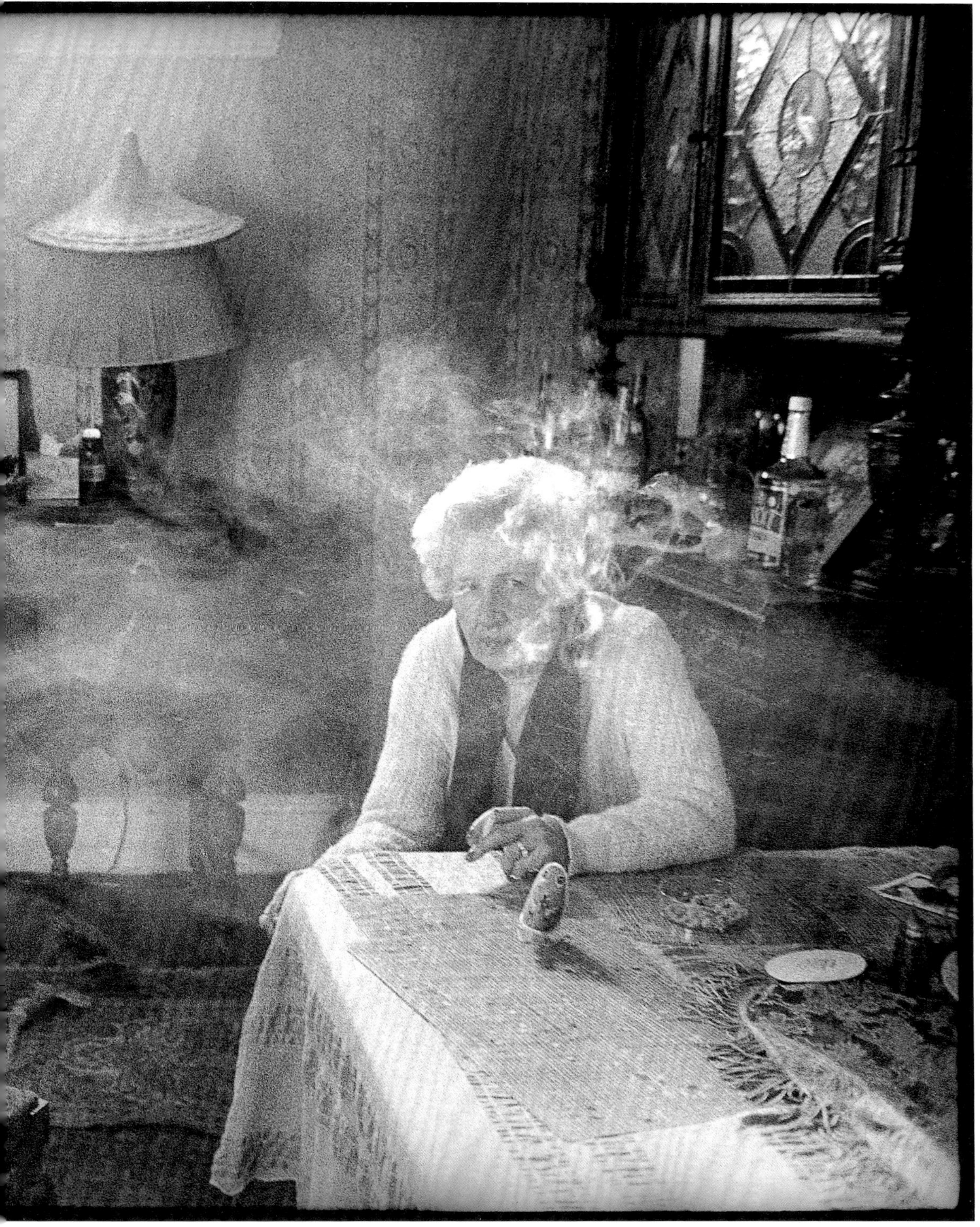

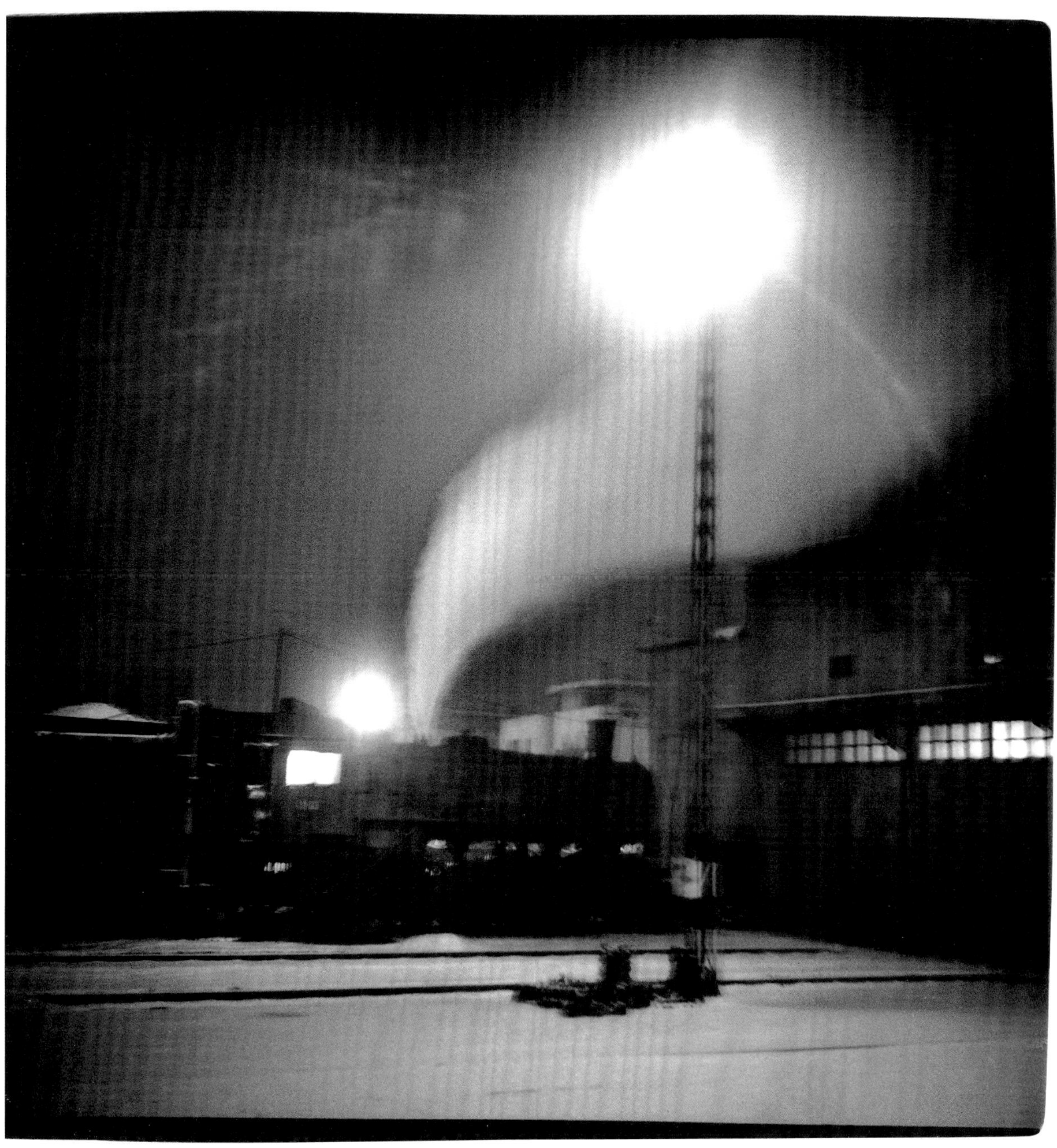

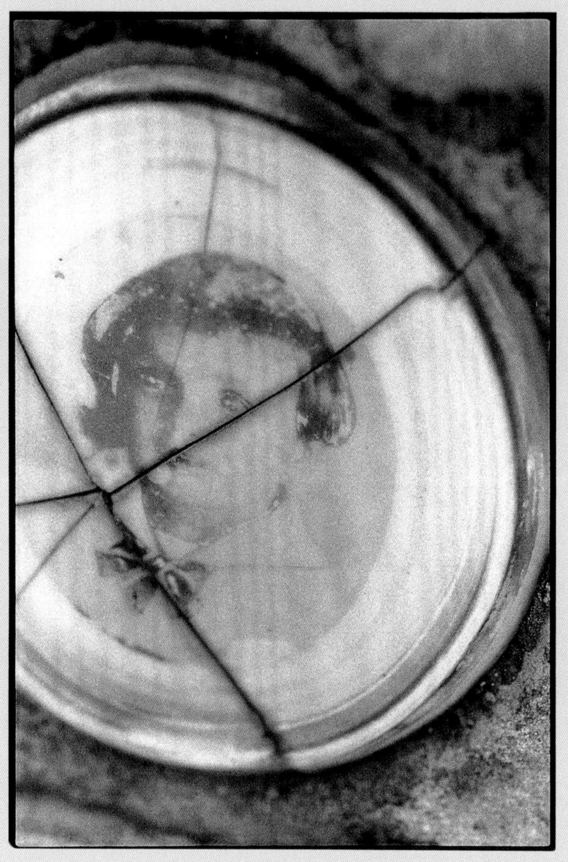

My first window was french and bare. From my pillow, tucked in safely, I waited and watched. Dust specks danced on rays of sun. Black smoke from chimneys rose like so many genies. Once, a blue parakeet flew in.

The night before each December 6, I placed my polished shoes between the double panes. By morning, Mikulas (Saint Nicholas) had filled one with candy and the other with twigs.

When I was six or seven I had a recurring vision. I would wake to the hypnotic smile of an Asian man with a wispy beard and no body. He beamed from the left corner of my window. Held by his gaze, I couldn't move but felt content.

One day I broke the spell. In my struggle to get up I fainted, and to my regret I've never seen him again.

The images in mirrors and windows never last. A puddle briefly holds reflections, but when I trap a vision through the lens of my camera it can't escape.

Wedded to their pictures, most frames perish with them. Those holding portraits of political leaders may be the exception. I was in Belgrade in 1992, after the Iron Curtain fell, and Yugoslavia was at war. There, still hanging on the wall of a bureaucrat's office, was the empty frame that had once held the portrait of Marshal Tito, himself the longtime frame for that discordant nation.

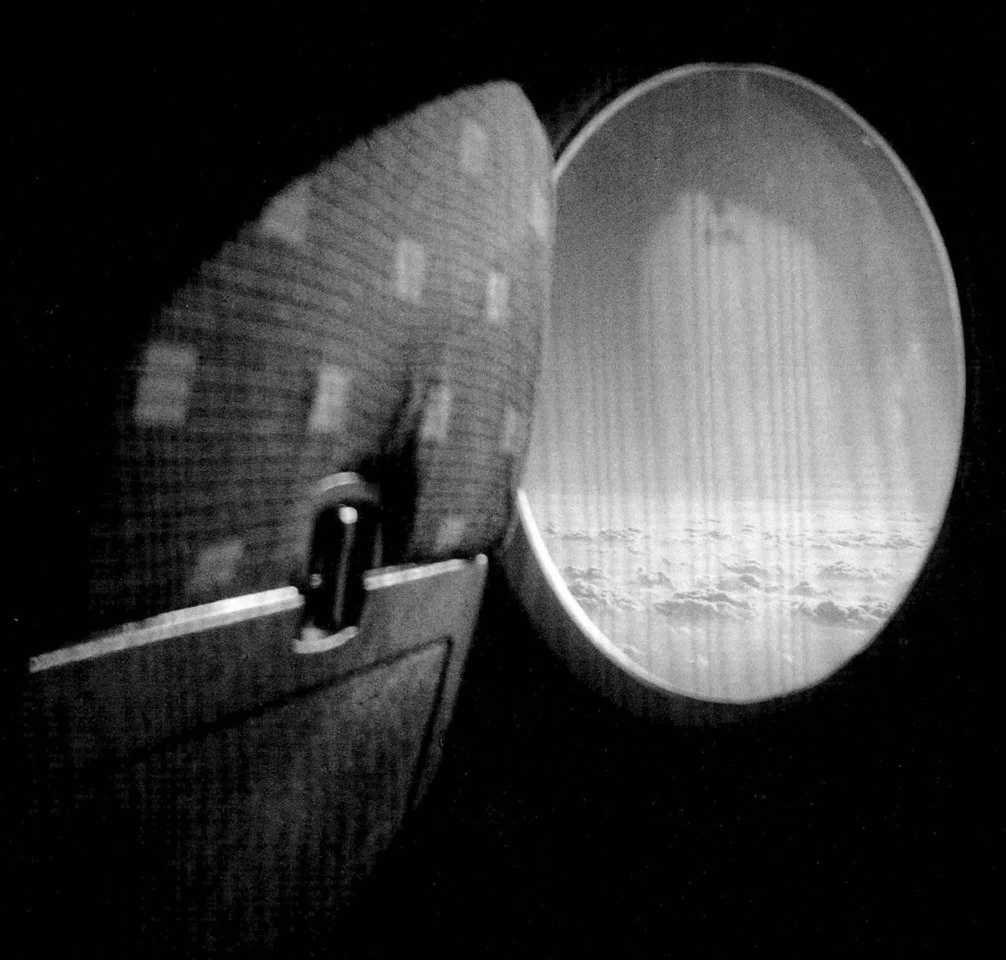

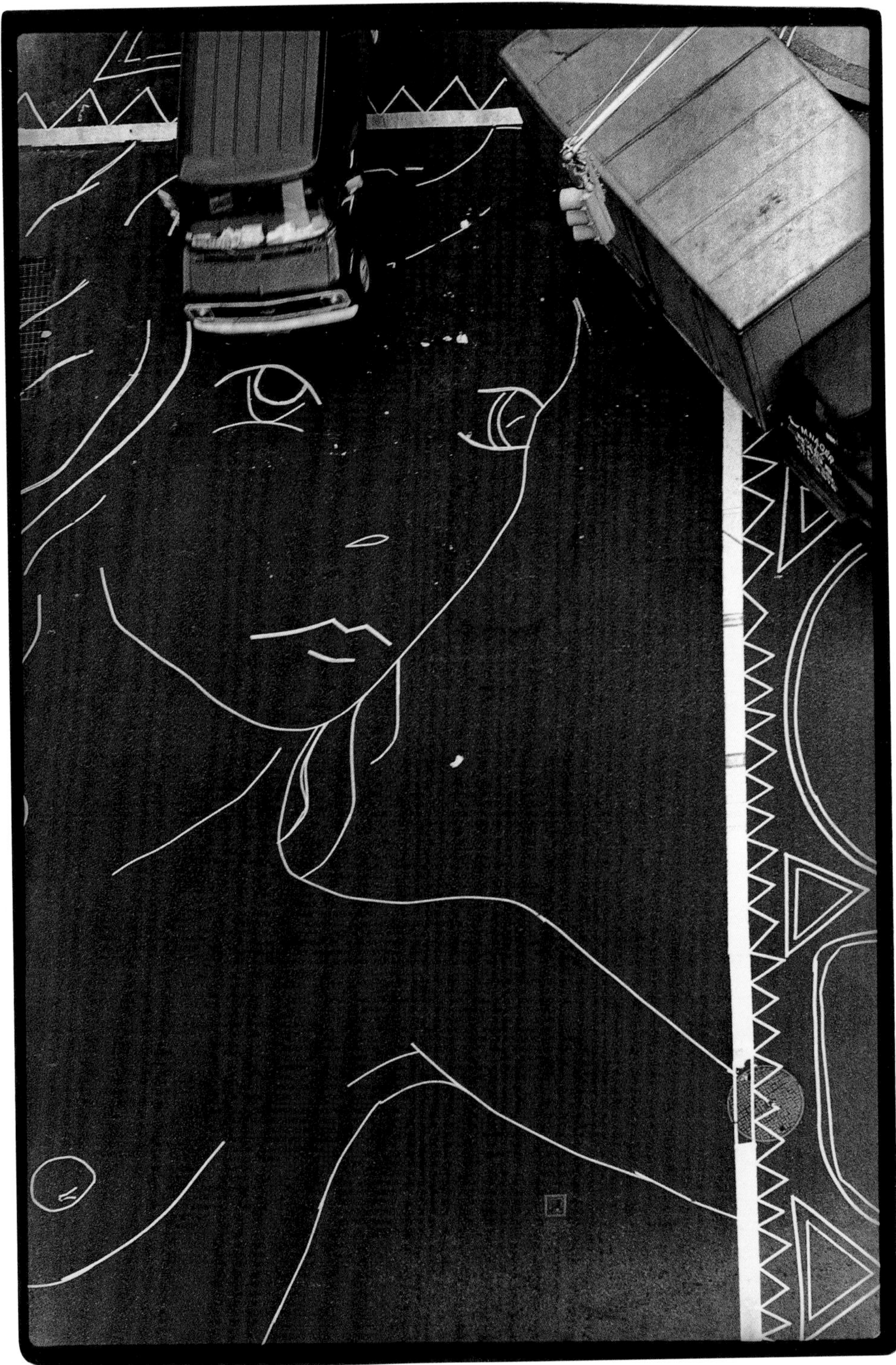

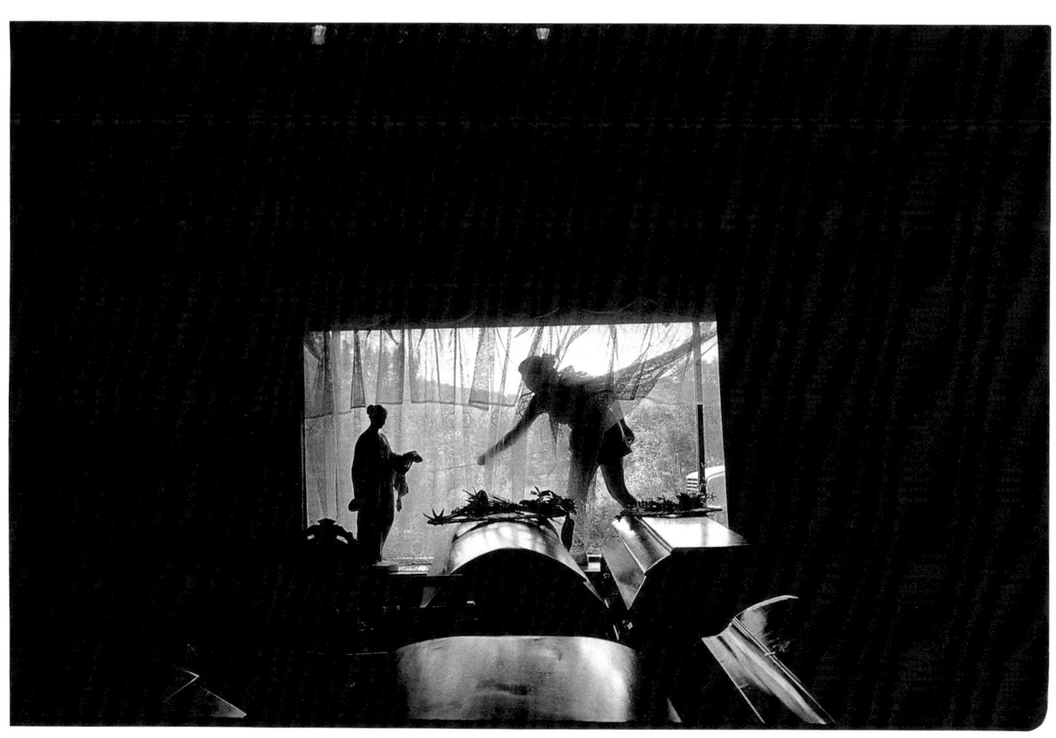

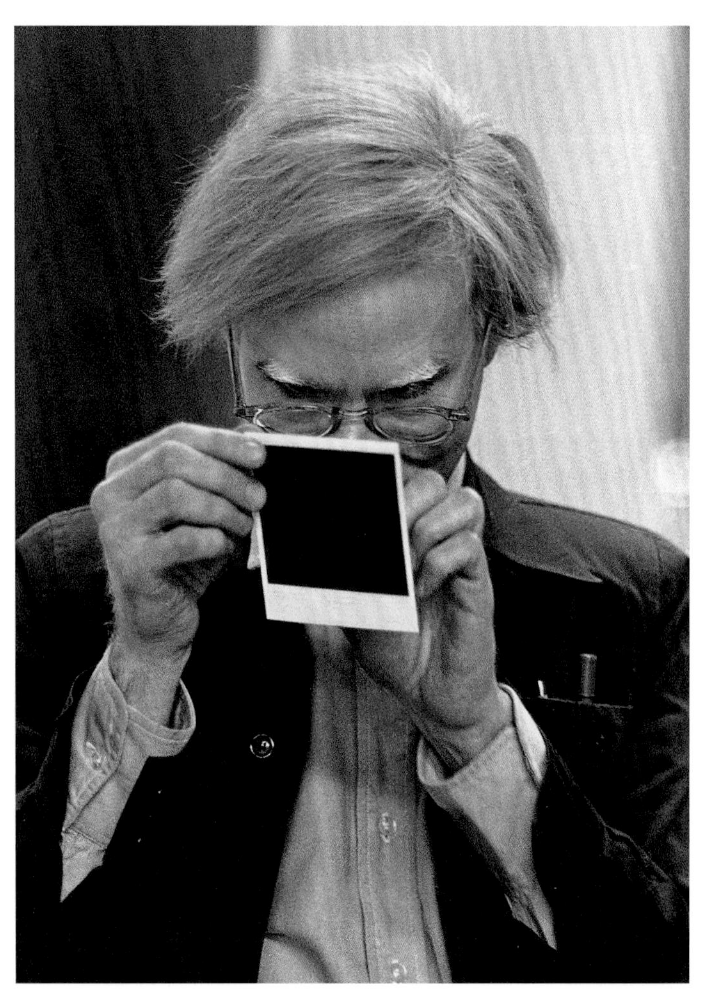

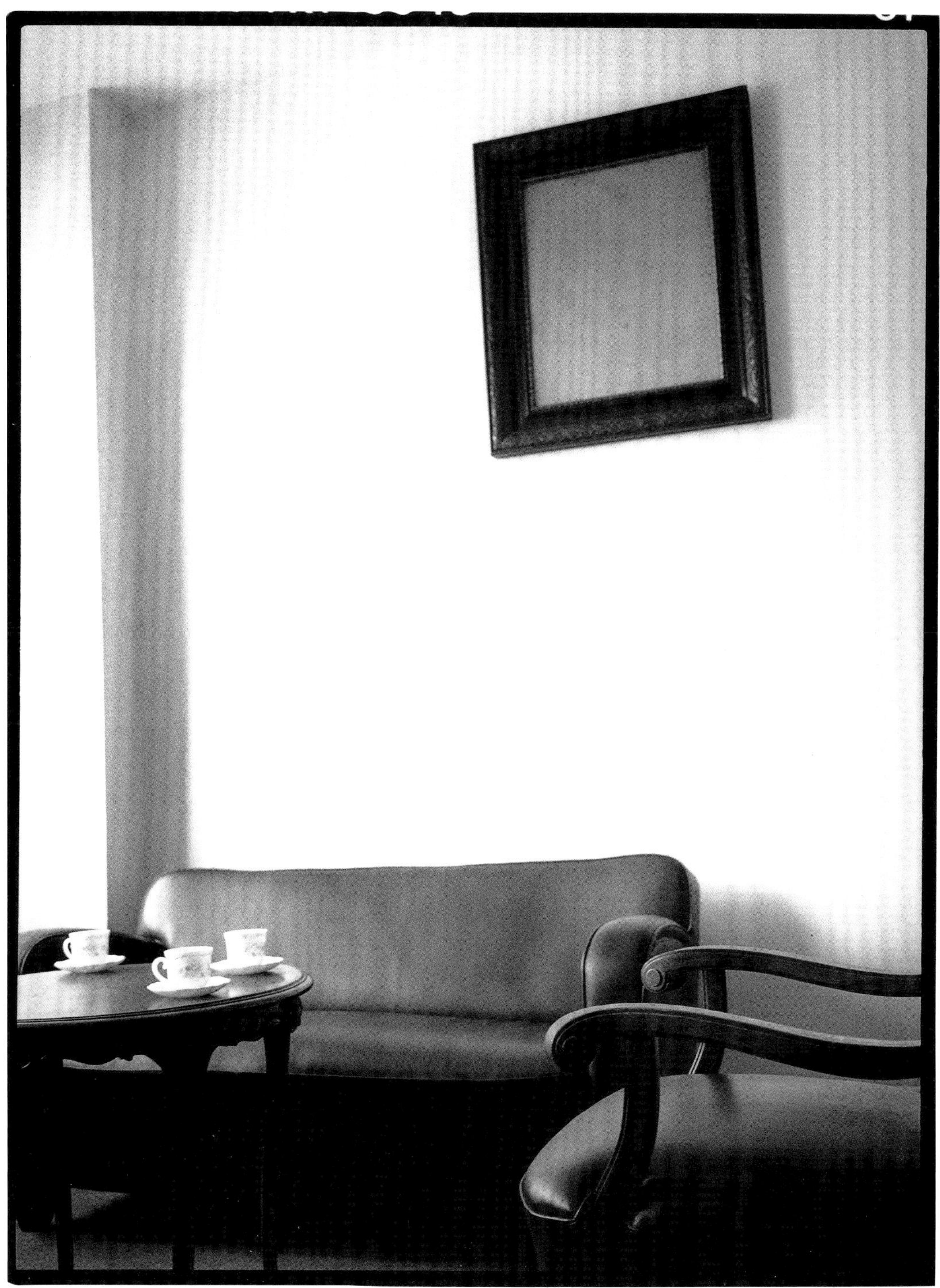

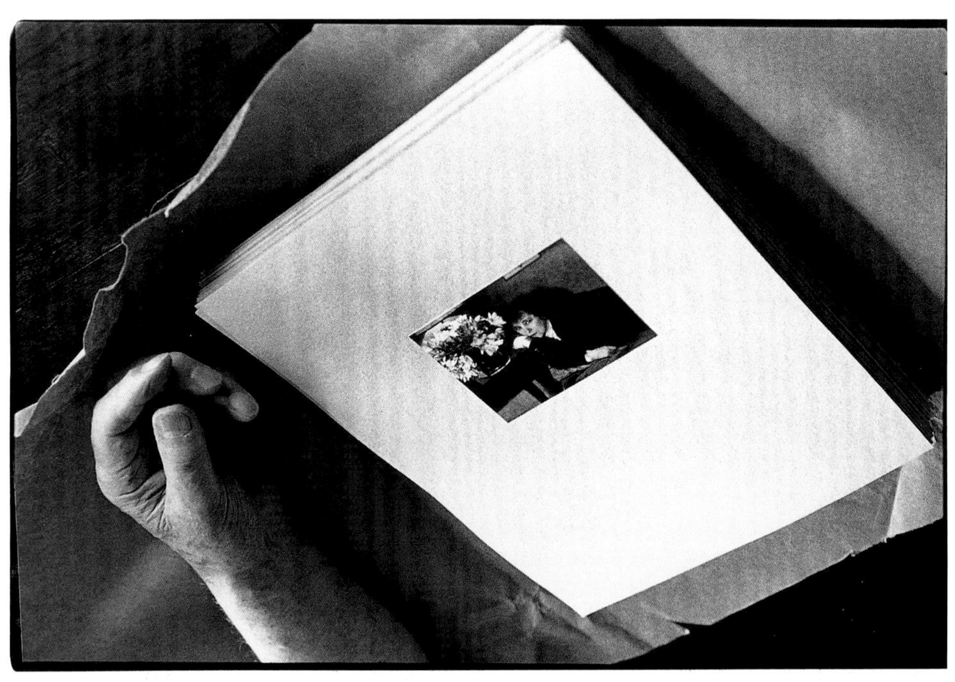

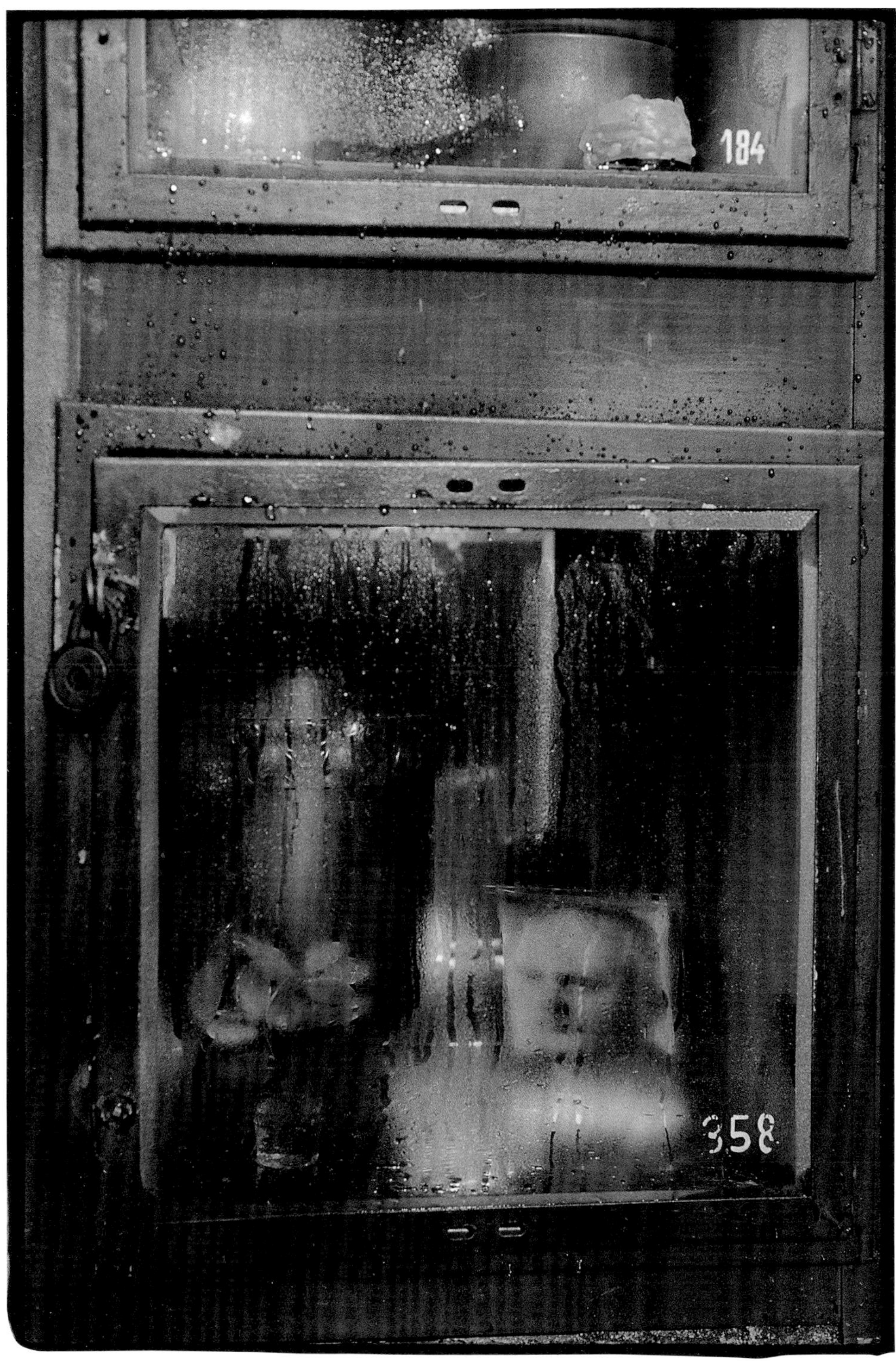
184
358

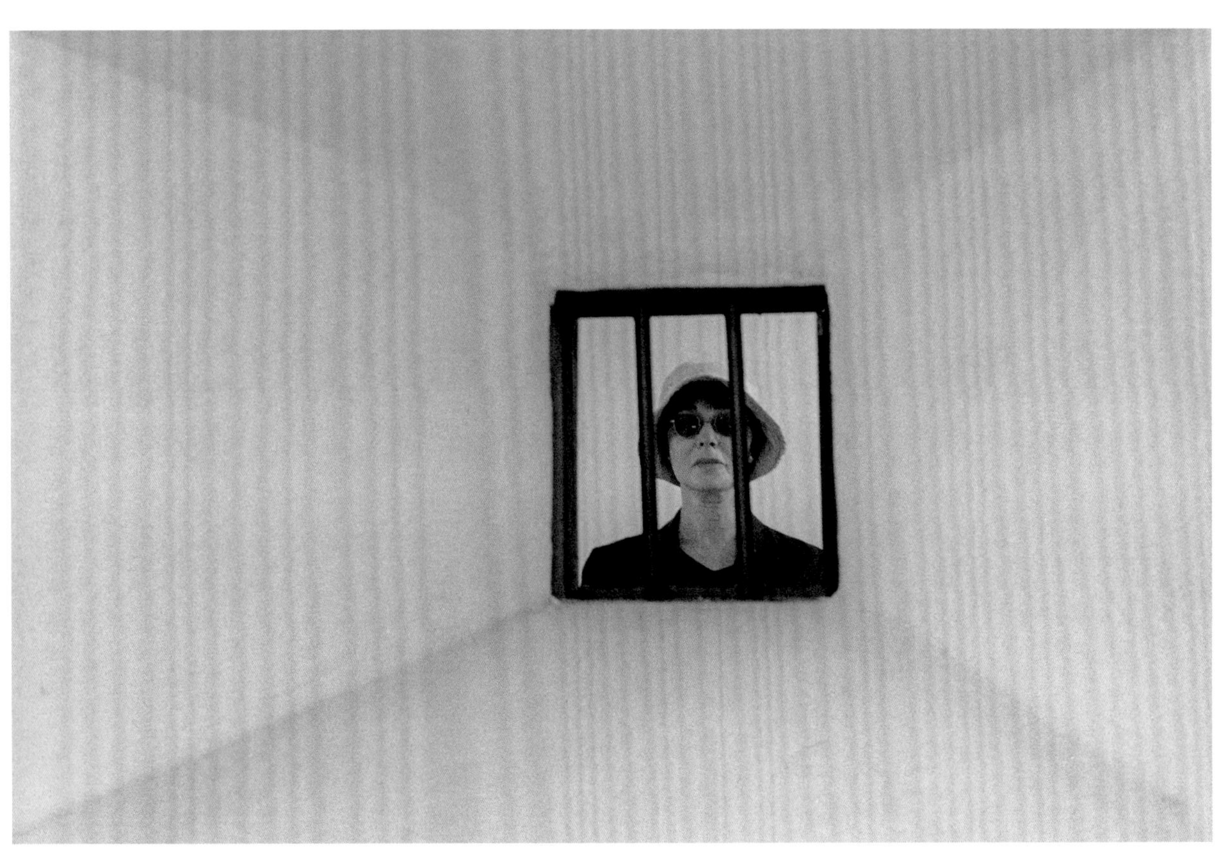

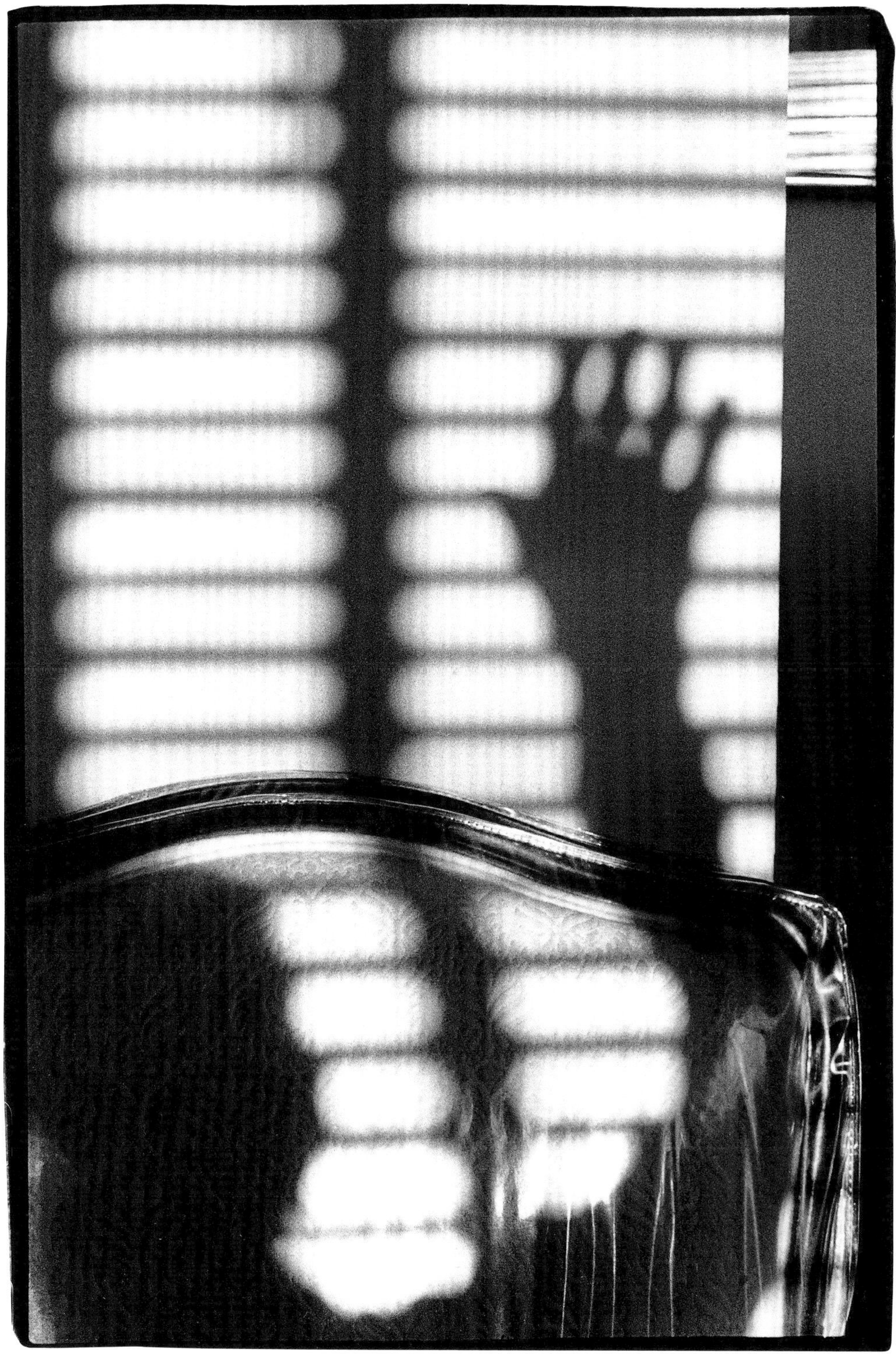

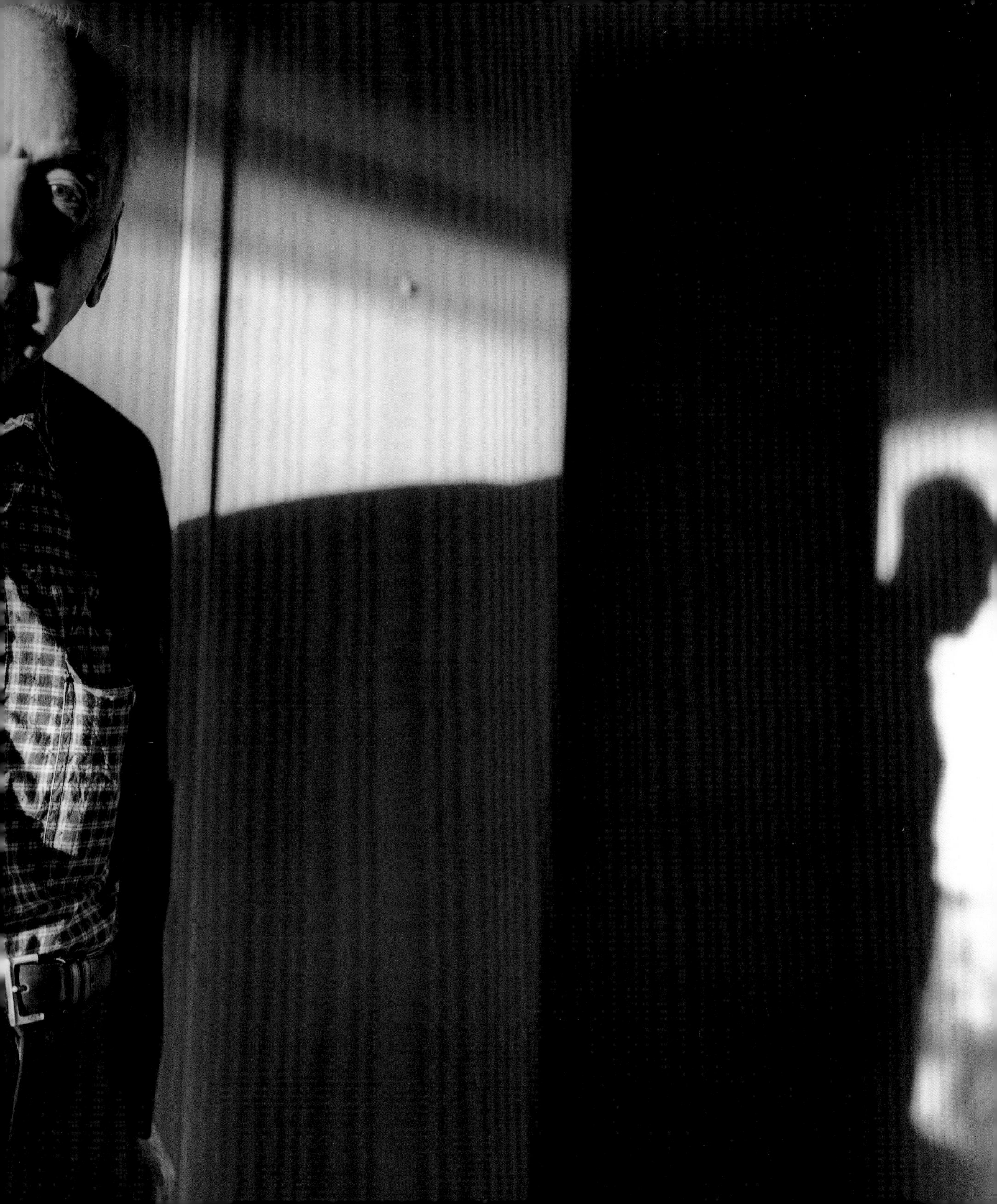

The past redoubles itself.

Has everything already happened?

Once, when I was small, I stood on a chair and rummaged through my parents' desk. I found a faded photograph of a little girl. She had a large bow in her hair and was standing on a chair. I thought it was me, but it turned out to be my mother.

Passing a store window I'm startled by my reflection; I look so crumpled and worn. I turn away. The specter follows, slinking along on glistening walls, insistently. On the ground she stalks me as my shadow. We used to be like twins. But I turned my back on her and set out to mirror the world.

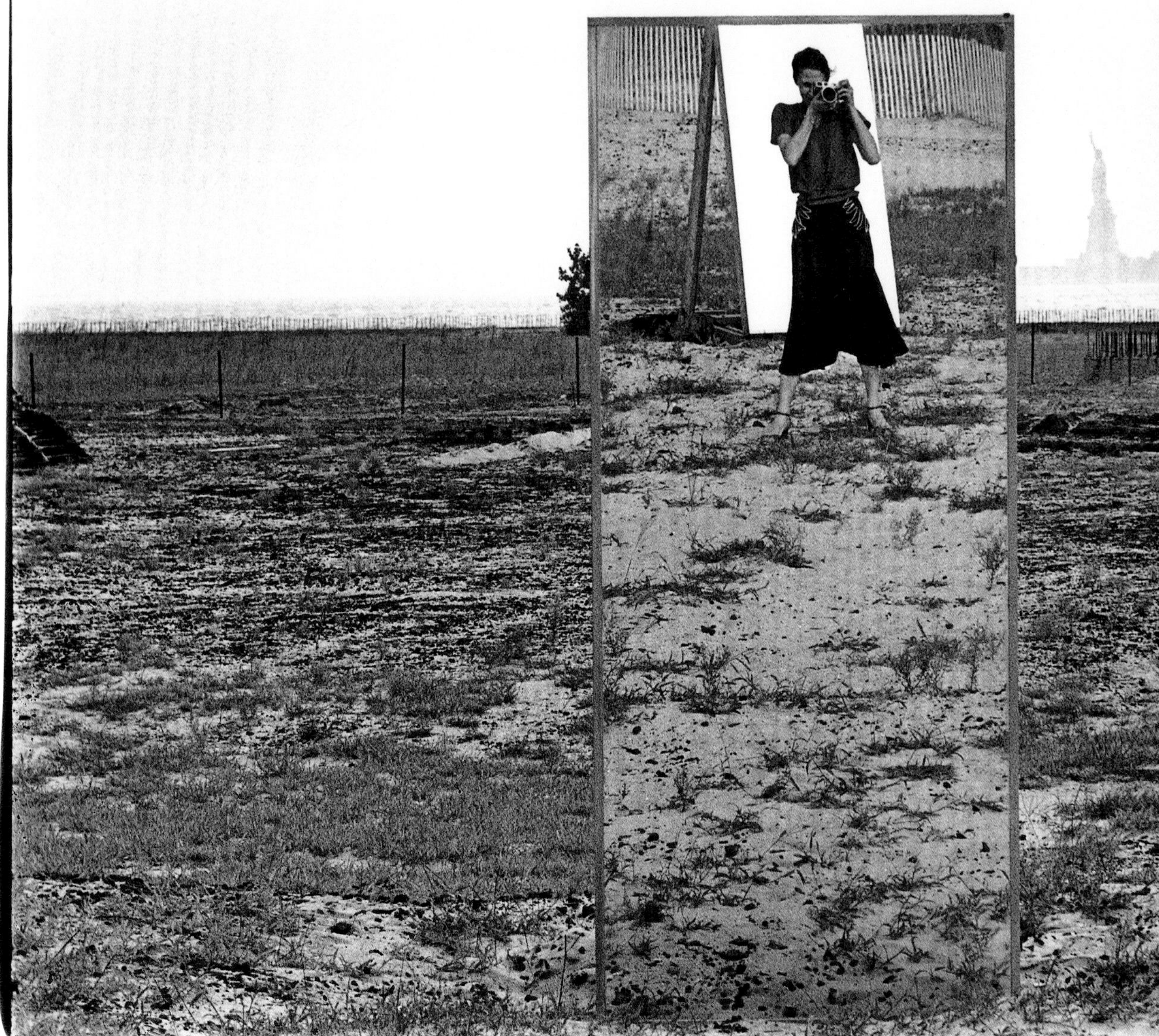

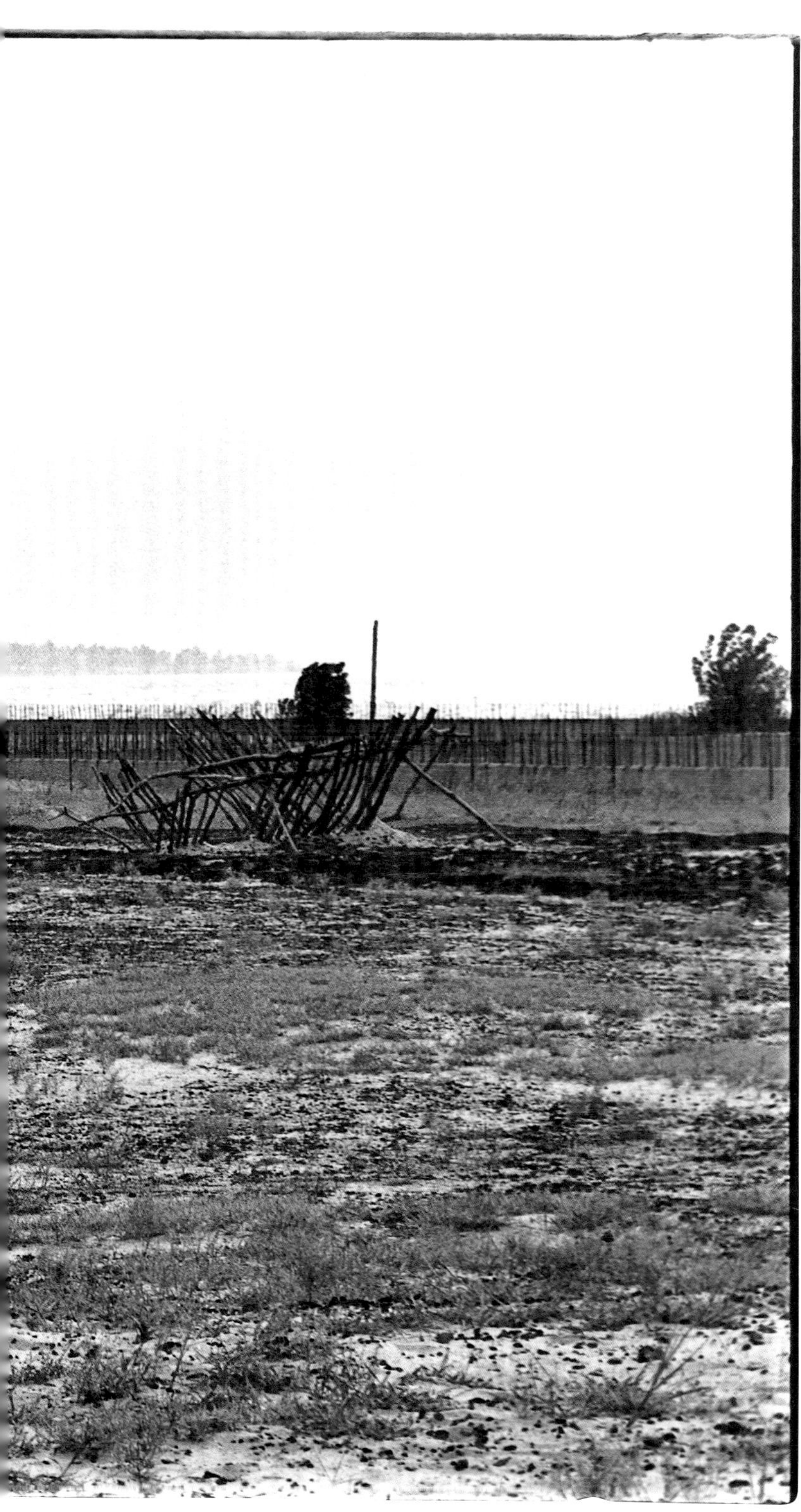

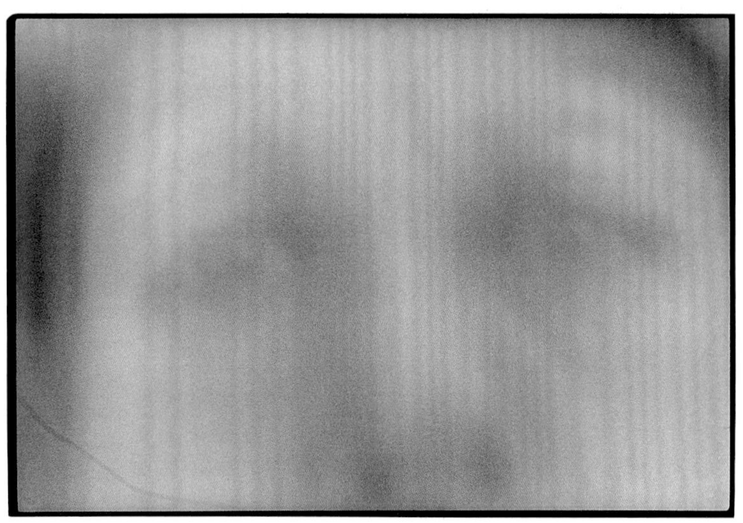

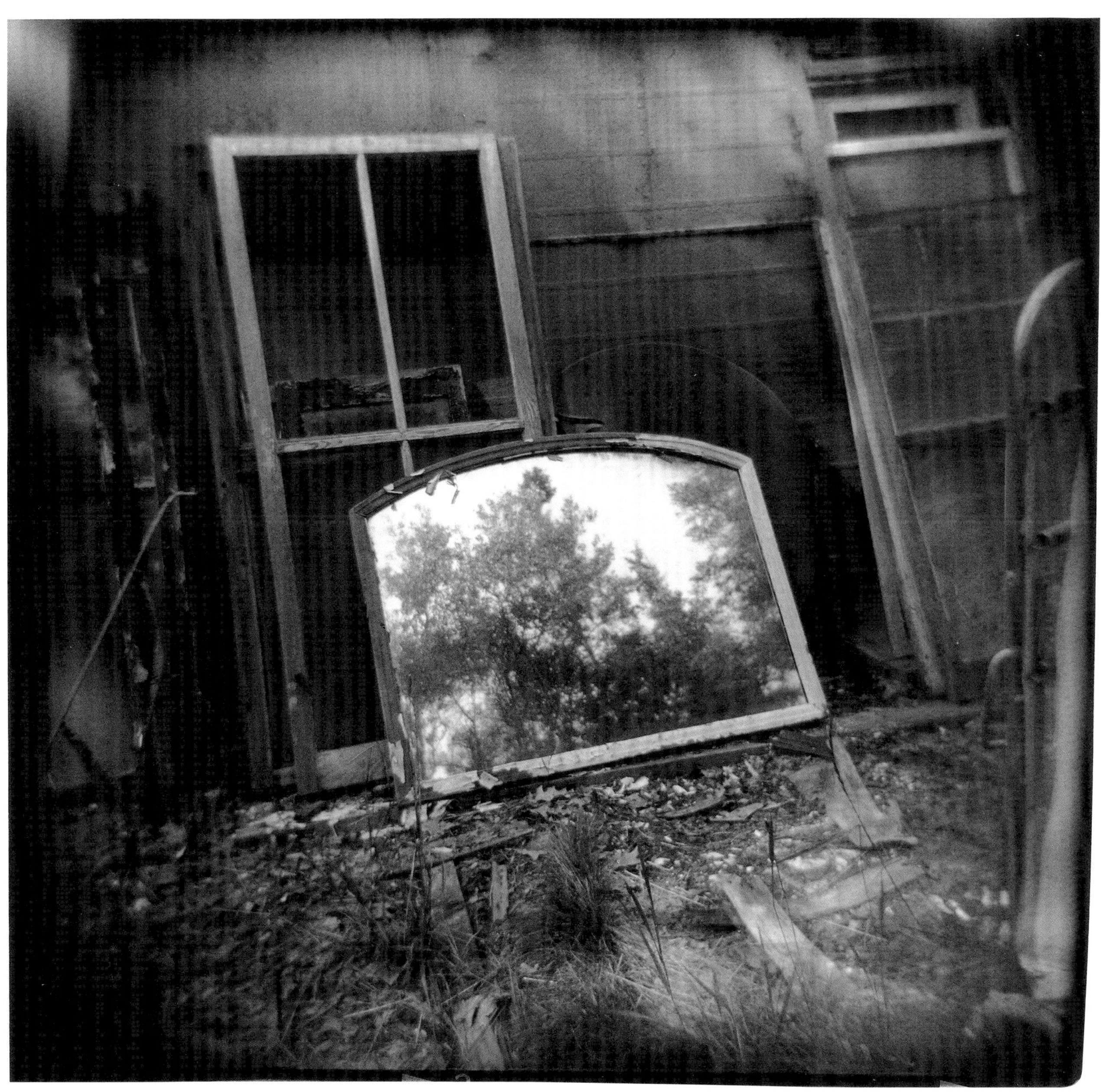

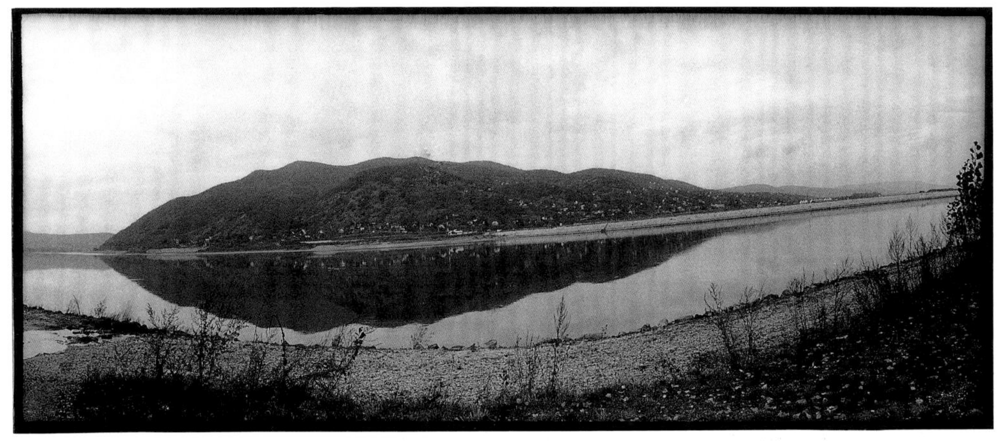

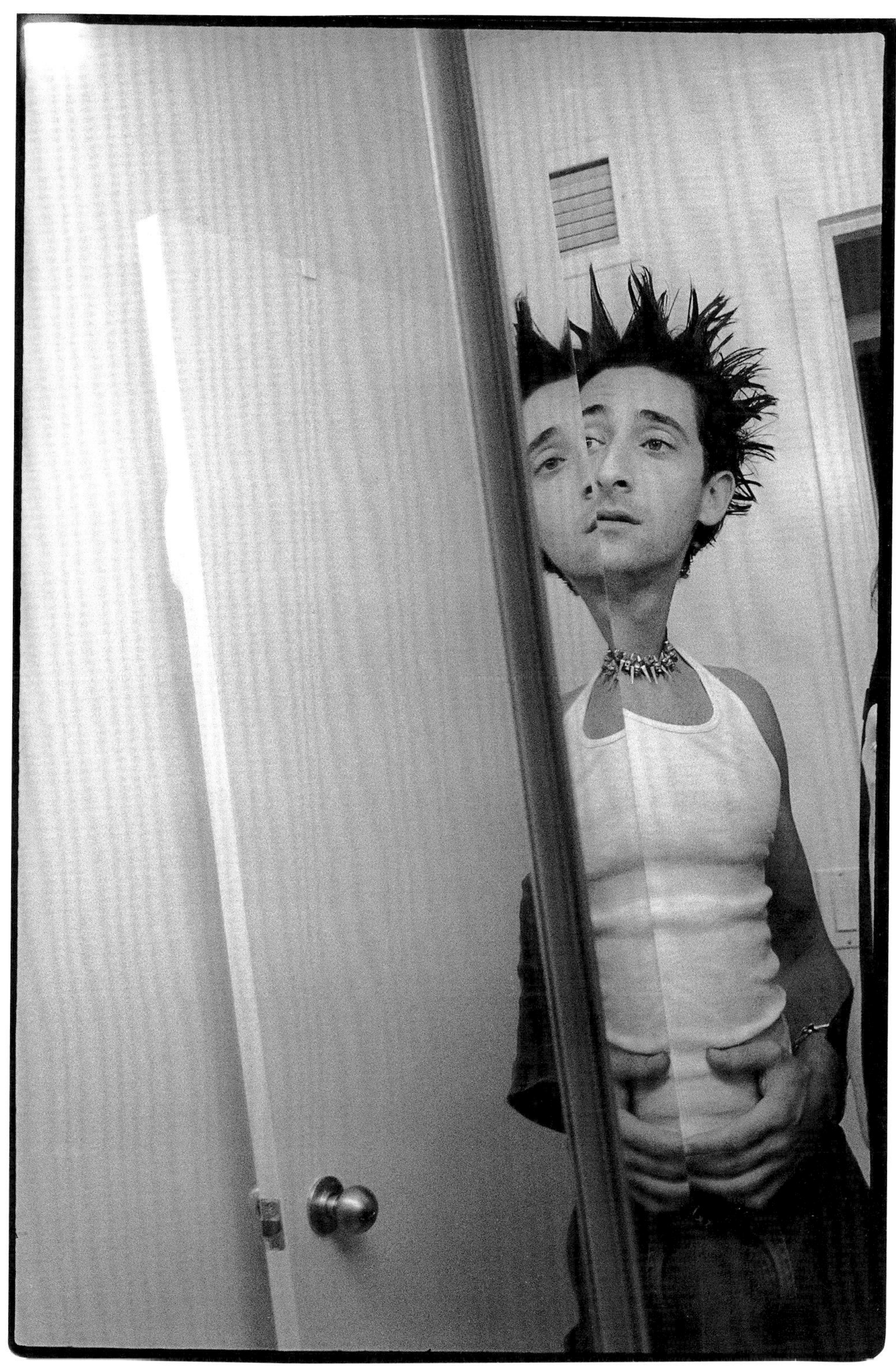

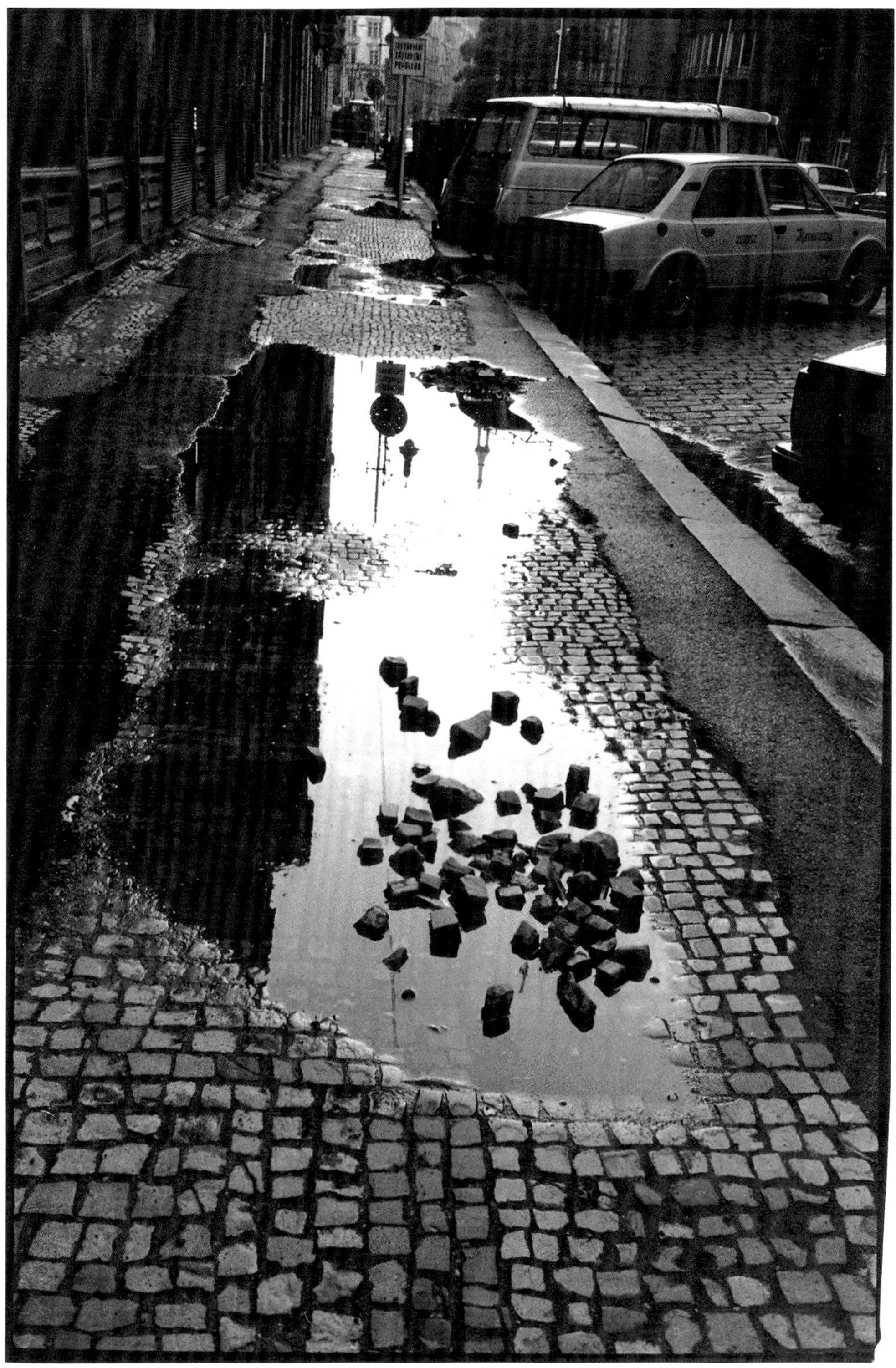

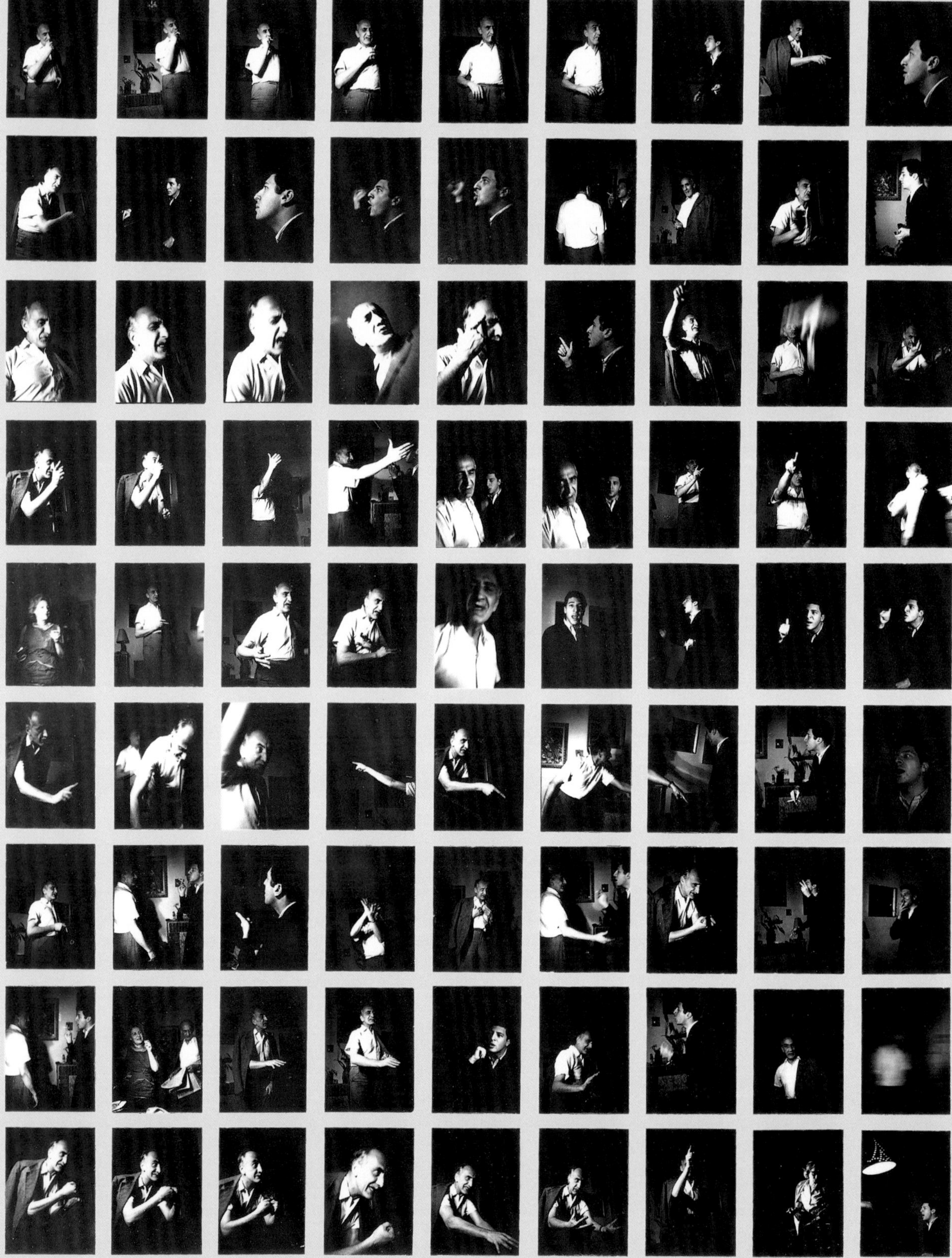

Robert the Hungarian lives in Central Park. He says it helps his memory to walk a figure 8 over and over again.

Long ago, my future husband Elliot and my father would engage in frequent, passionate debate. Their fights usually ended in a draw. They agreed on nothing; they argued anyway.

A mother in Florida used to take Polaroids of her son. Now that he's been murdered she takes Polaroids of his grave.

At a Red Sox game, I overheard a young autograph seeker: "Mr. Vaughn! . . . Mr. Canseco! . . . Mr. Clemens!" When no one came, he wailed "ANYBODY!"

At the heart of every obsession is a howl. There is no great accomplishment without it. Who isn't driven? What Nabokov said about art is true of stamp collecting, fans, and every other compulsion: "It's a relief from the itch of being."

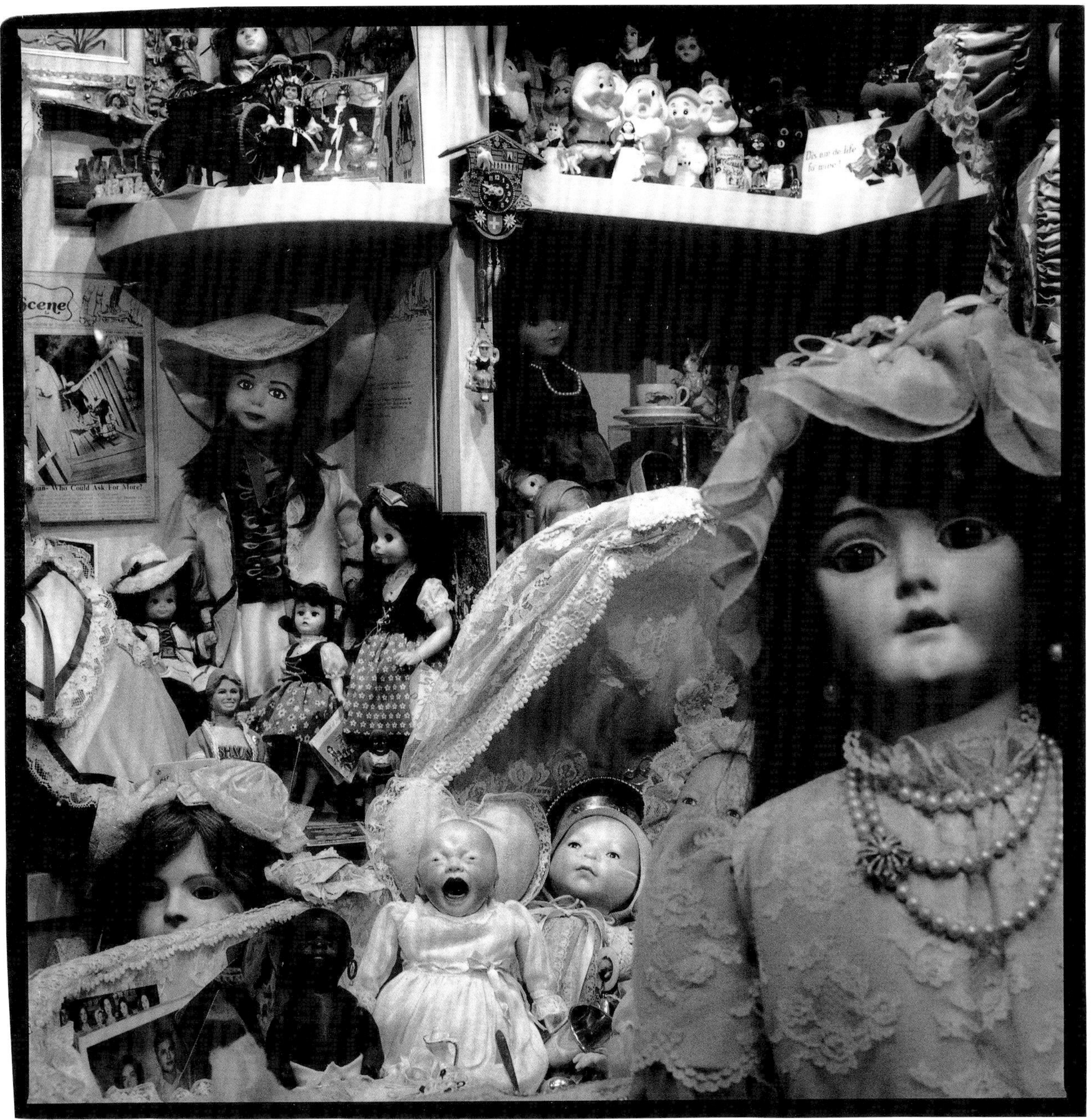
Scene

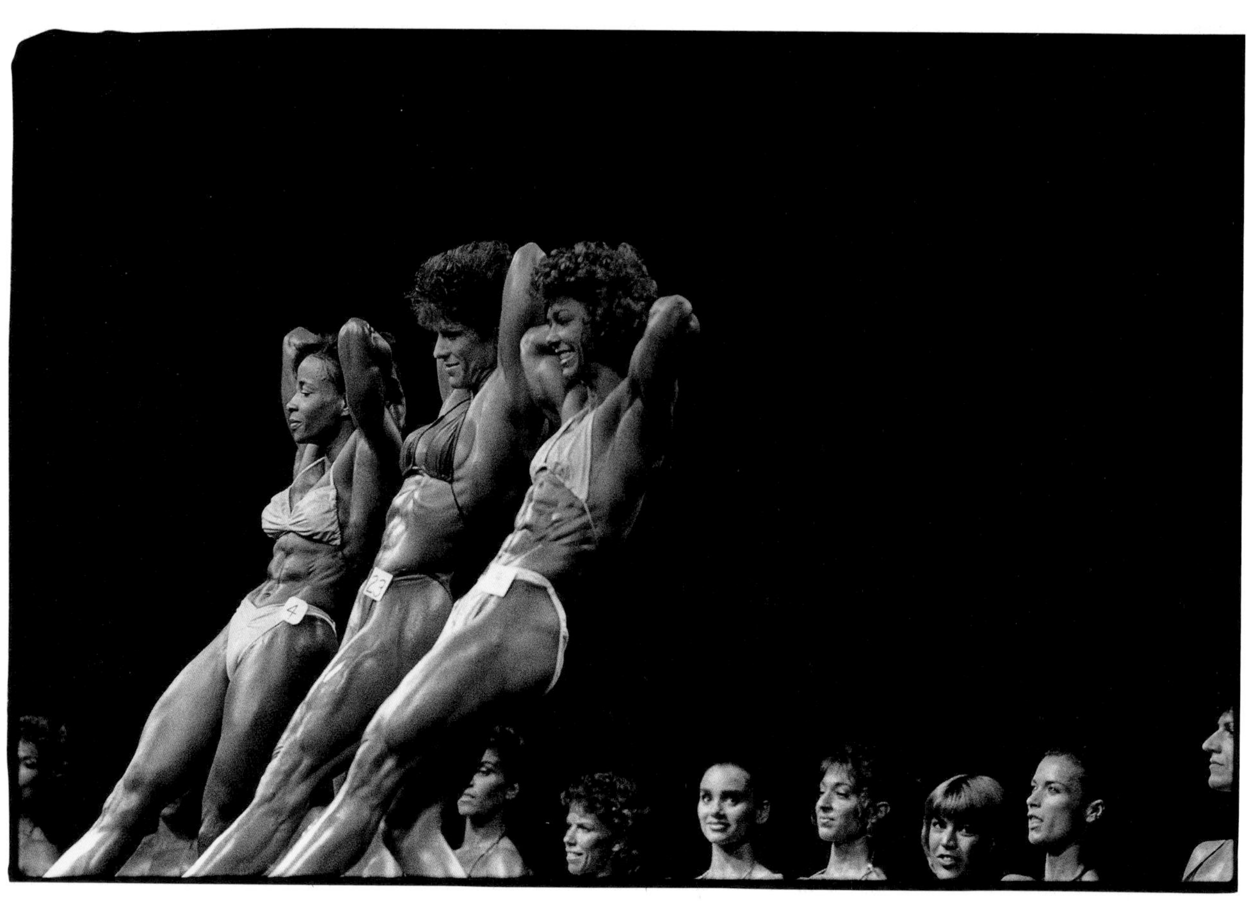
4
23

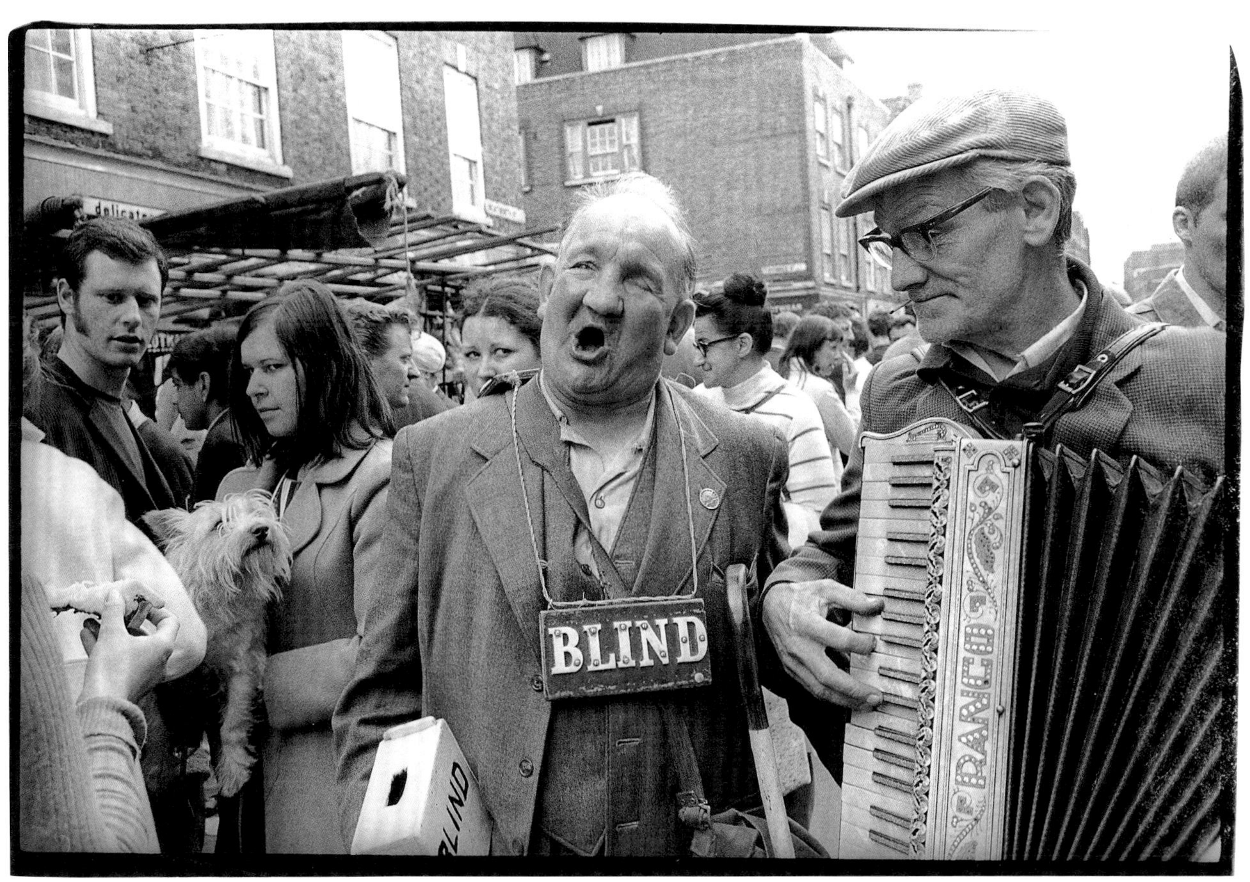
BLIND

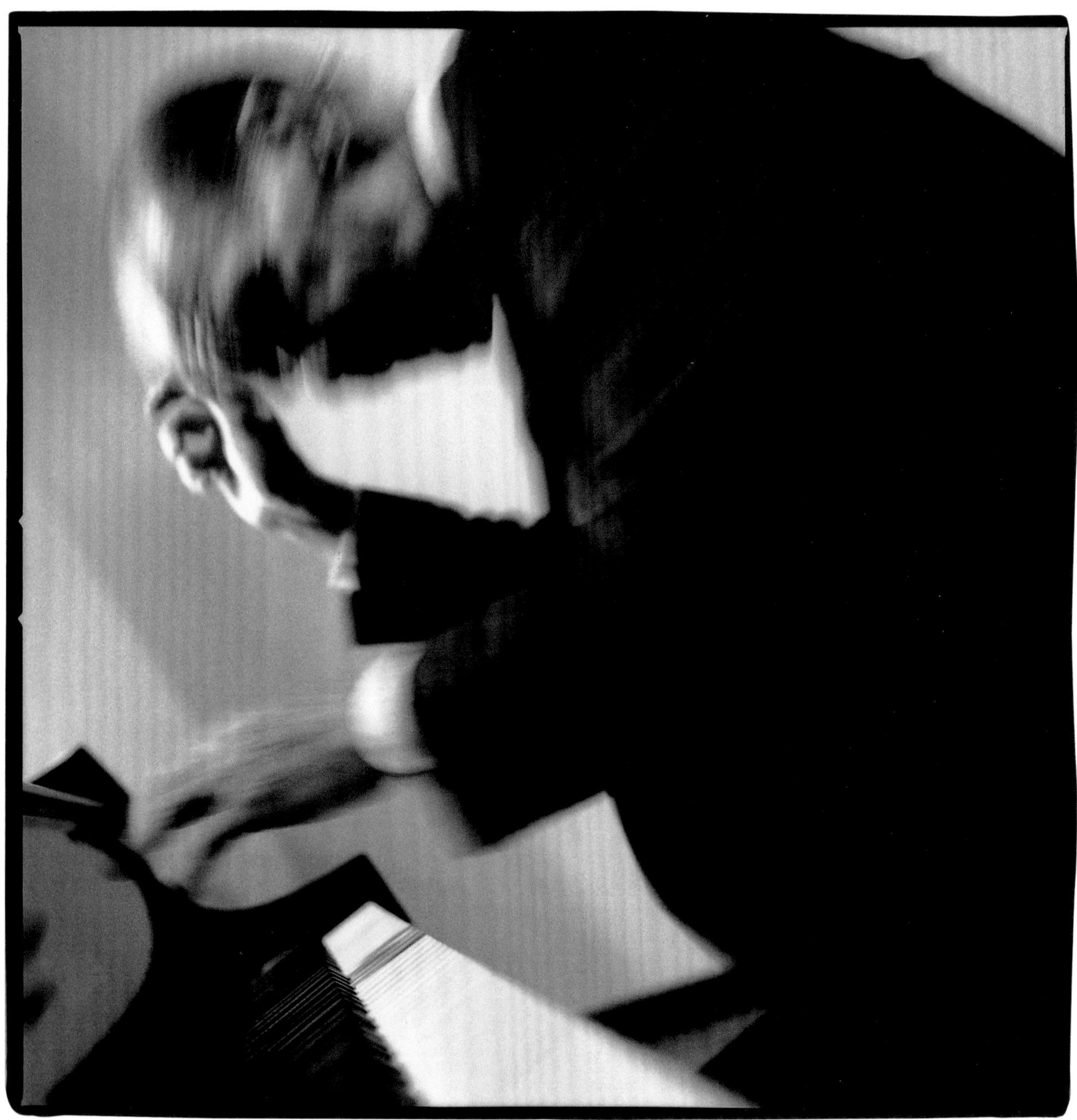

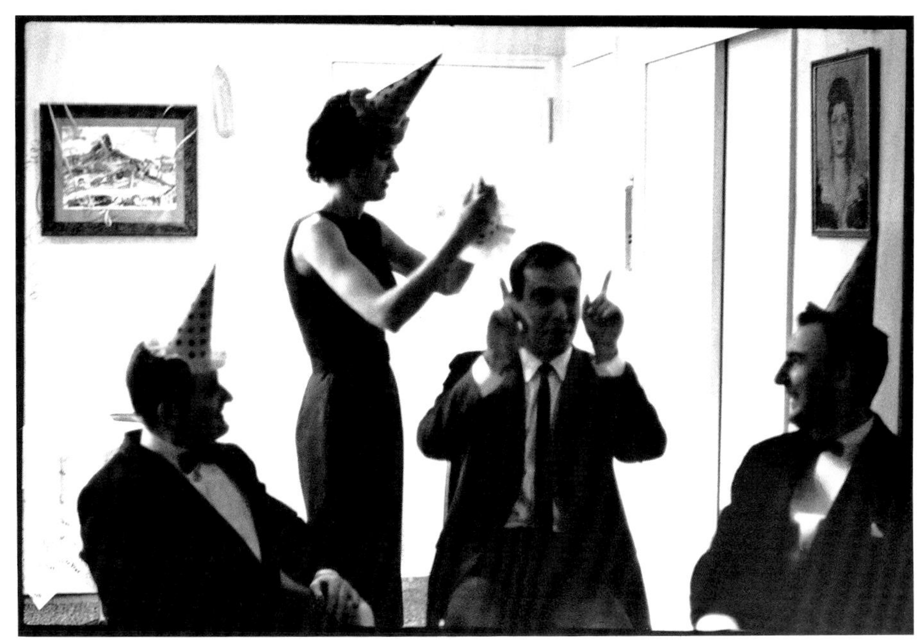

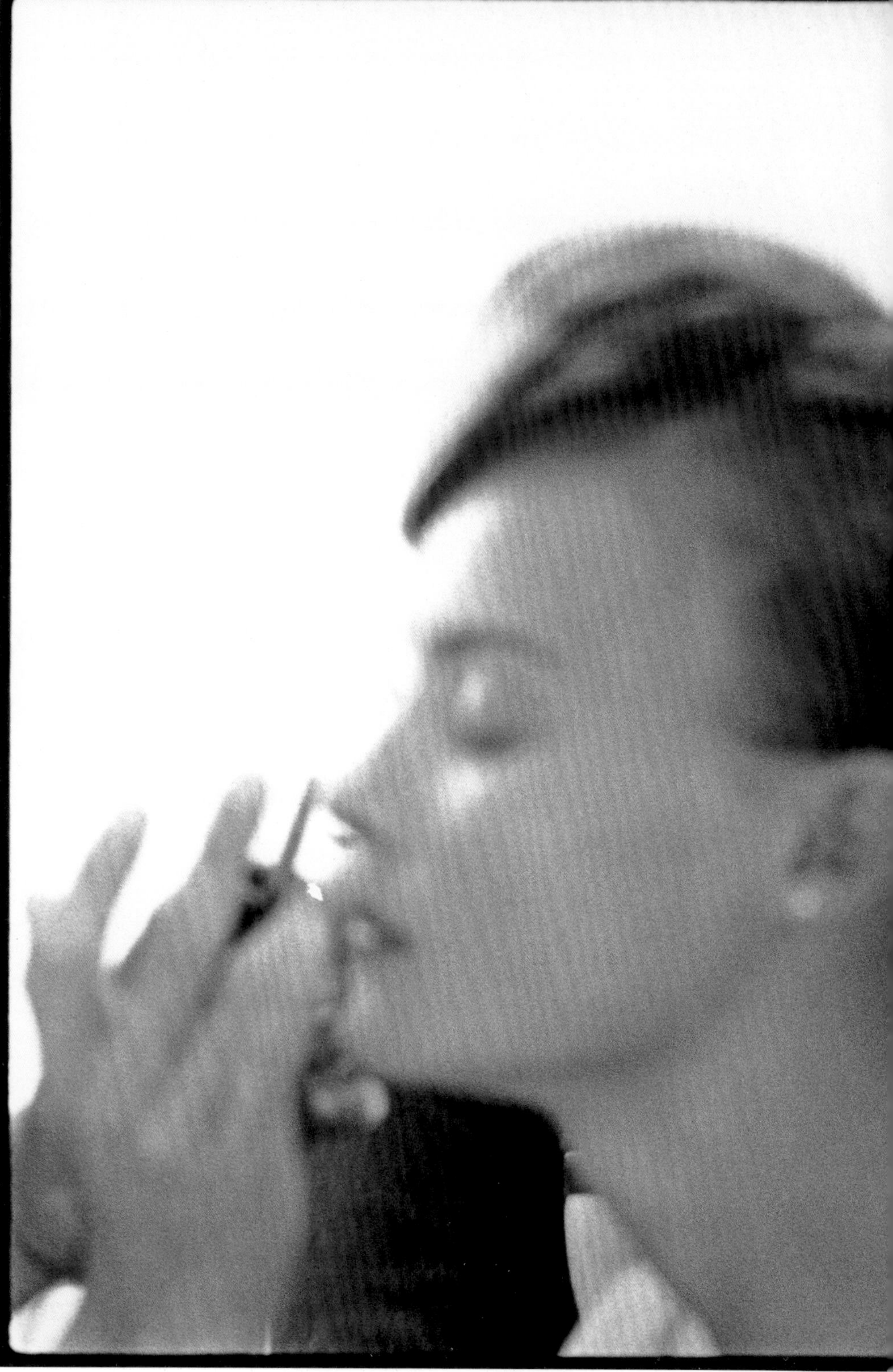

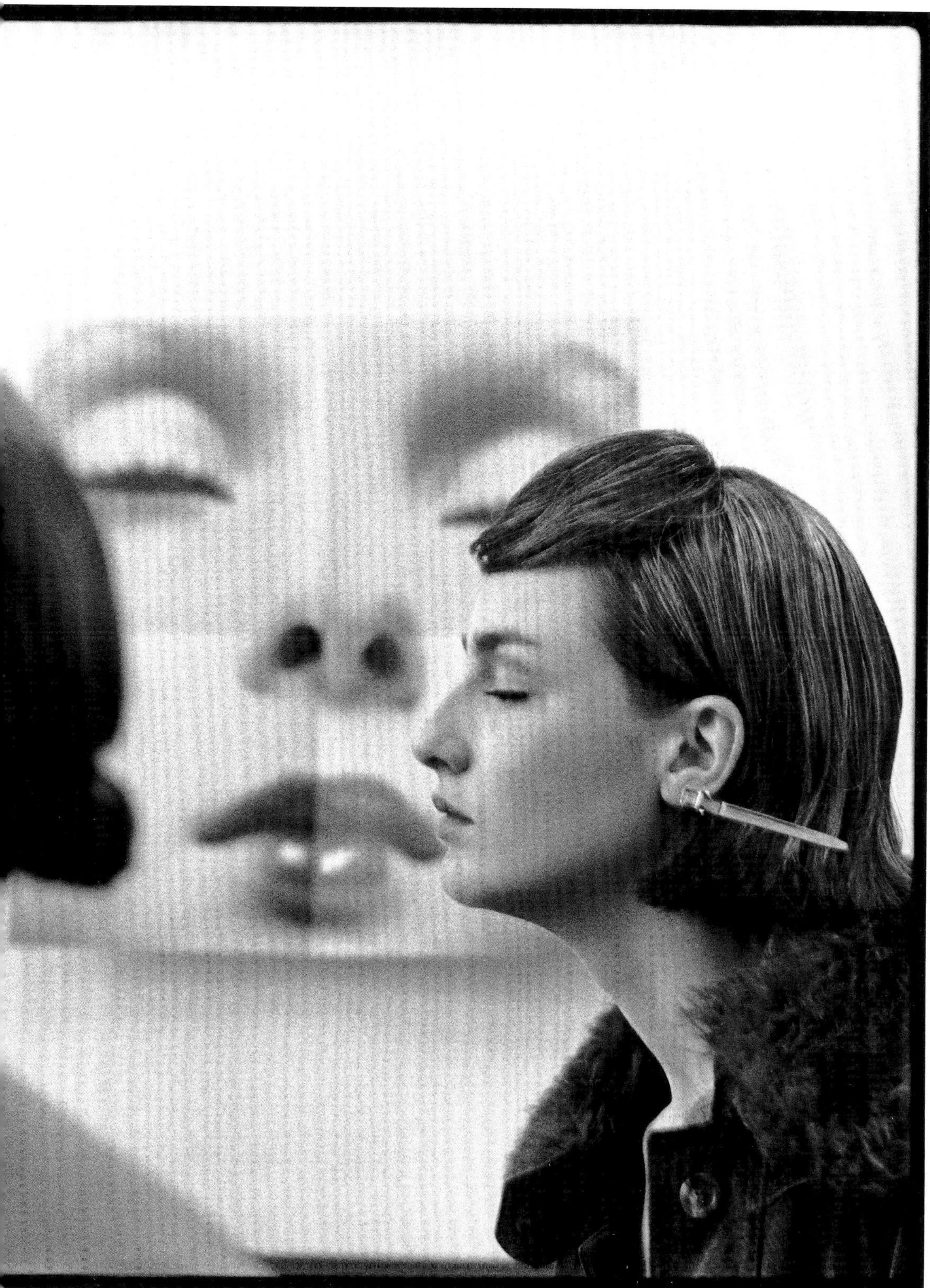

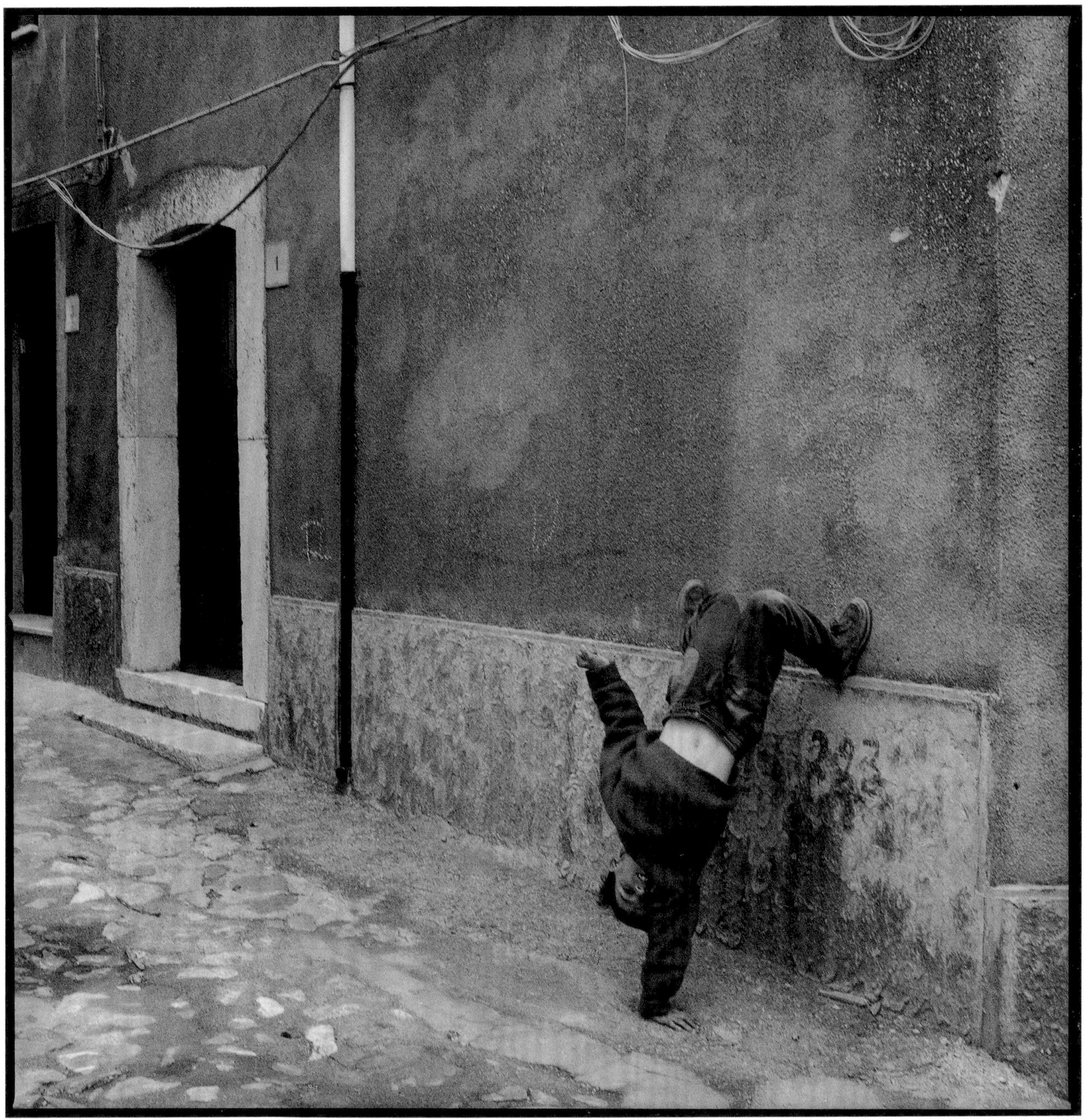

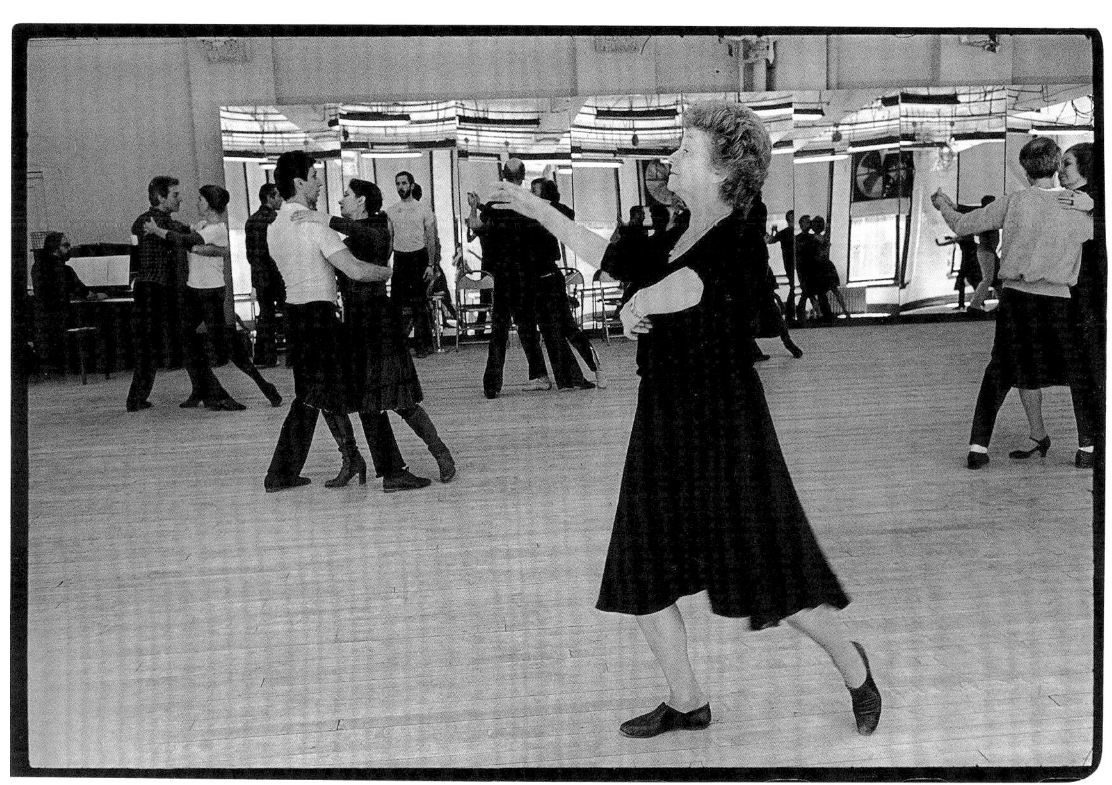

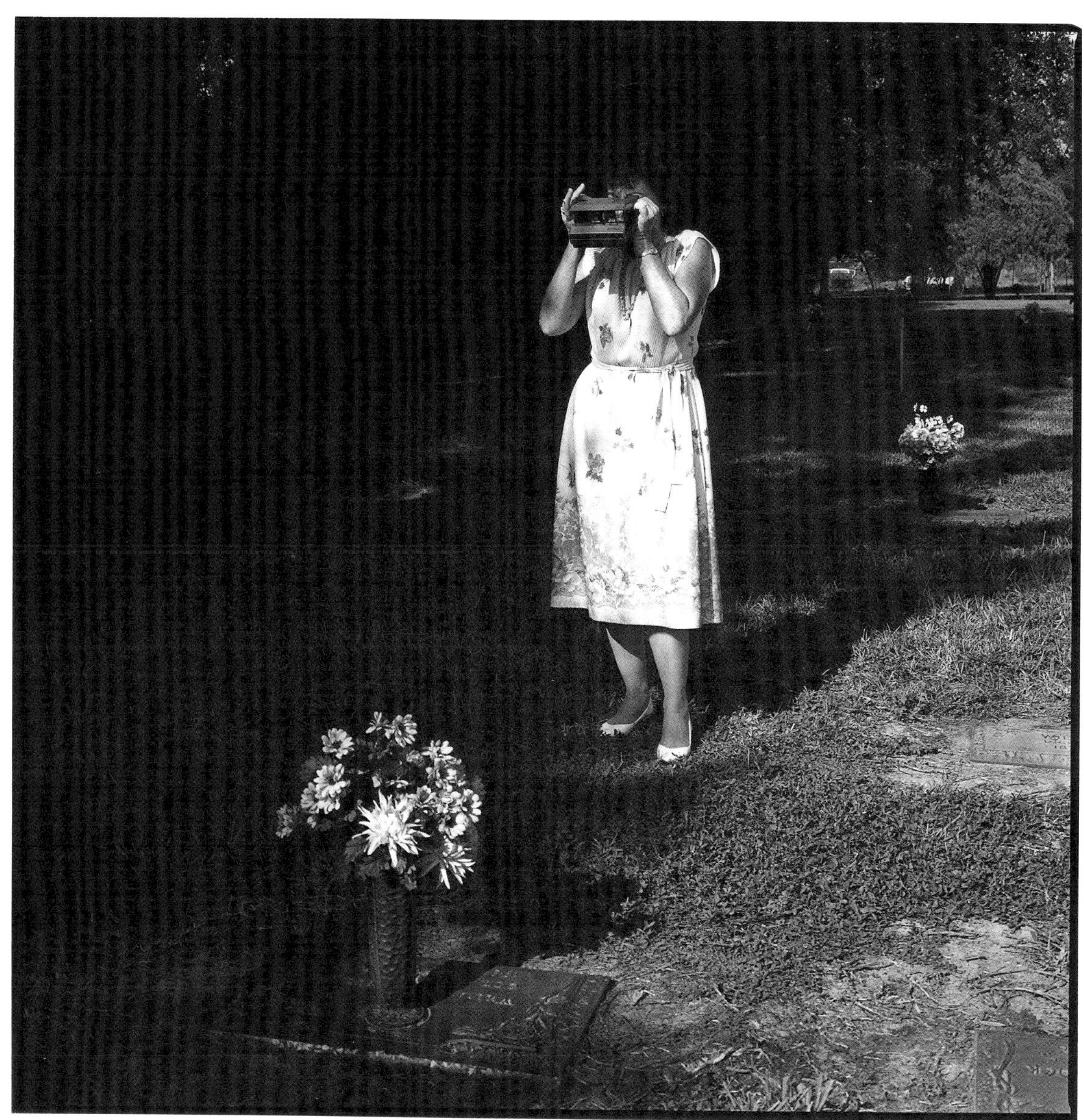

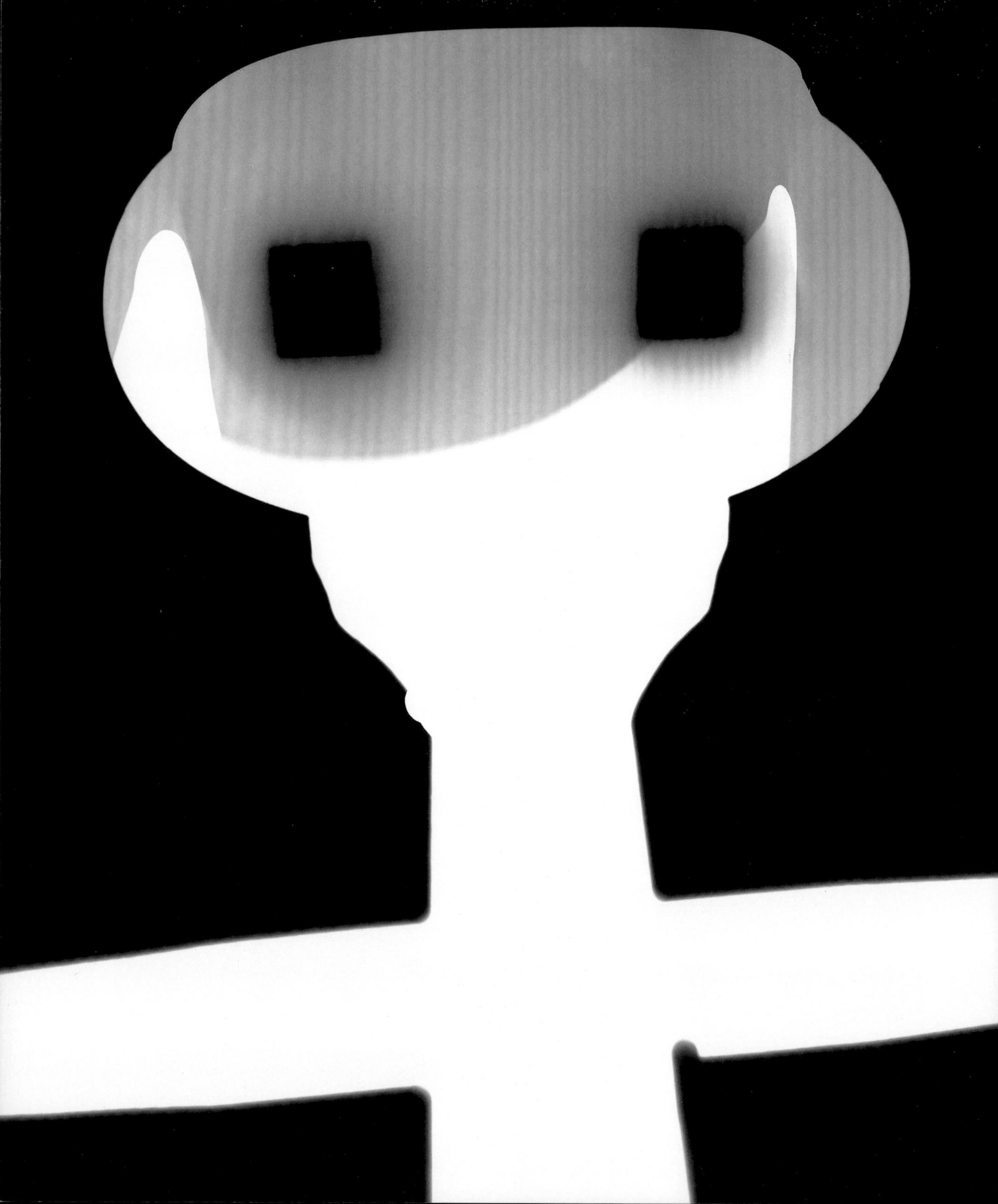

The small bridesmaid fixes her eyes on the hands of the photographer, who is focused on the groom and his father. The son has an open gaze; the father sits looking inward; a little way back, the brother-in-law is zooming in. In this web of looks, all the players are held in momentary gestalt.

There are looks that connect, looks that divide, and looks to die for. There are hungry looks that strip you, looks that kill, evil eyes, and healing glances.

Those who like to be looked at wait for those who like to look; artists will keep their favorite models for years.

I often wish I were invisible: I could see and not be seen. I wouldn't have to reveal myself. I would record in a picture looks deep as the dark and connections entwining as crisscrossing railroad tracks. But then I wouldn't be part of it and why would I care?

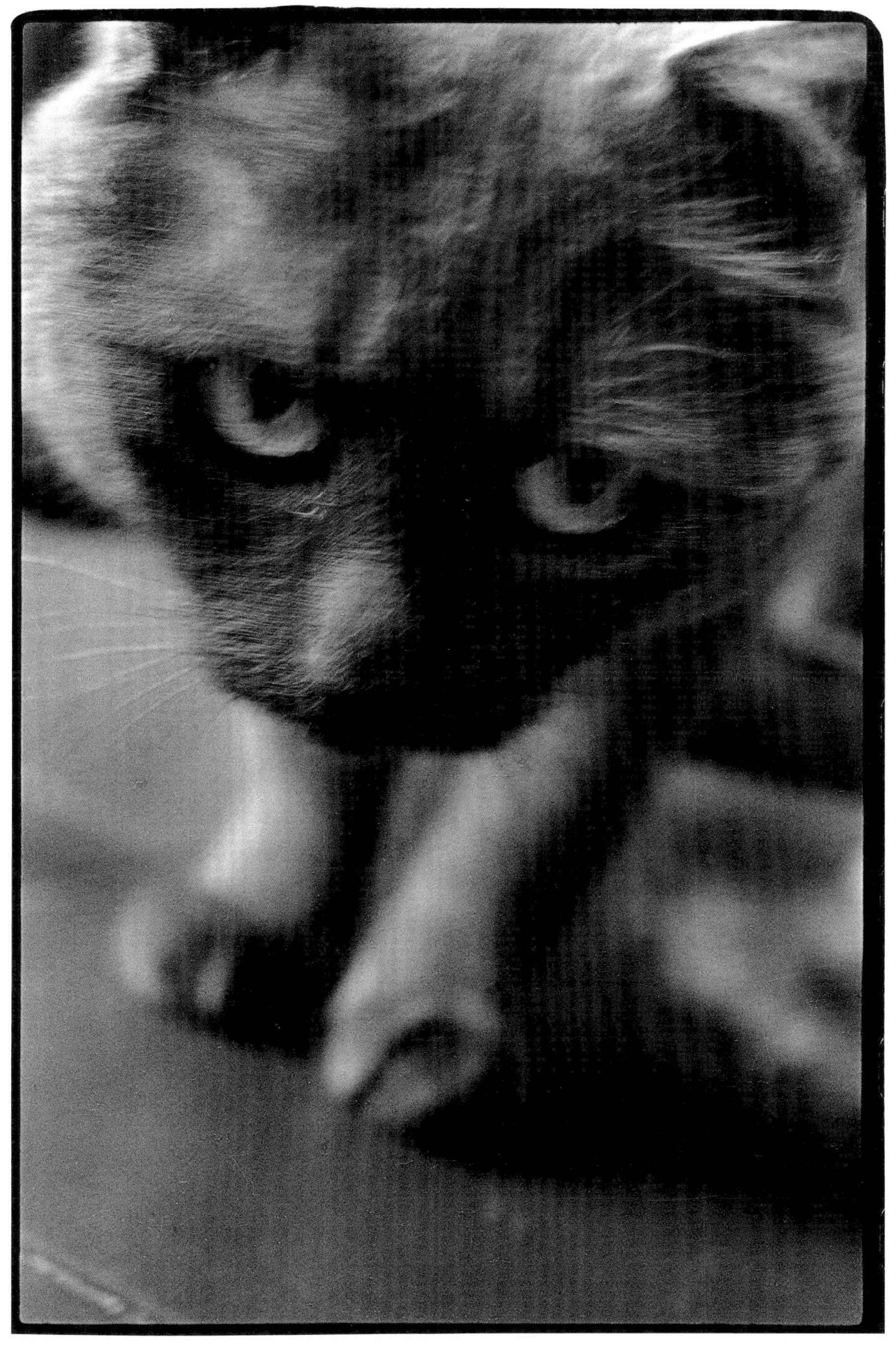

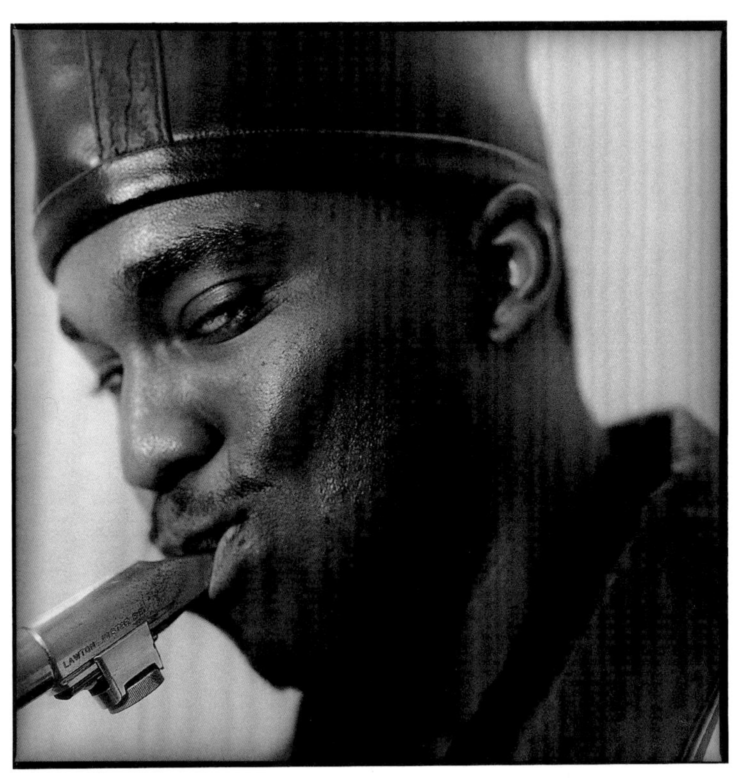
LAWTON

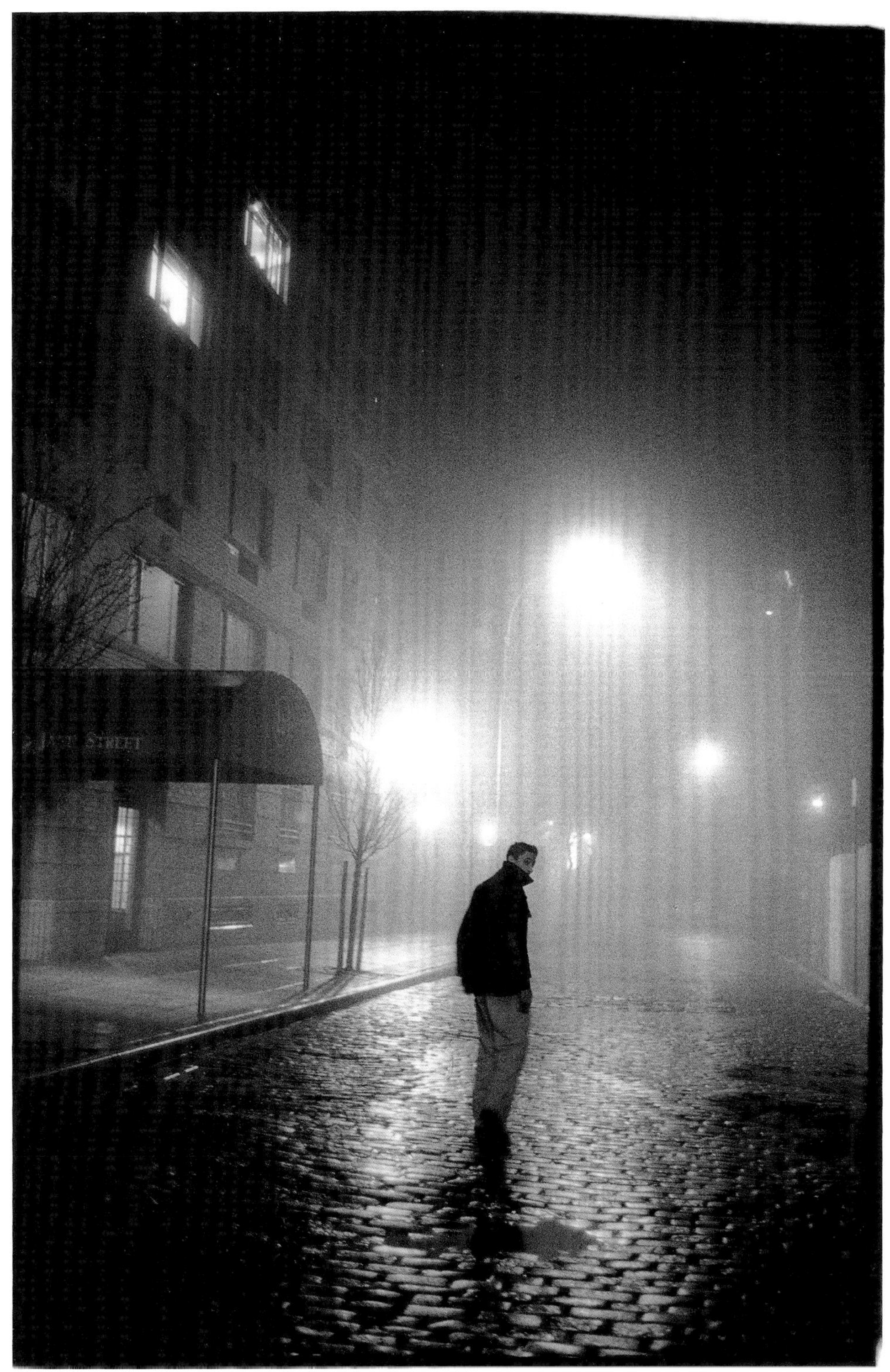
STREET

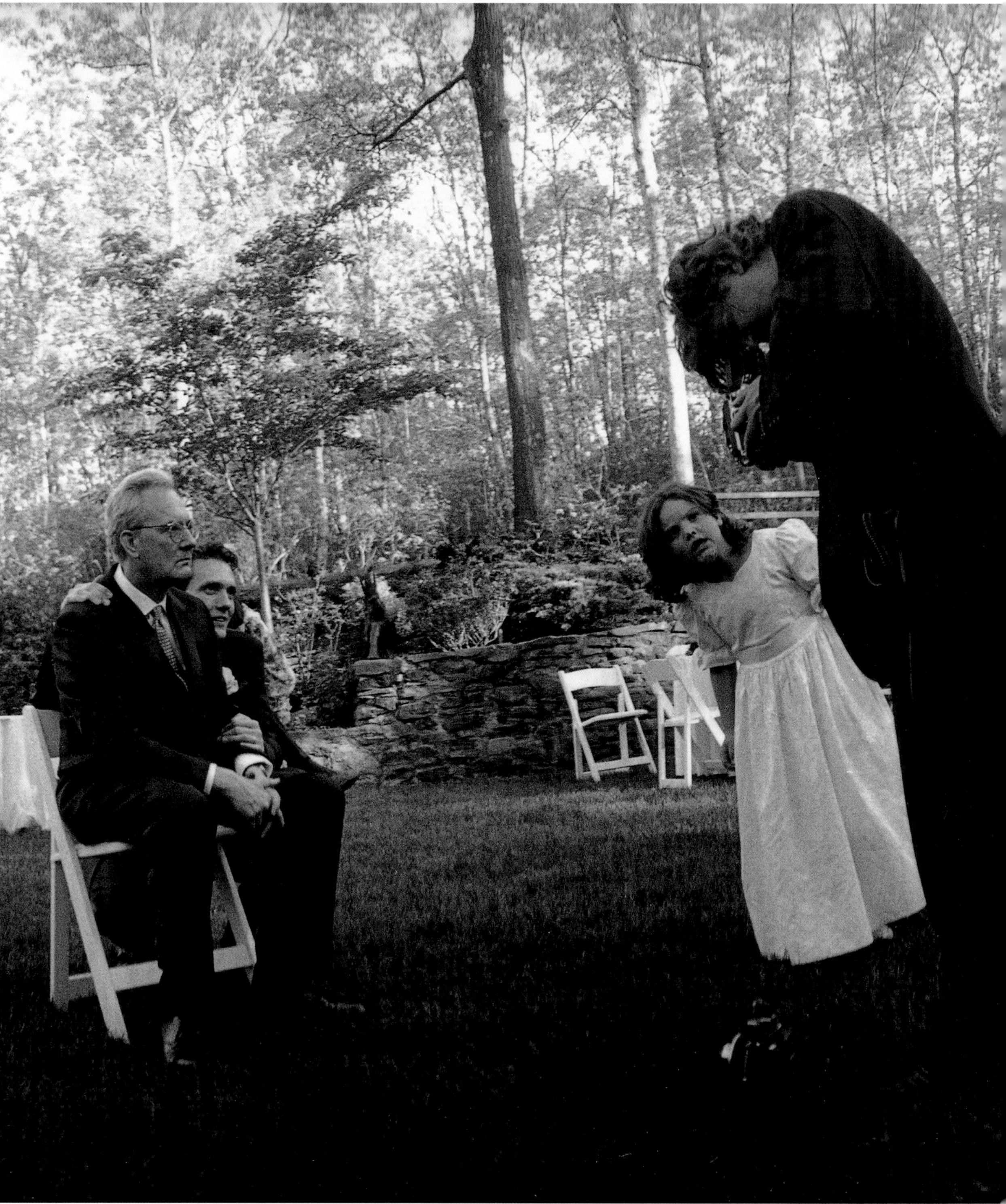

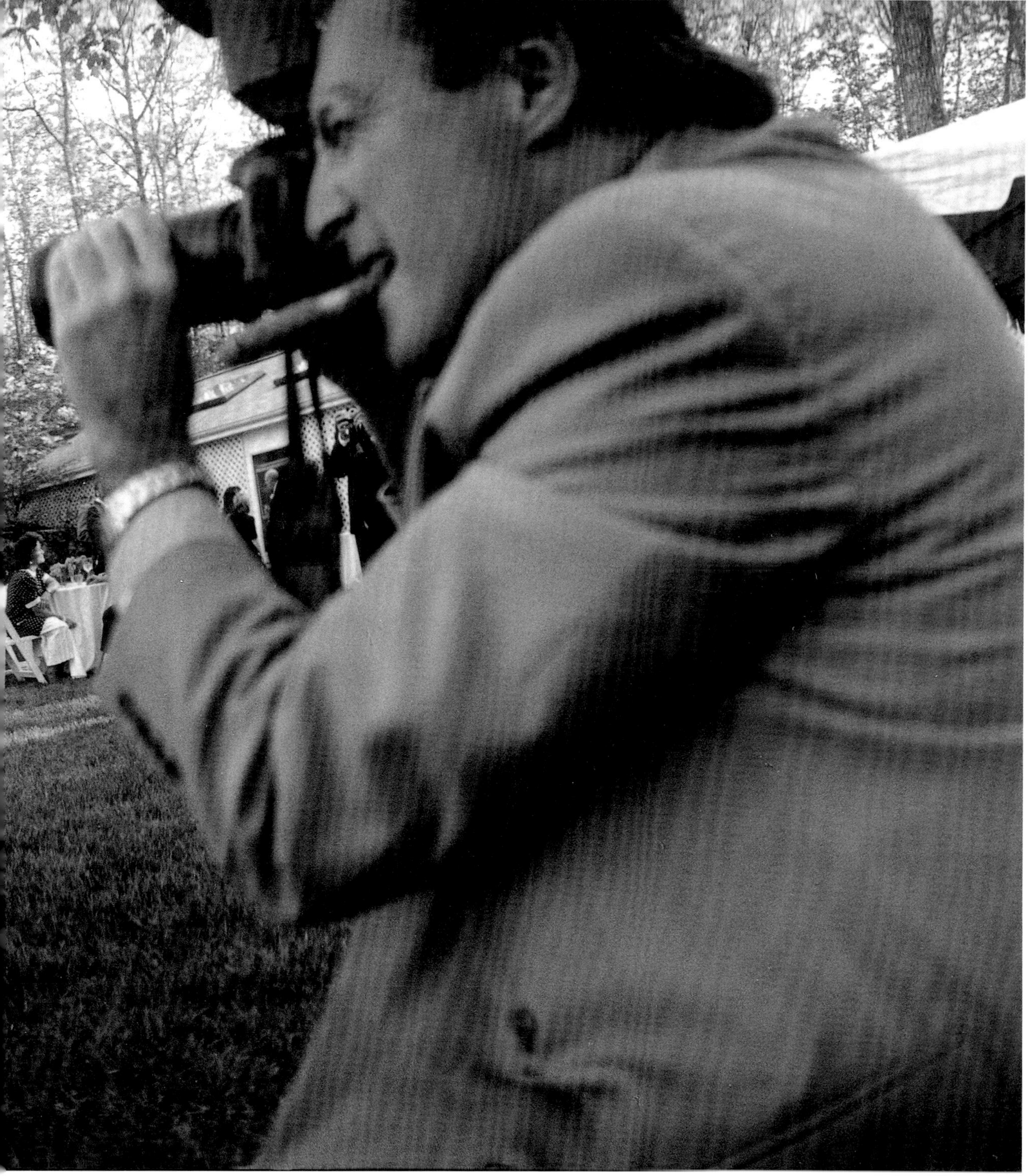

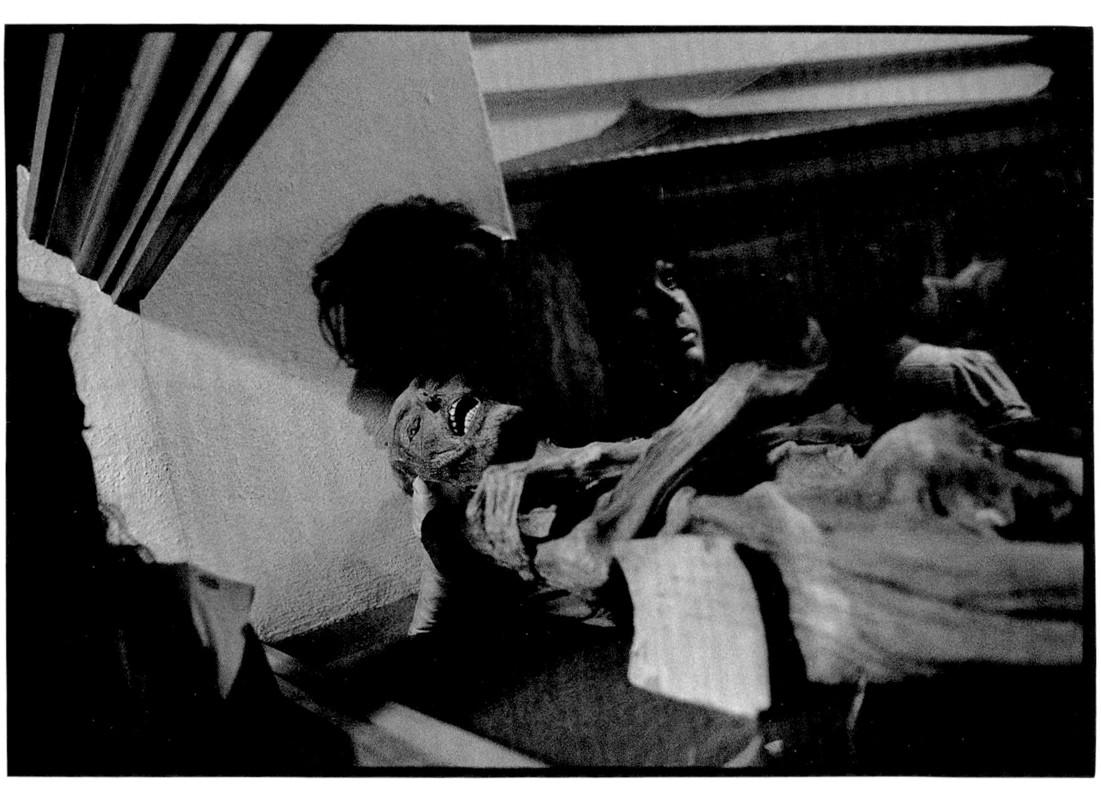

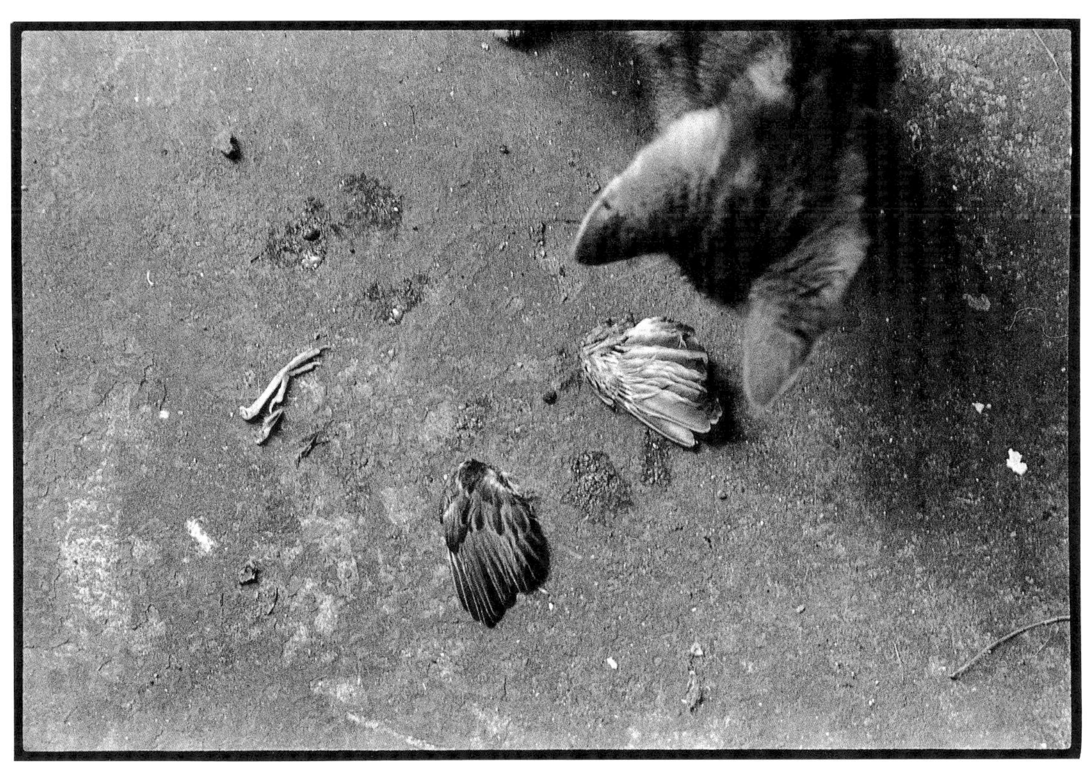

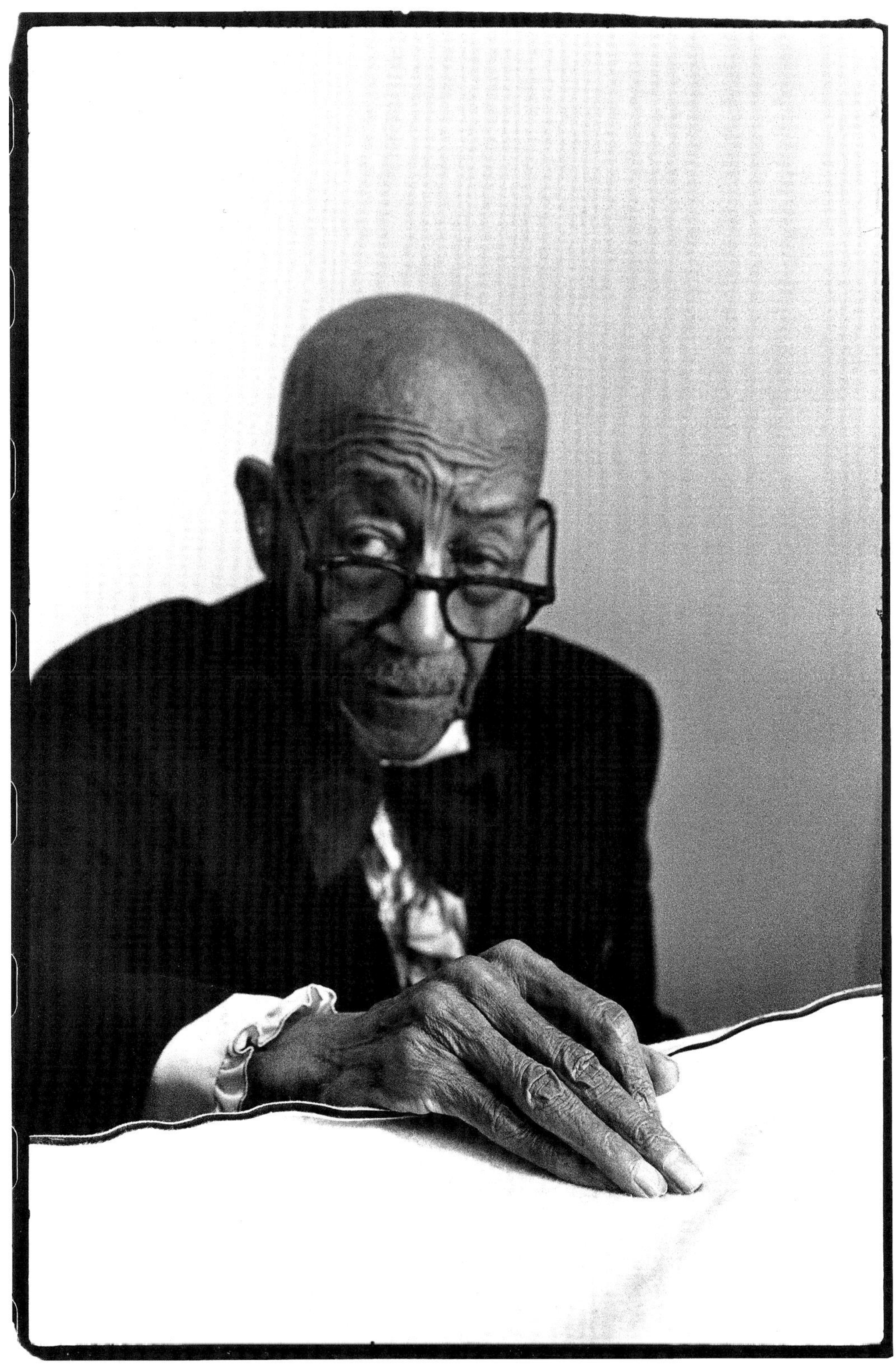

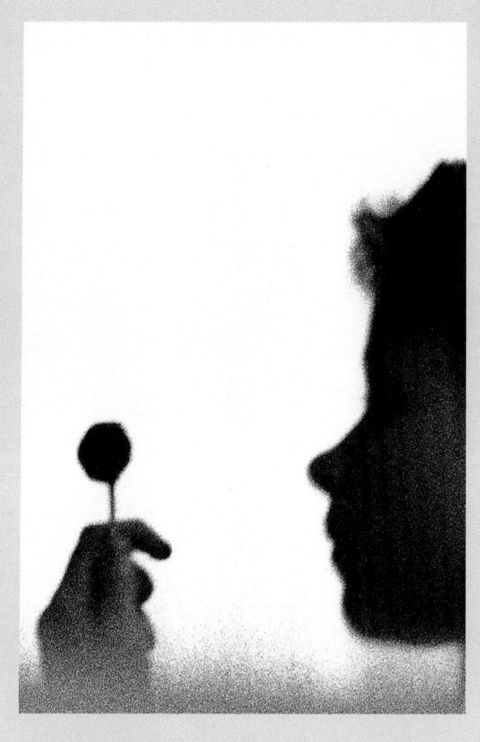

"Take a picture!" said Yolanda as she exposed her pregnant belly between floors in the elevator of the Condé Nast building. What mischief, to show off her natural roundness in the Temple of Style.

roundness in its spherical perfection surpasses fashion. It signals power and mystery. Like a seed, it connotes beginning, center, creation. Who can resist touching a Buddha belly or rubbing a bald head?

"A circle closed again" my mother would say when something got resolved. Finding something, losing a friend, the death of someone dear are a closing of the parenthesis, an end or a beginning.

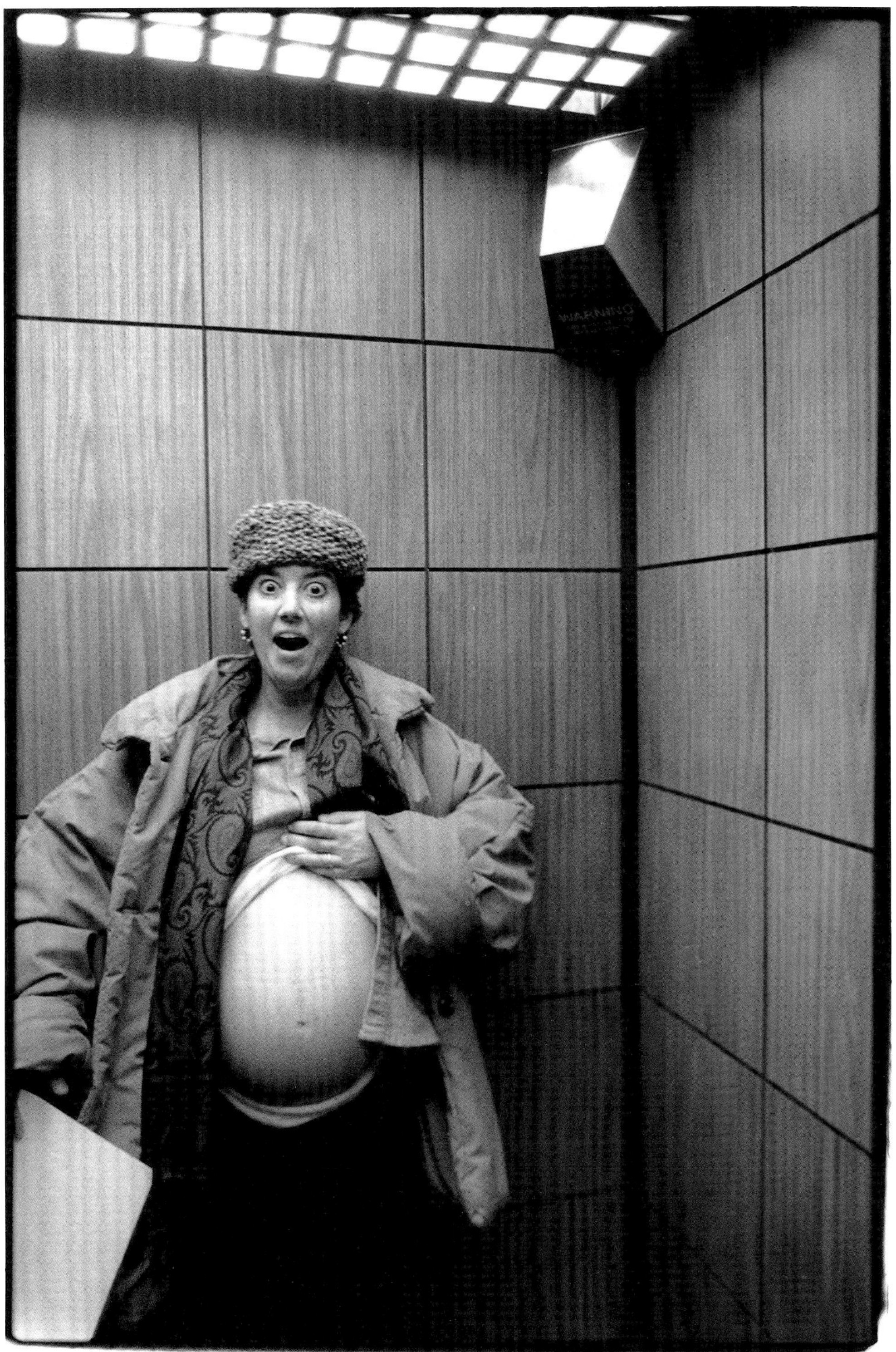
WARNING

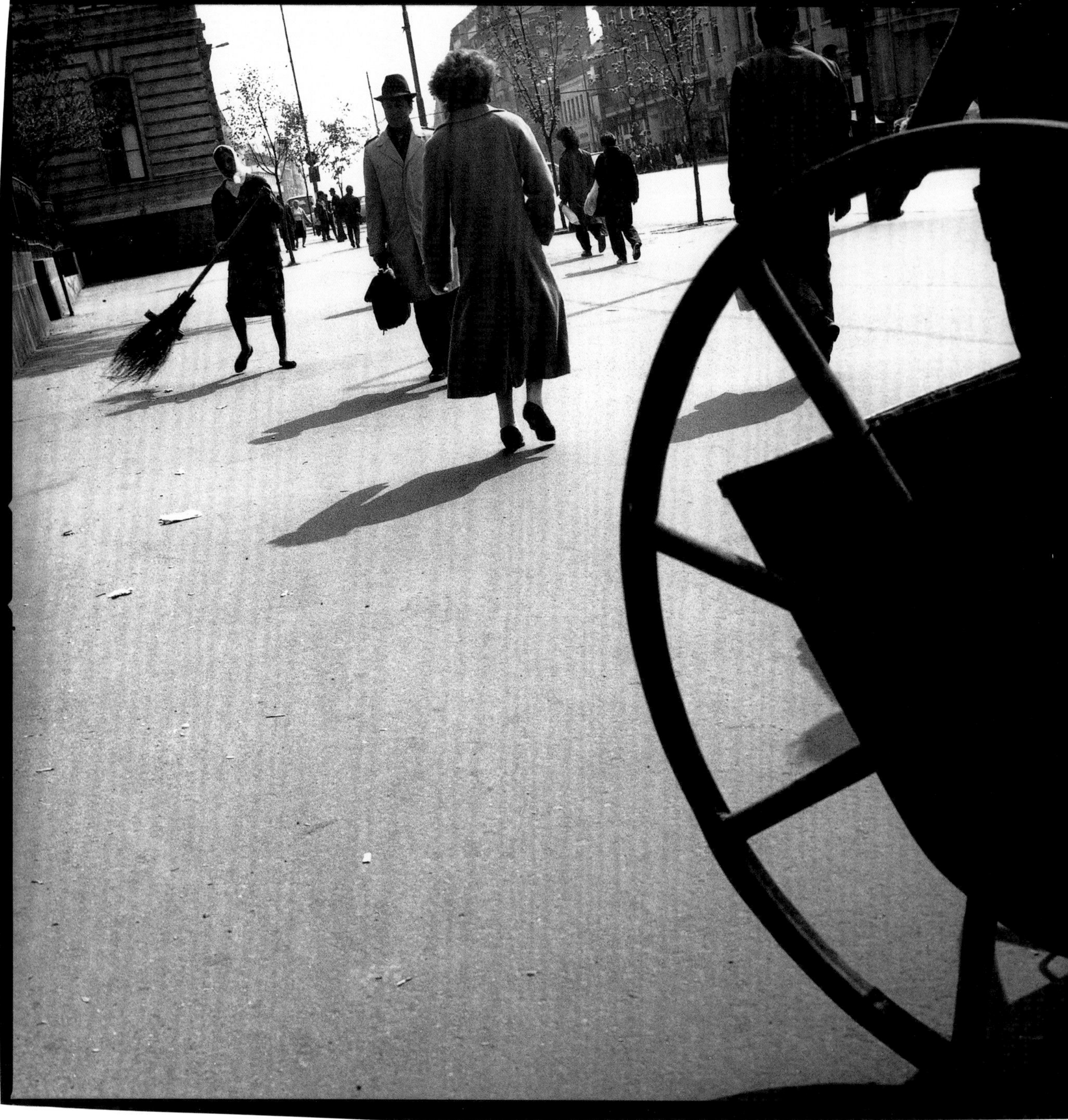

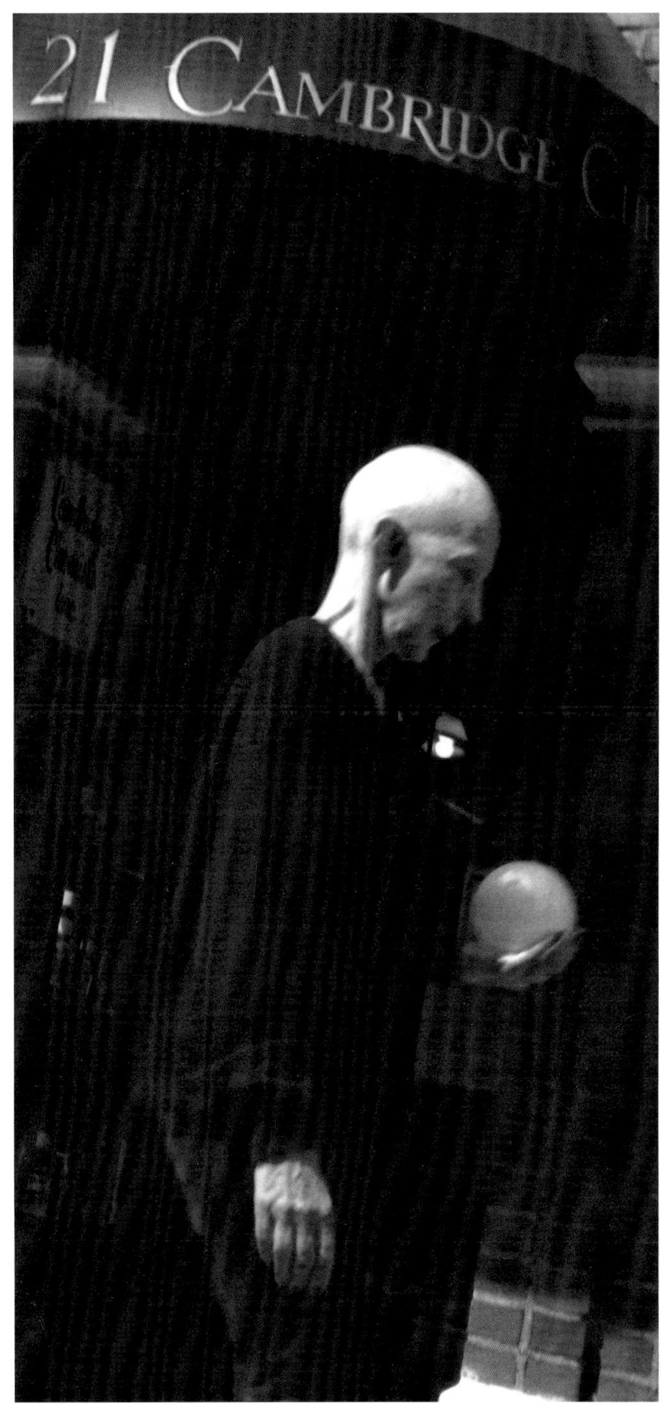
21 Cambridge

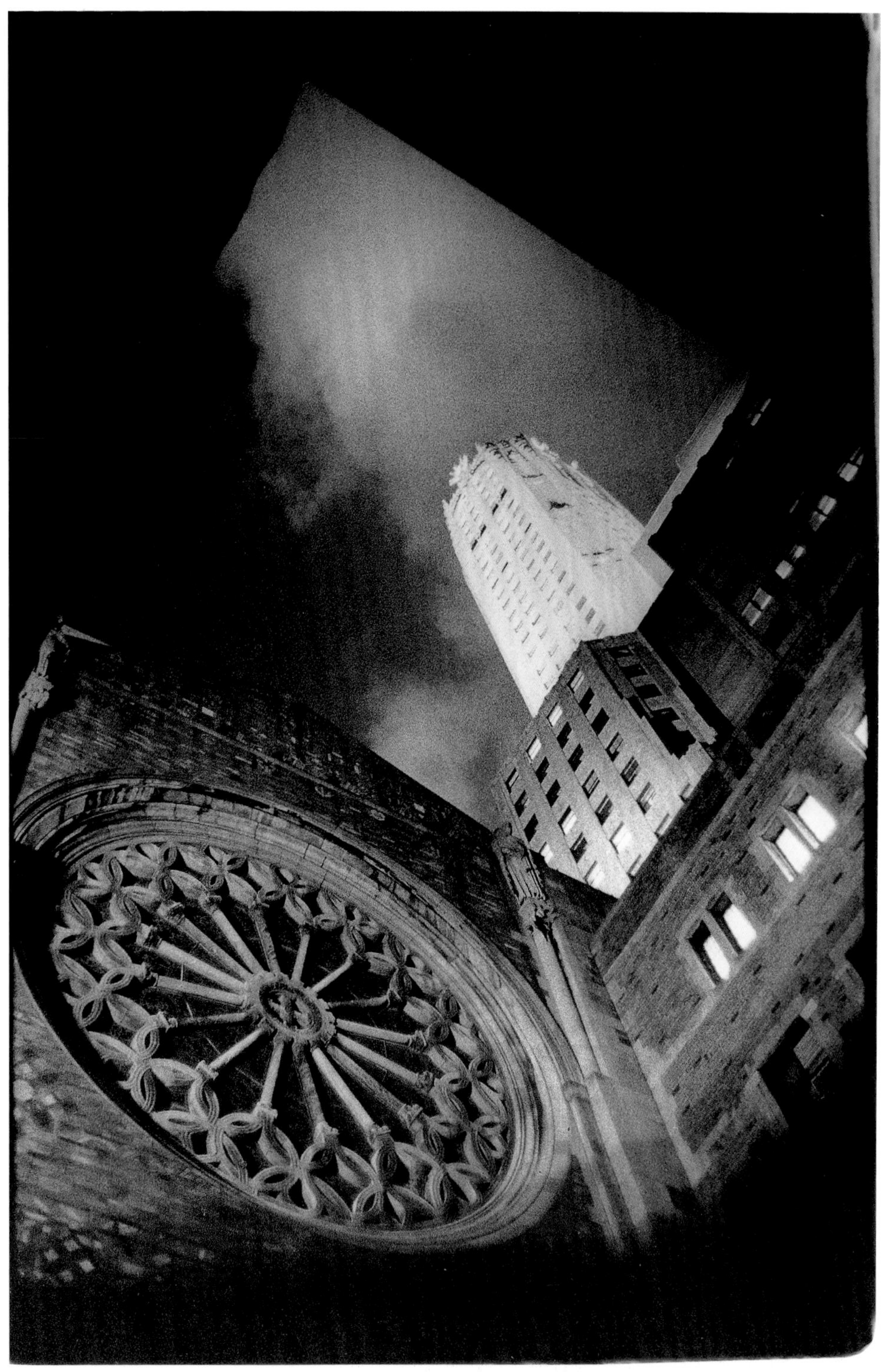

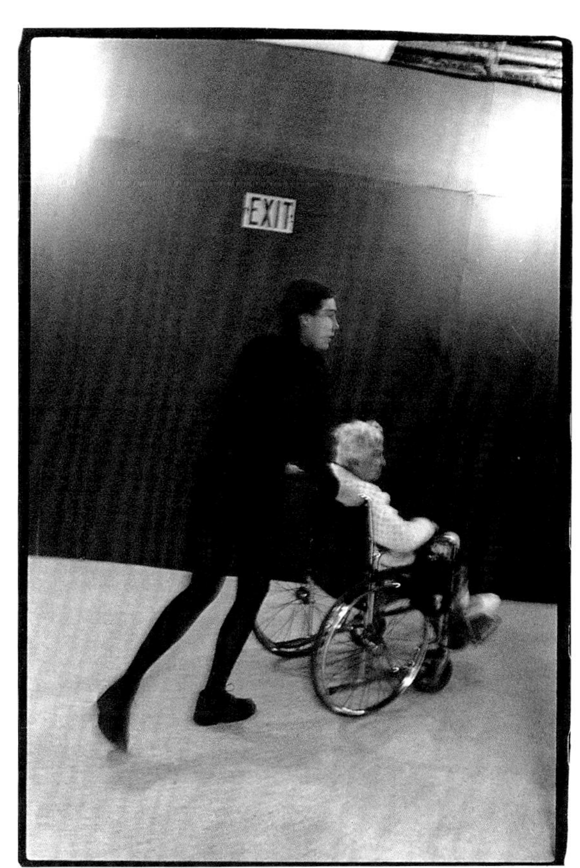
EXIT

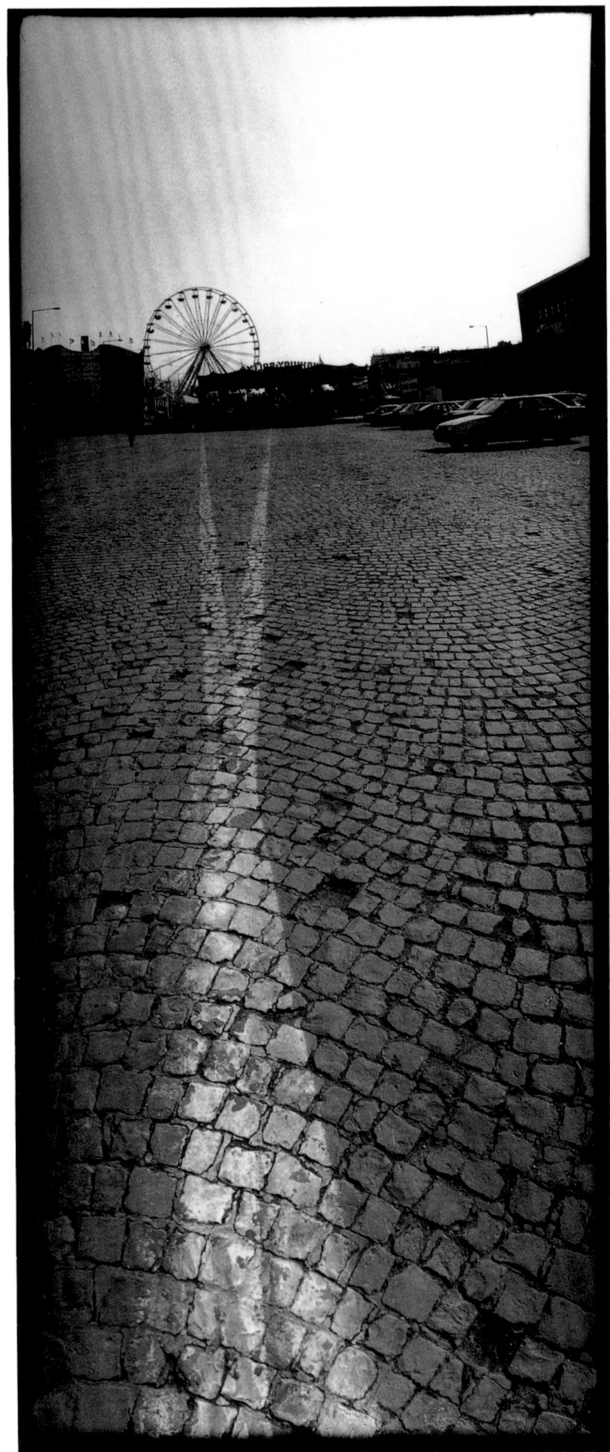

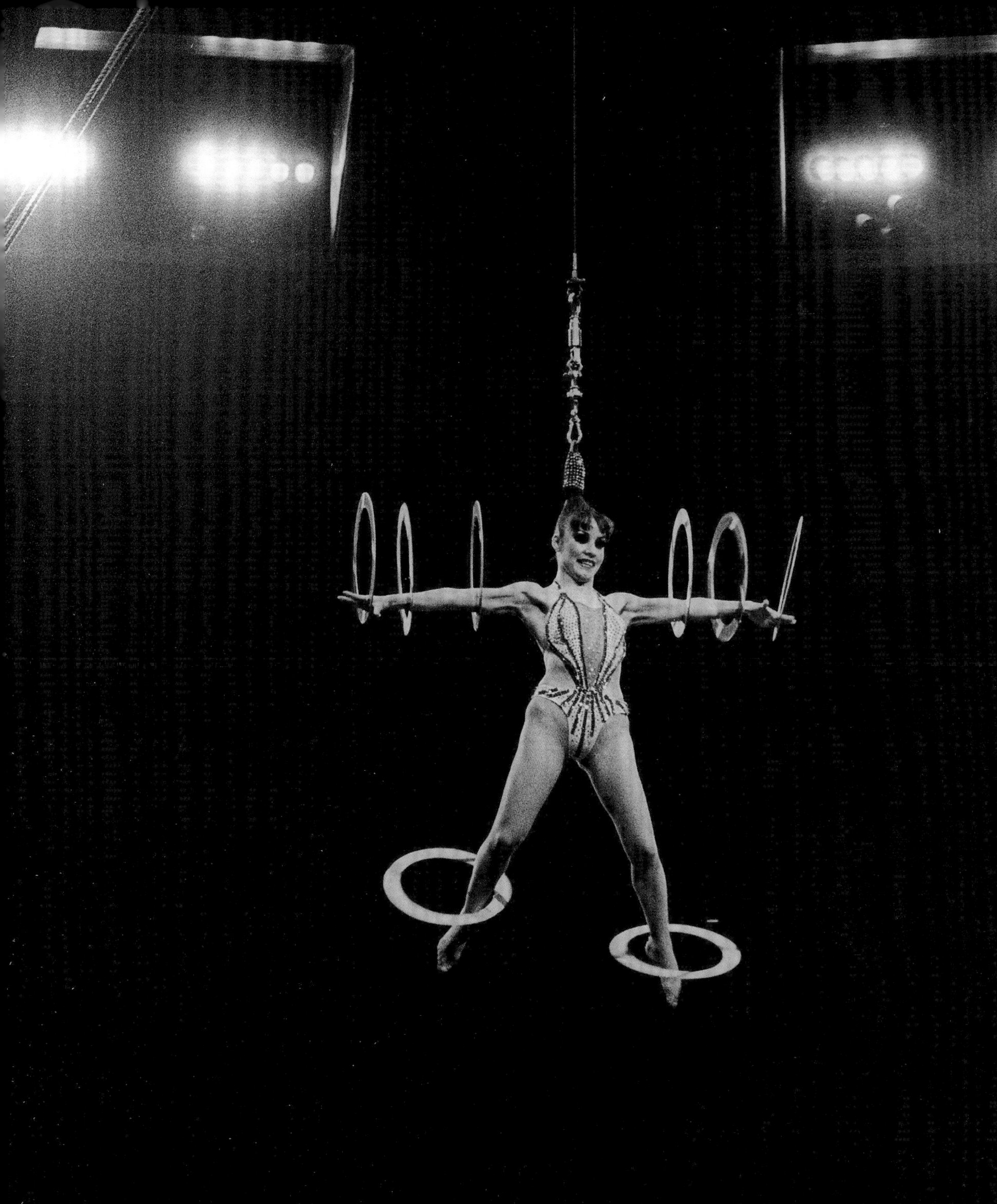

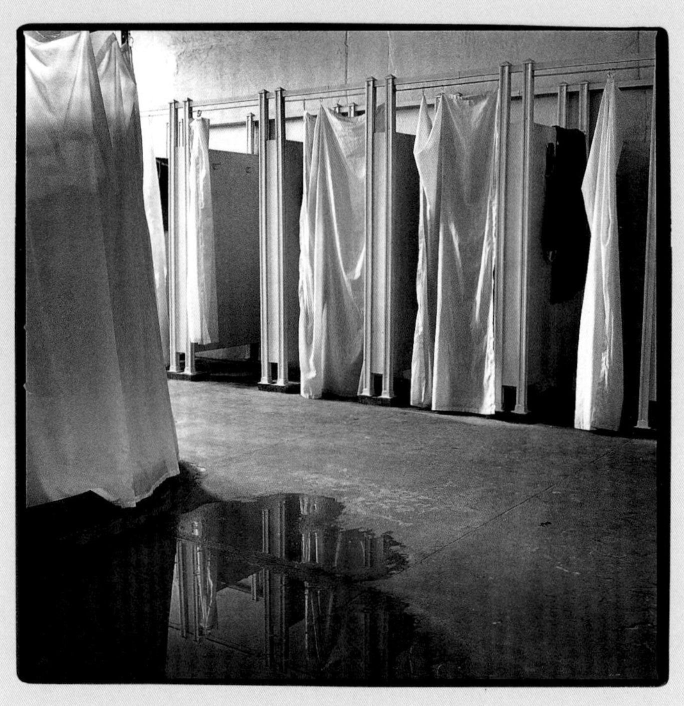

Anonymous is a statue in Budapest erected to the memory of unsung poets. He sits in a park in his hooded robe with his head in deep shadow, and I, as a child, always tried to catch a glimpse of his face.

Not far from the statue, at the entrance to the Metro, a figure sat in rags, only her hand visible. She chanted without end "I am a poor sick old woman." I begged my mother to help her. She wouldn't. The next night I had a nightmare. We were inside the station. There were trains on either side of the platform. When the doors of one opened the old woman snatched a child from her mother's arms and, rollerskating across the platform, hung the child in the straps of the opposite train. I pulled on my mother's coat because I knew I was next. She wouldn't listen. Then I woke up.

But not all veils hide monsters of hopelessness. While grab bags and gifts seldom live up to expectations, somewhere under the cover of snow lies a peach pit from which a tree will sprout. I'm with Christo; I like shrouds. Under each fold, as beyond each word, is a secret, a chance to hide-and-go-seek.

In a photograph, you cannot peel back the shades of gray; below the emulsion is whiteness: the alchemy is in the coating.

That's a wrap.

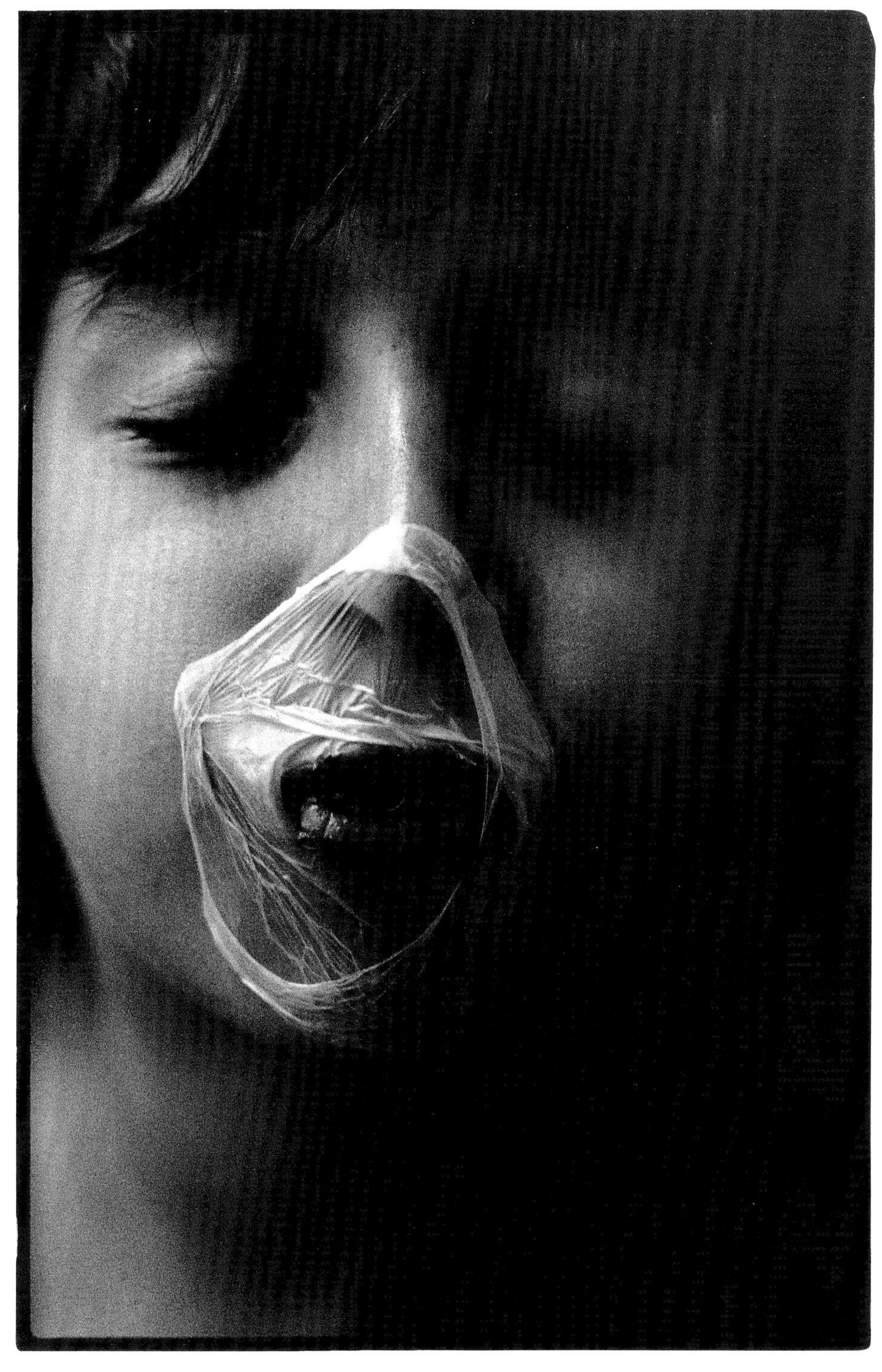

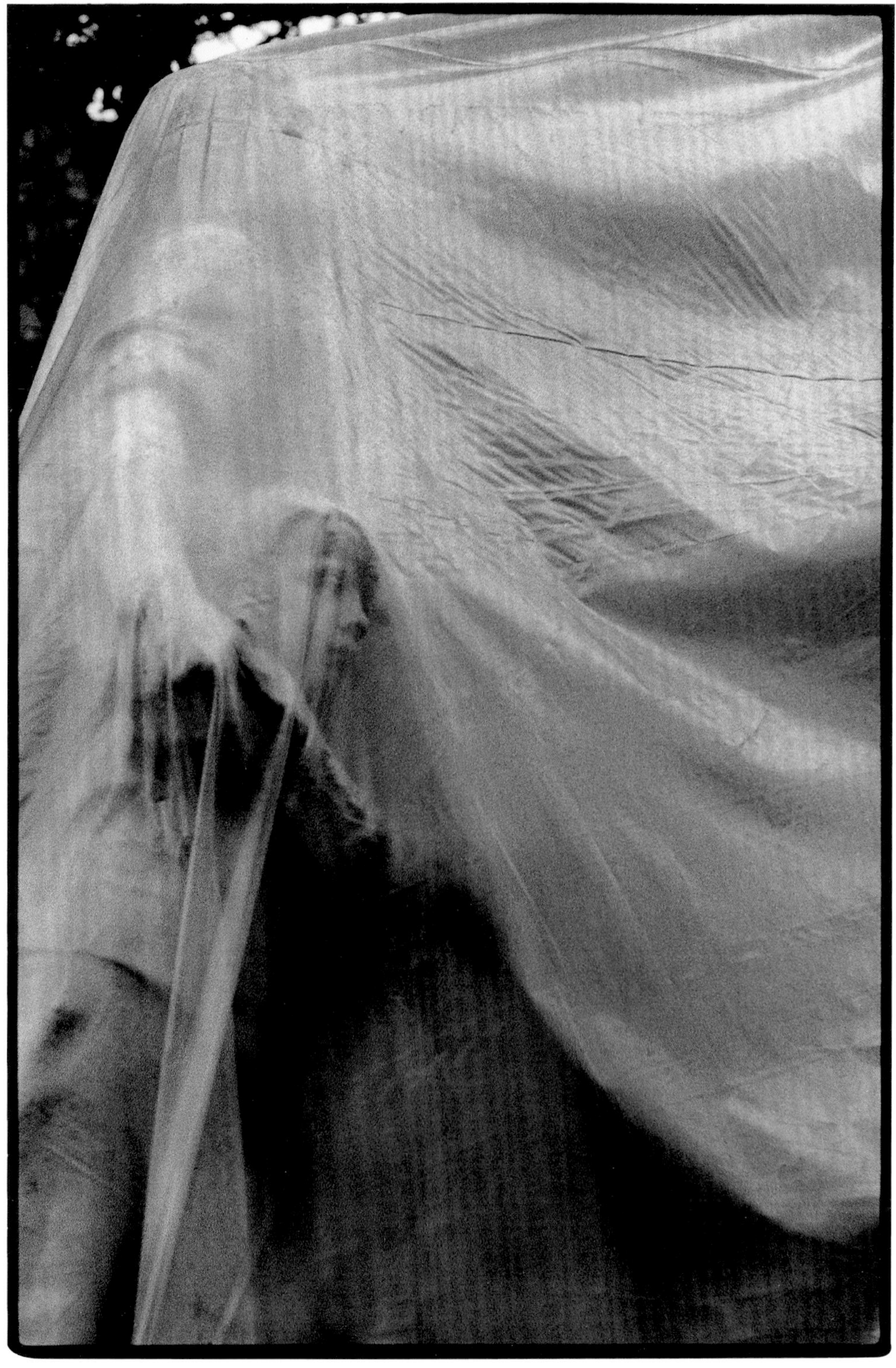

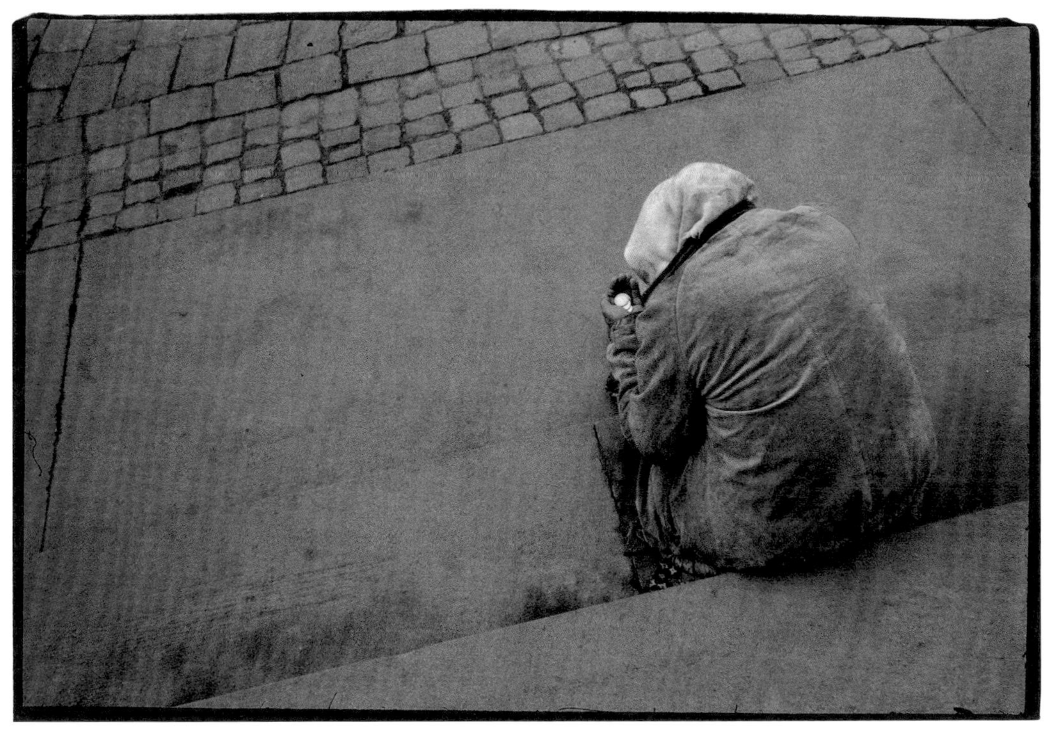

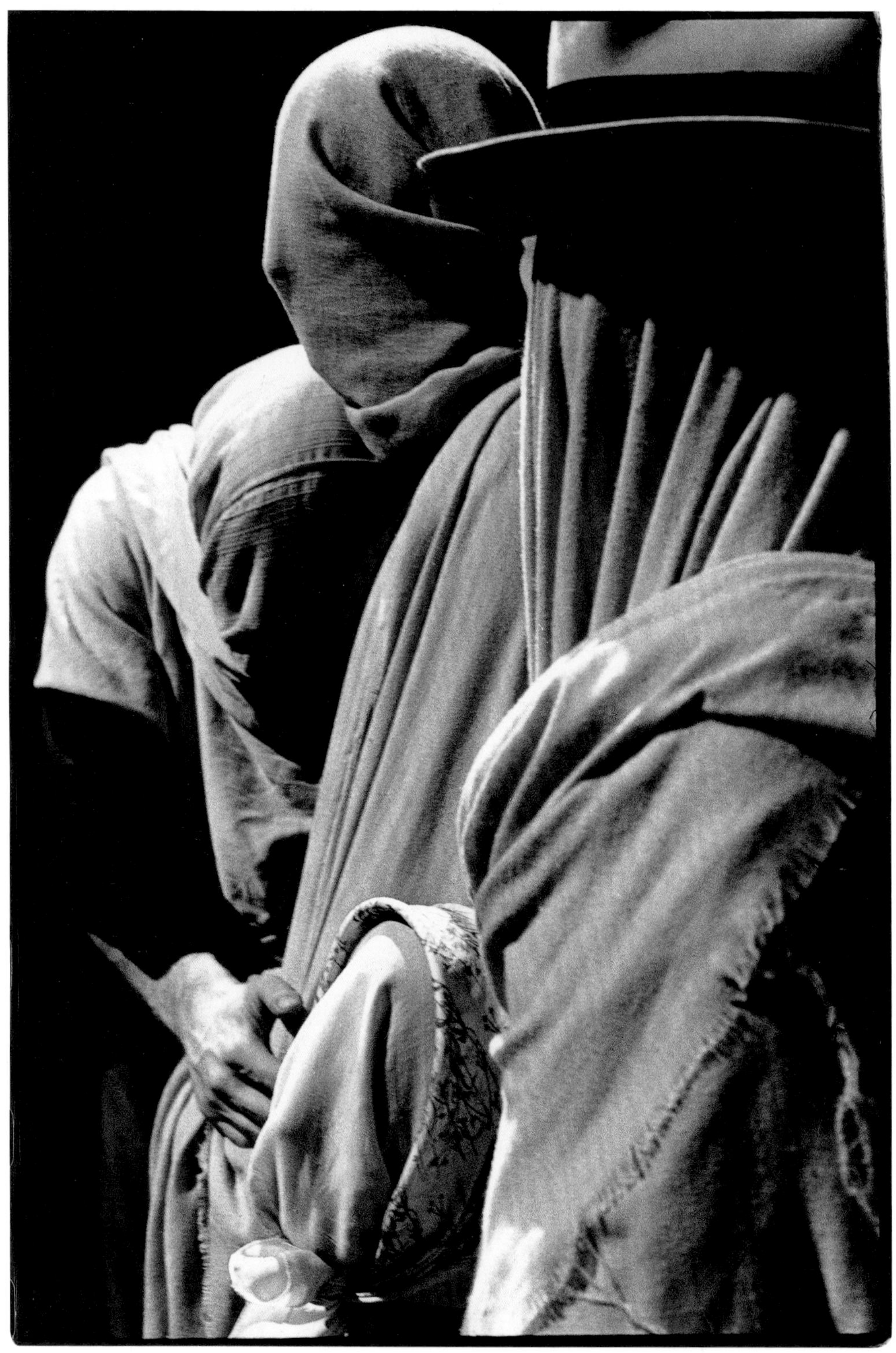

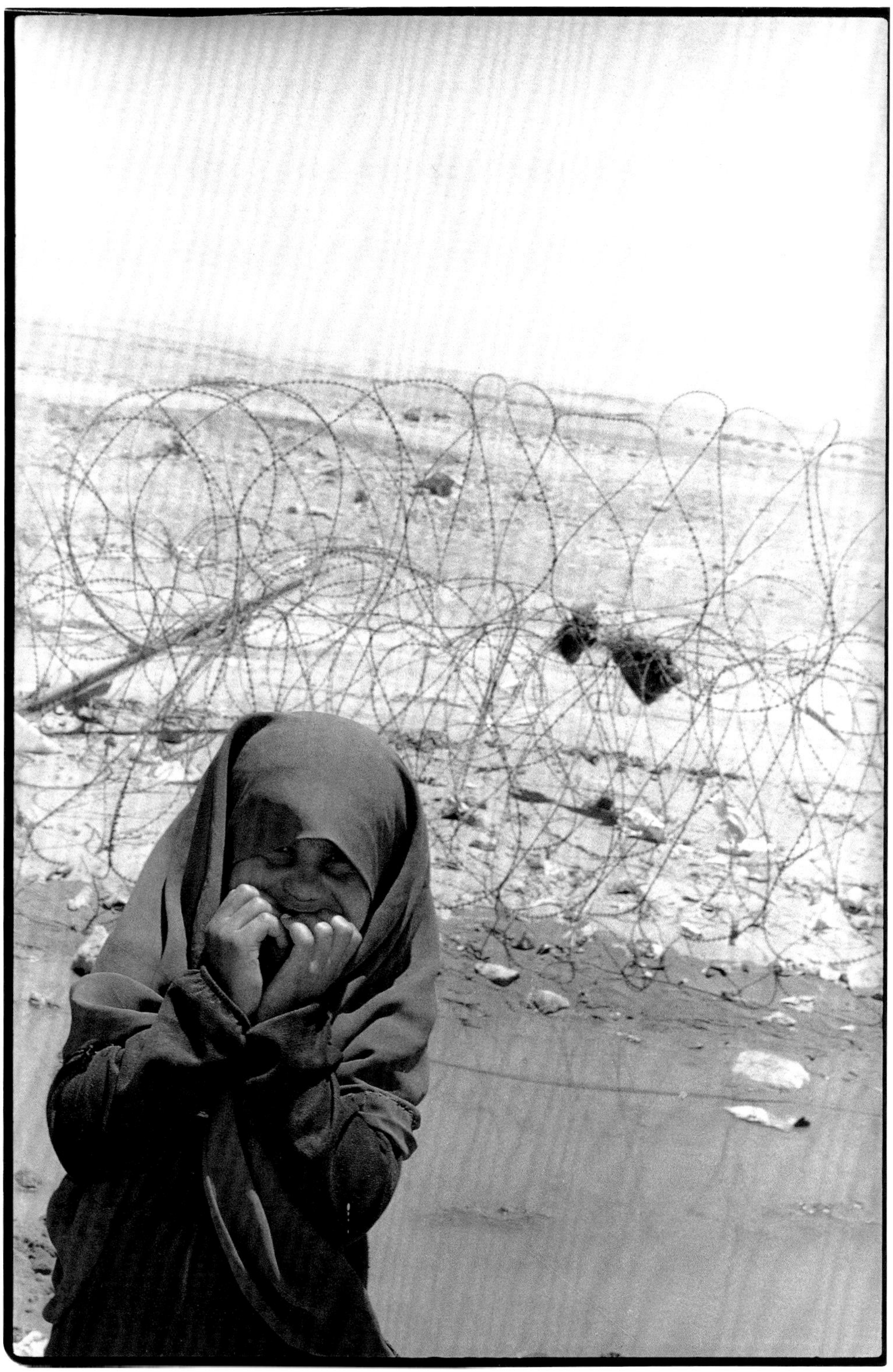

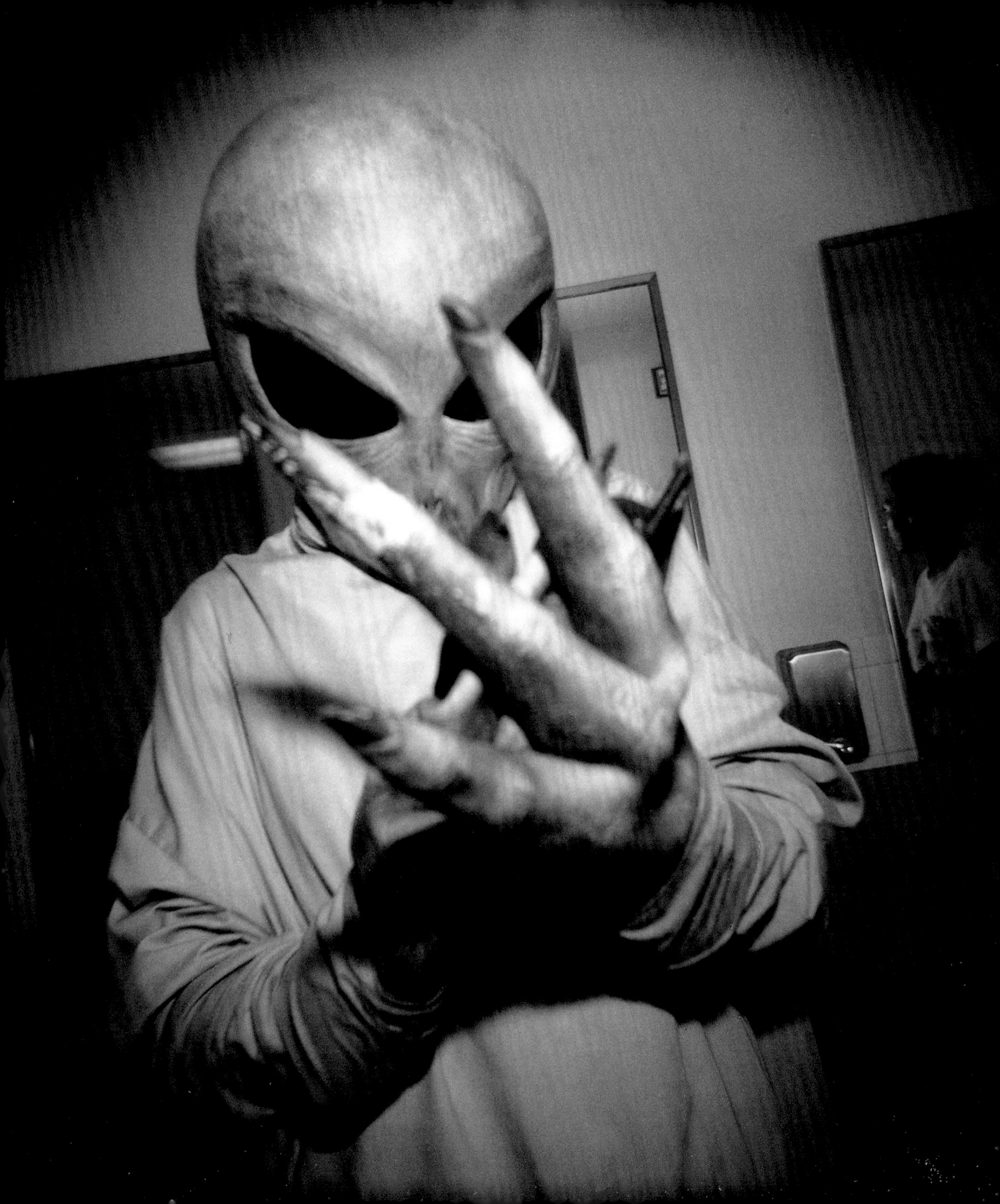

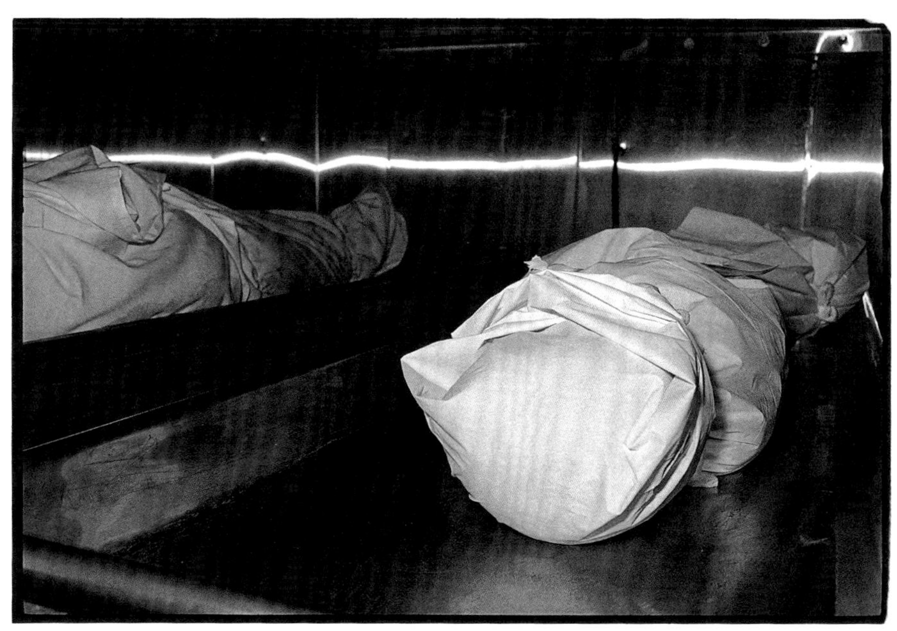

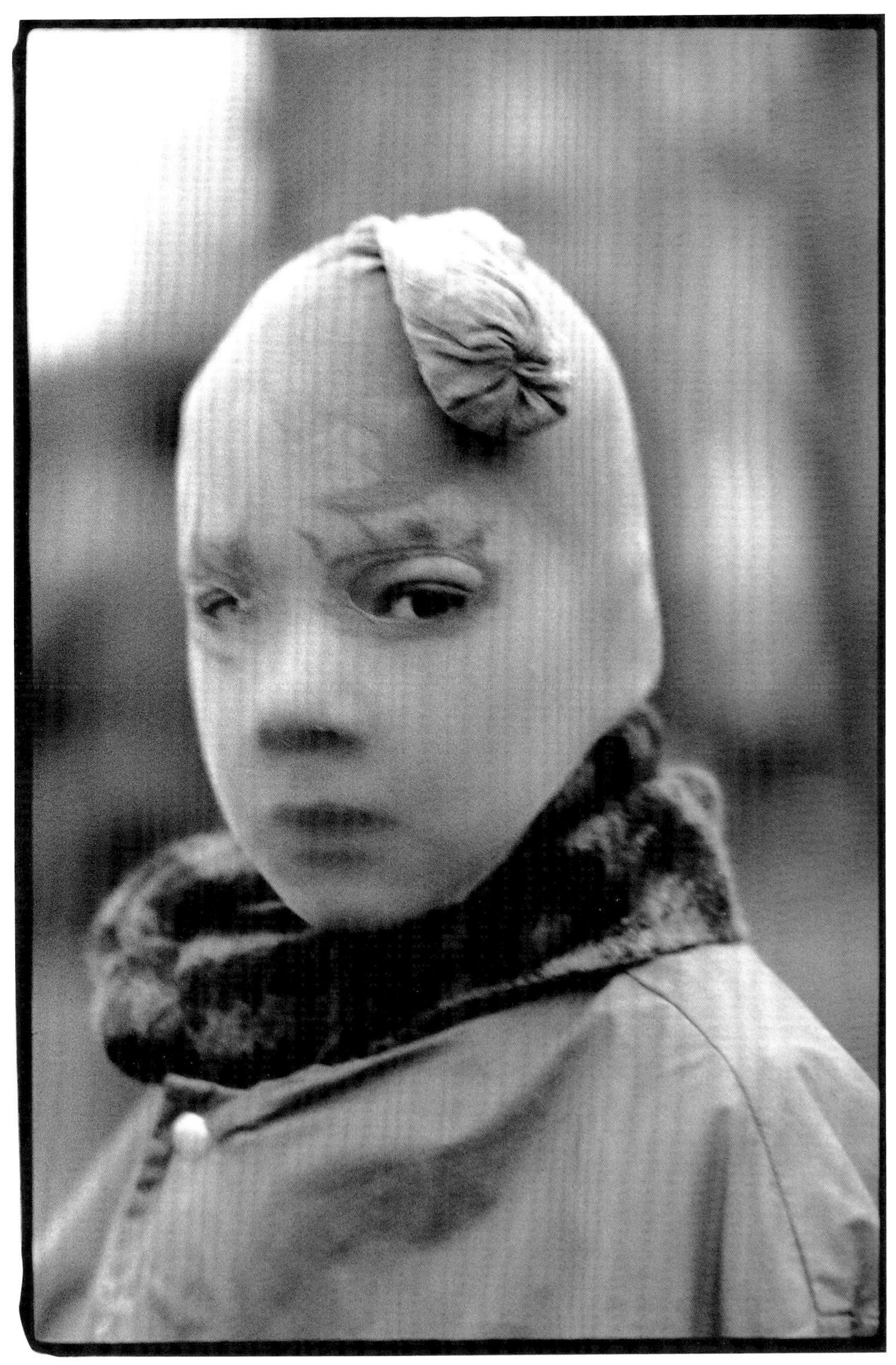

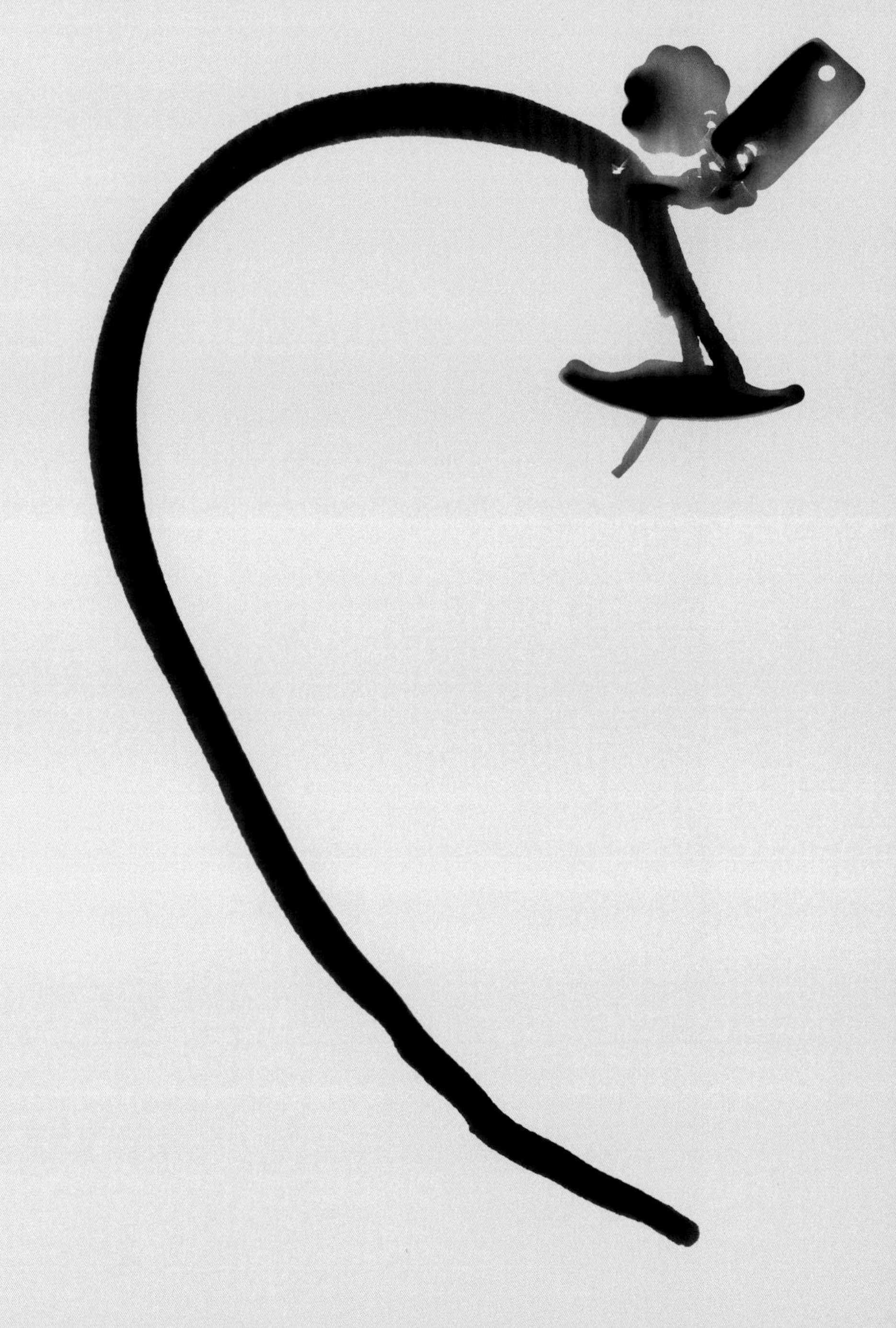

My great-aunt Klári, unable to part from Pici, her pet chihuahua, after he died, had him stuffed and kept his little body on the mantel.

There weren't any **pet cemeteries** in Hungary in those days. There are many in the States. The epitaphs are unabashedly sentimental. No need for decorum: the animals understand and the visitors do not judge.

When we shoveled earth over Poco,
I took one last photo.
I hoped to keep her soul,
but instead only preserved my sorrow.

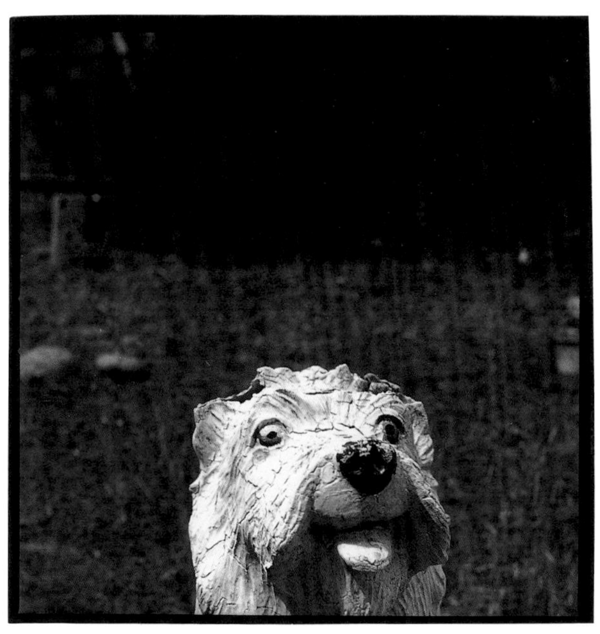

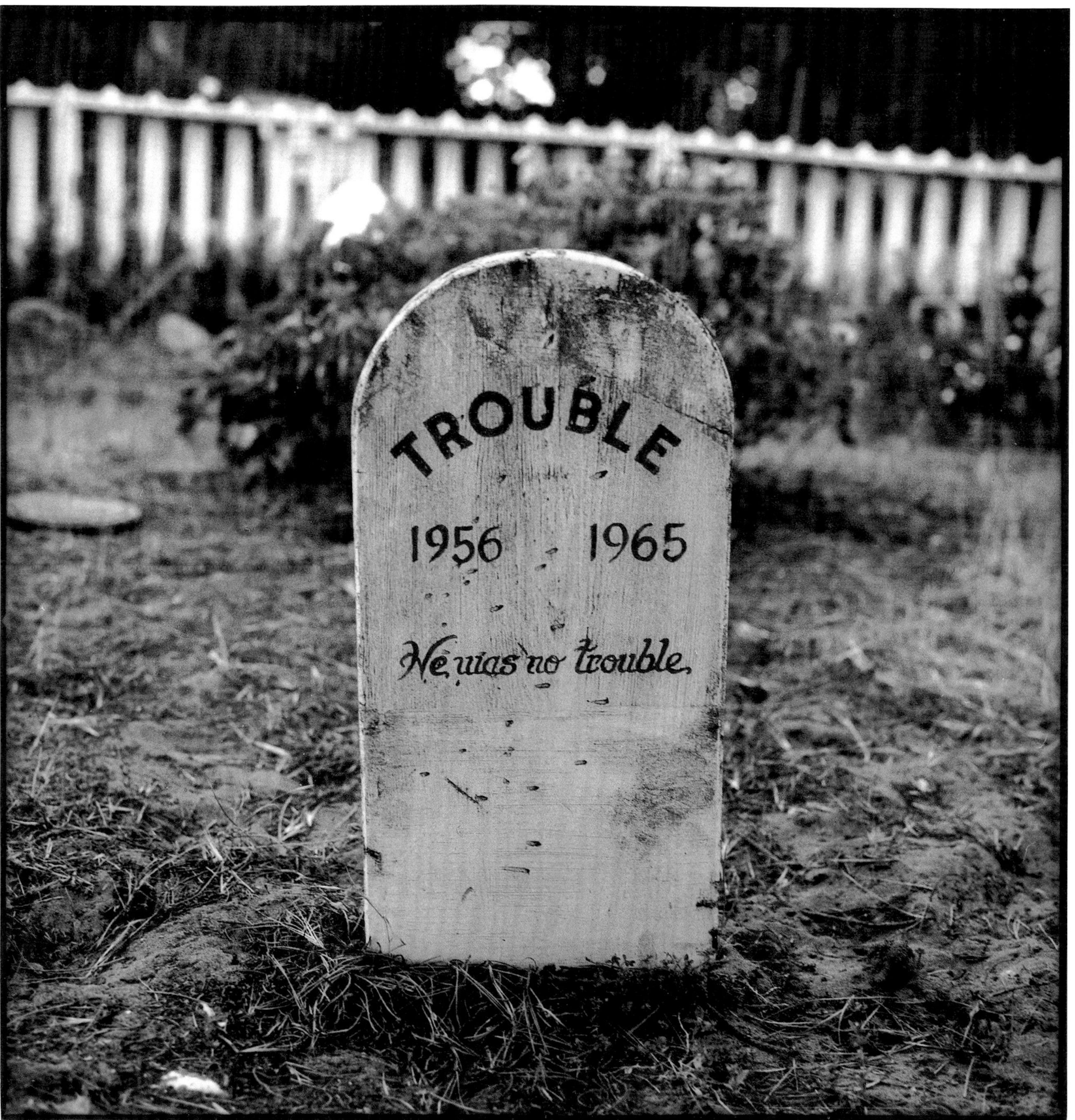
TROUBLE
1956 1965
He was no trouble

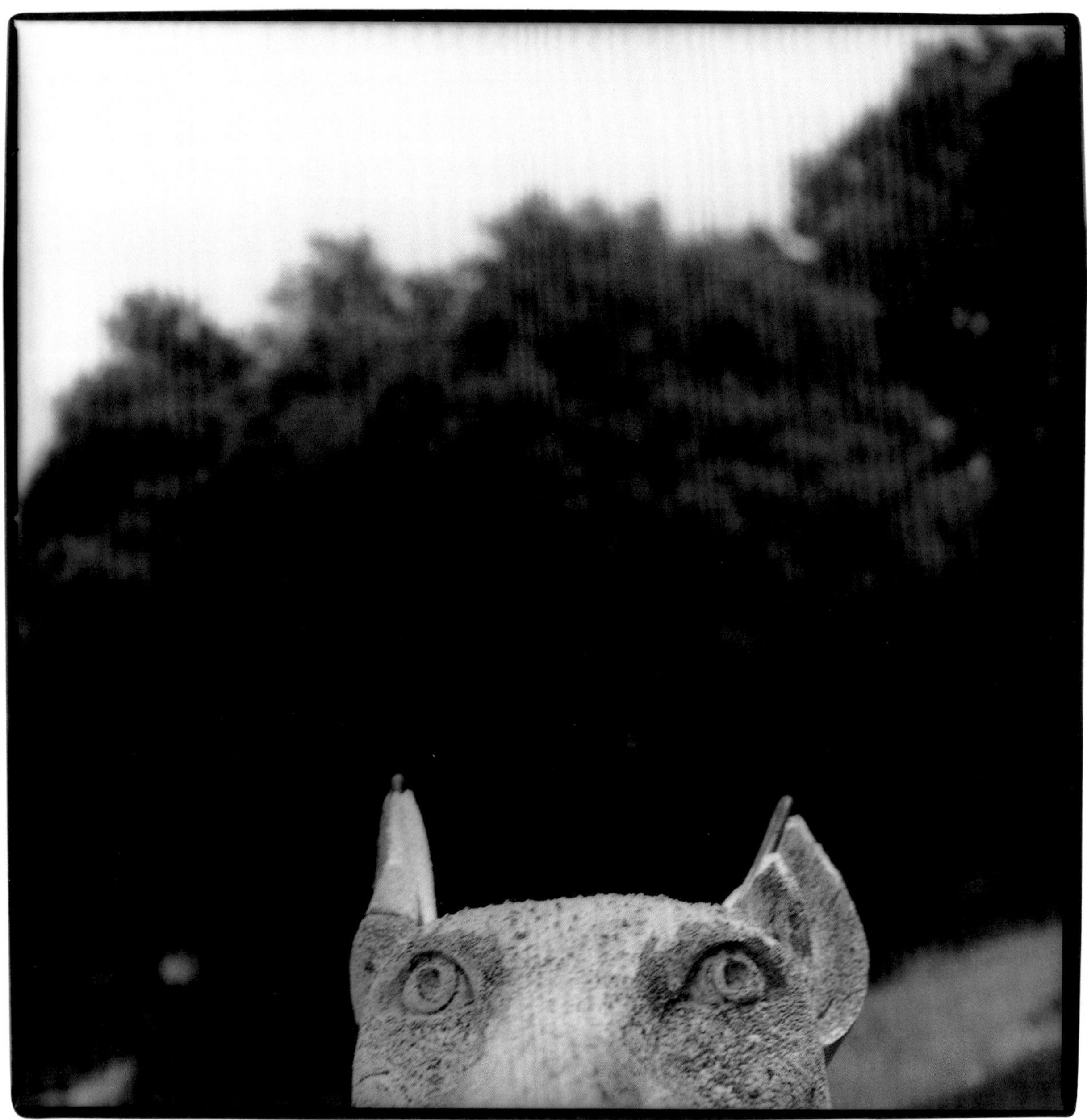

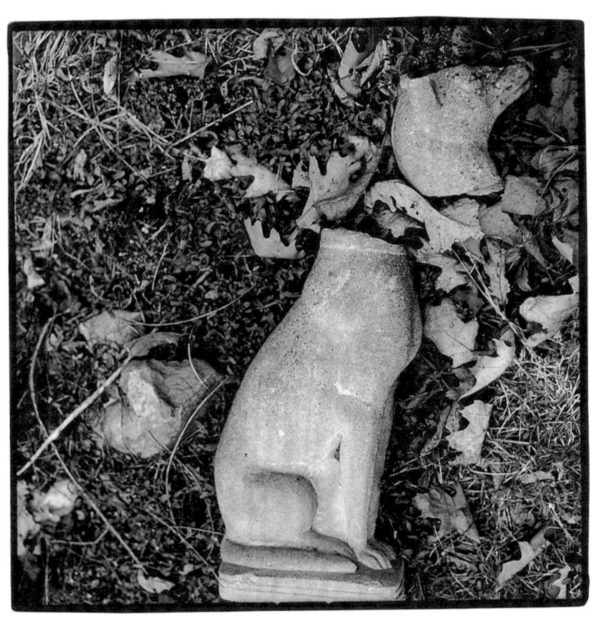

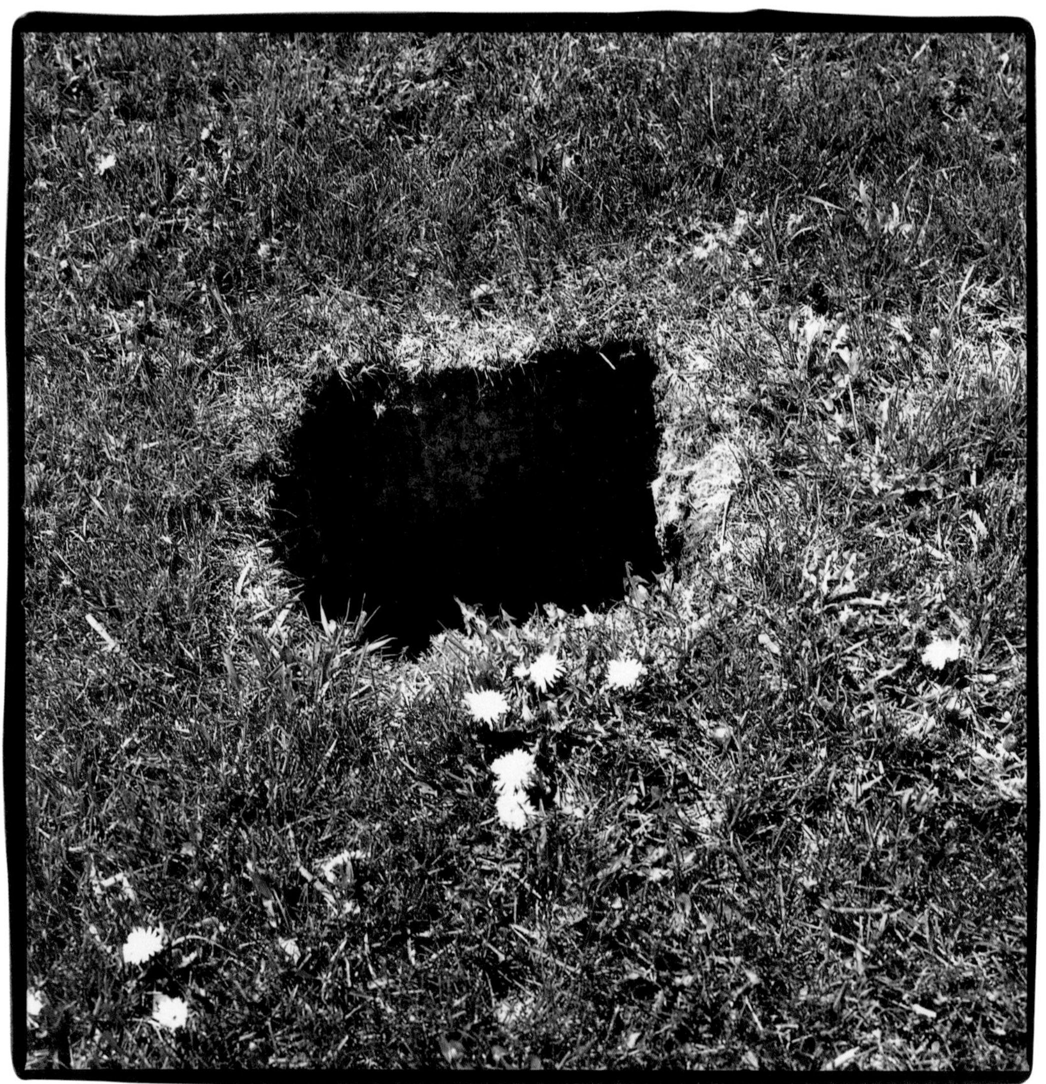

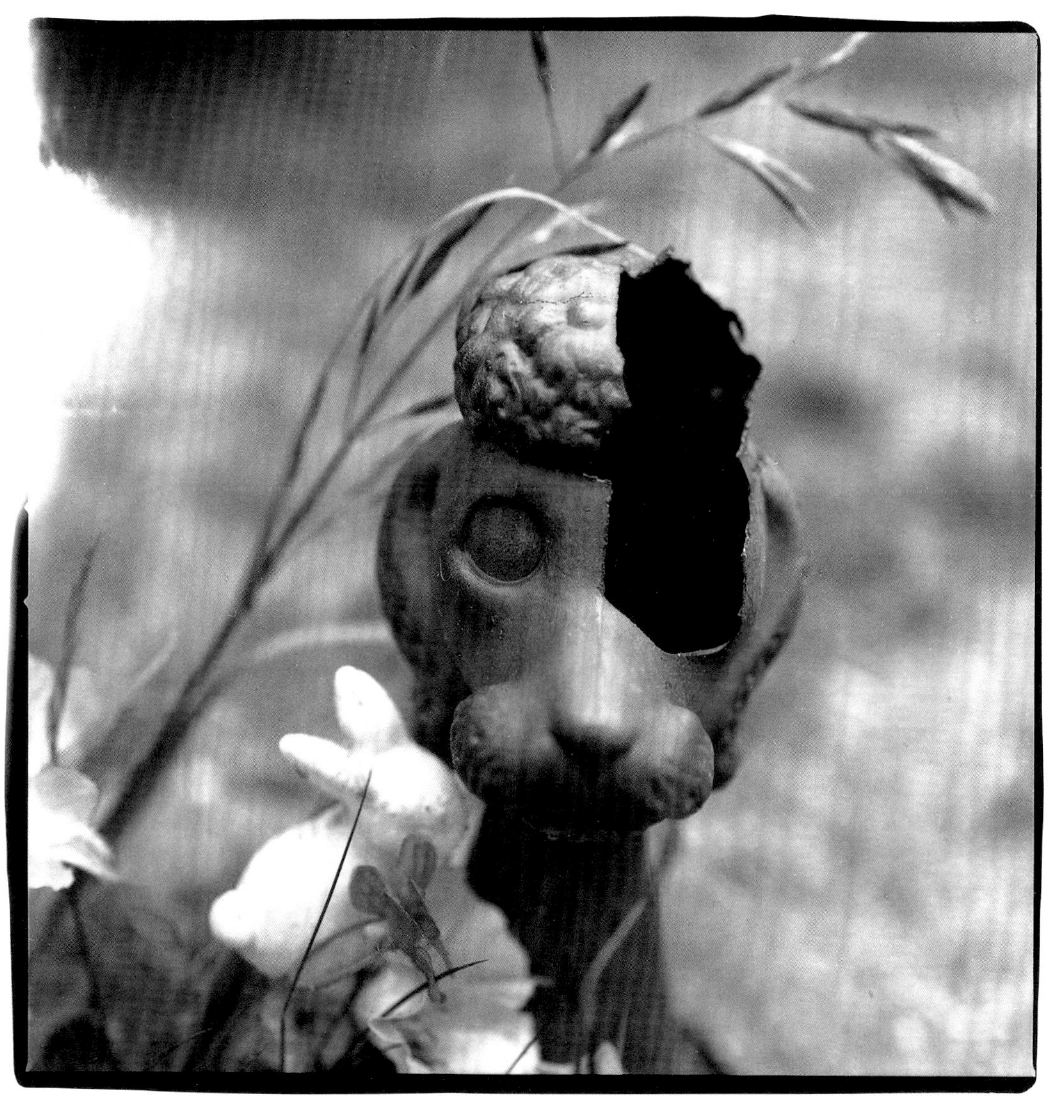

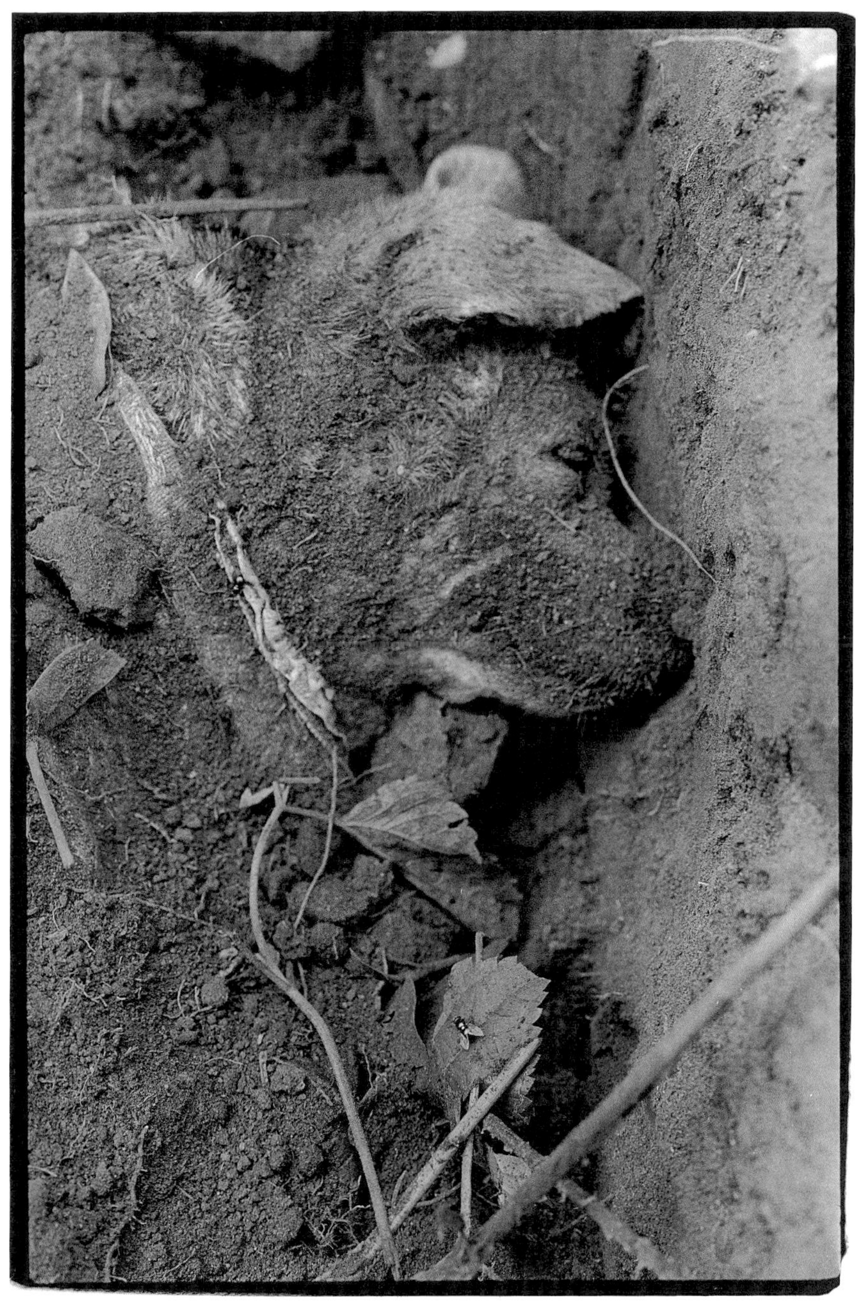

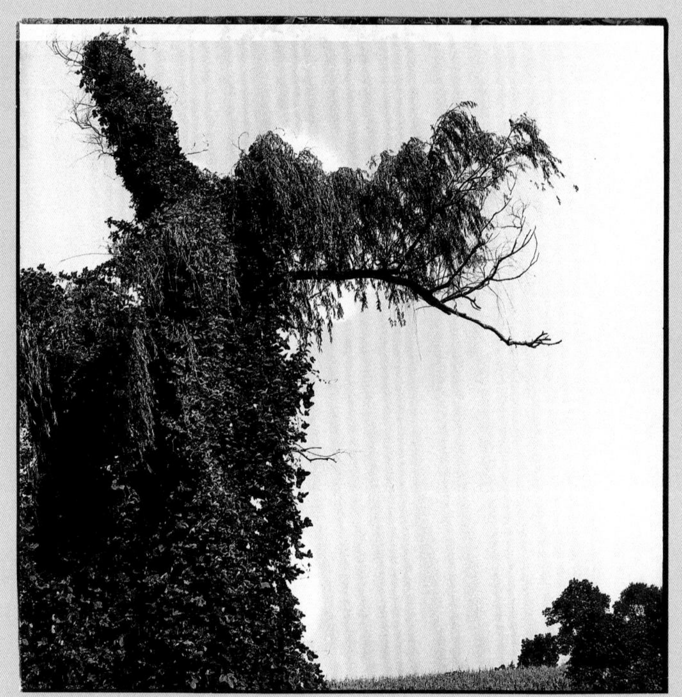

Once I photographed an old man who lived across from Three Mile Island. Every morning, flanked by the gnarly trees he had planted in his youth, he stood at his gate and measured how much radiation there was that day.

Trees don't talk; like spirits, they whisper.

Every year, my father picked autumn foliage in the Buda Hills. Later, when we came to America, he brought home his fall bouquet from an upstate forest. After he died the tradition stopped.

One year I forgot to weed; now I have a forest in my backyard.

Several years ago, in October, when my mother was very ill, on the ledge outside her building lay some maple branches, as if placed there for me. They were pink and gold and already dry. I brought them to her. Surprised when she saw them, she asked who they were from—but we both already knew.

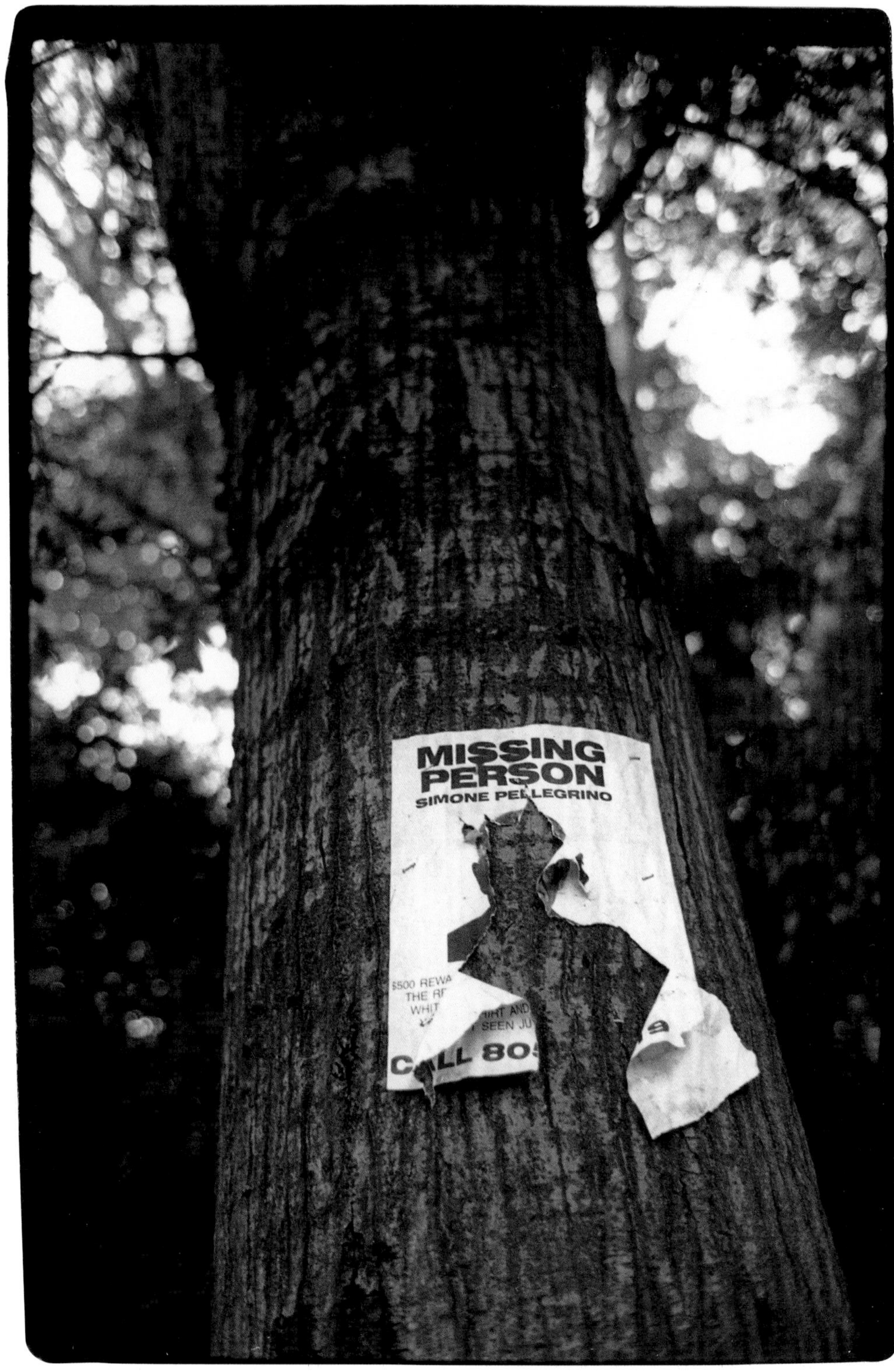
MISSING
PERSON
SIMONE PELLEGRINO
$500 REWA
CALL 80

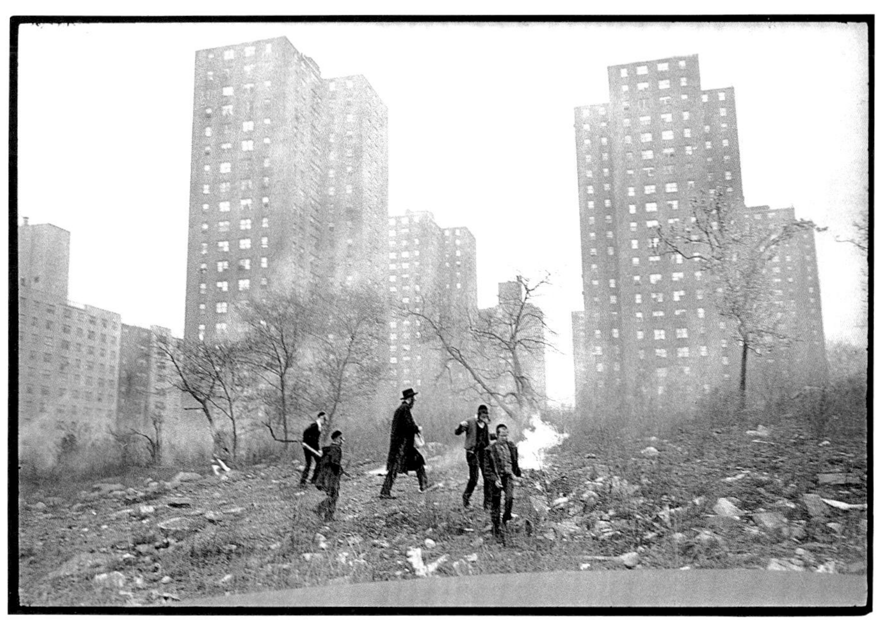

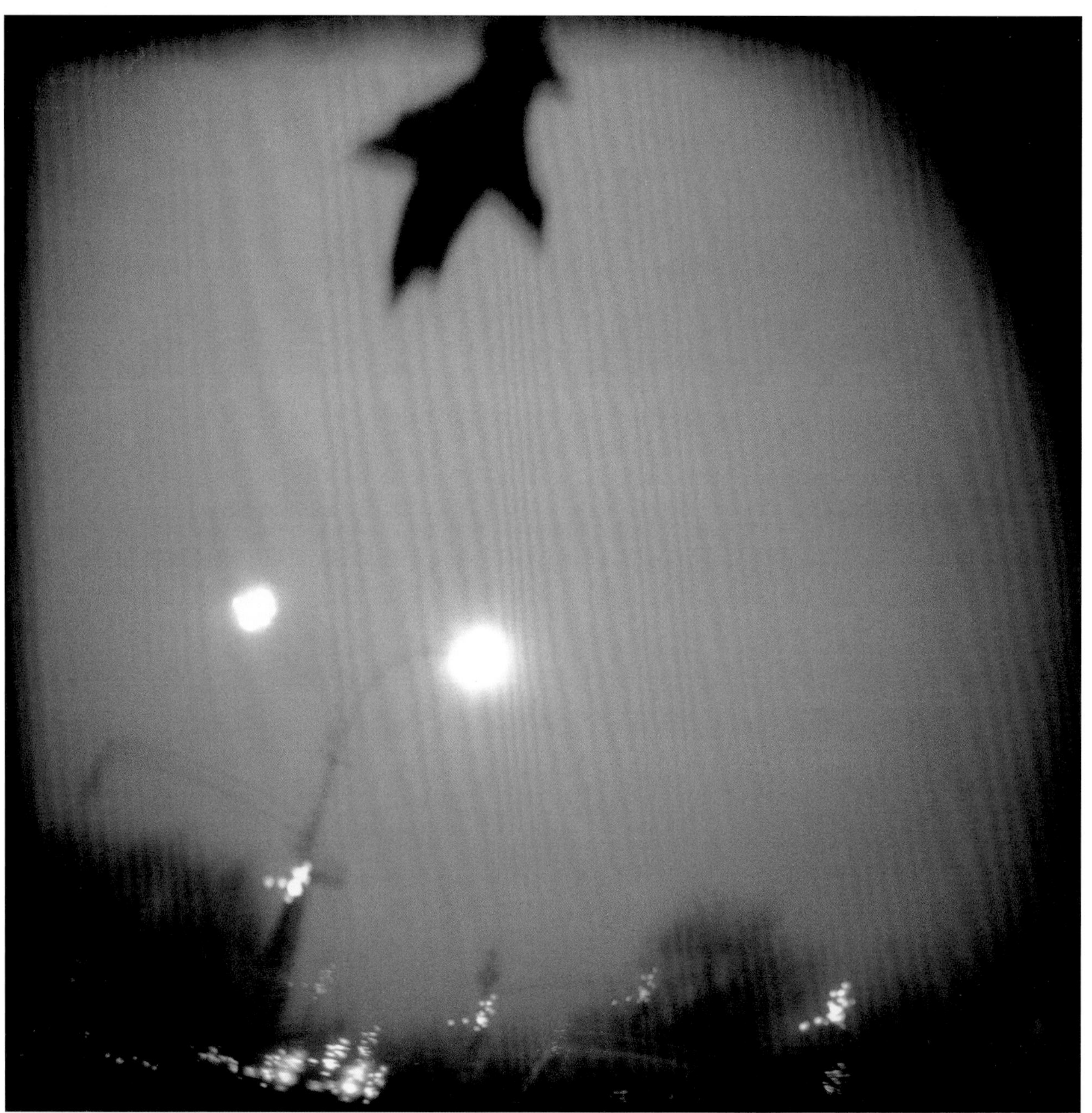

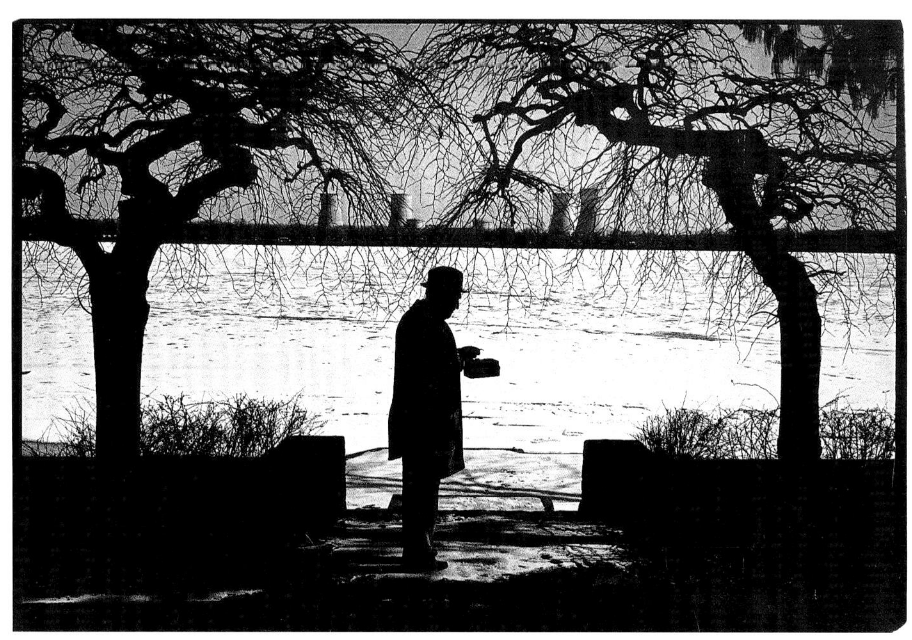

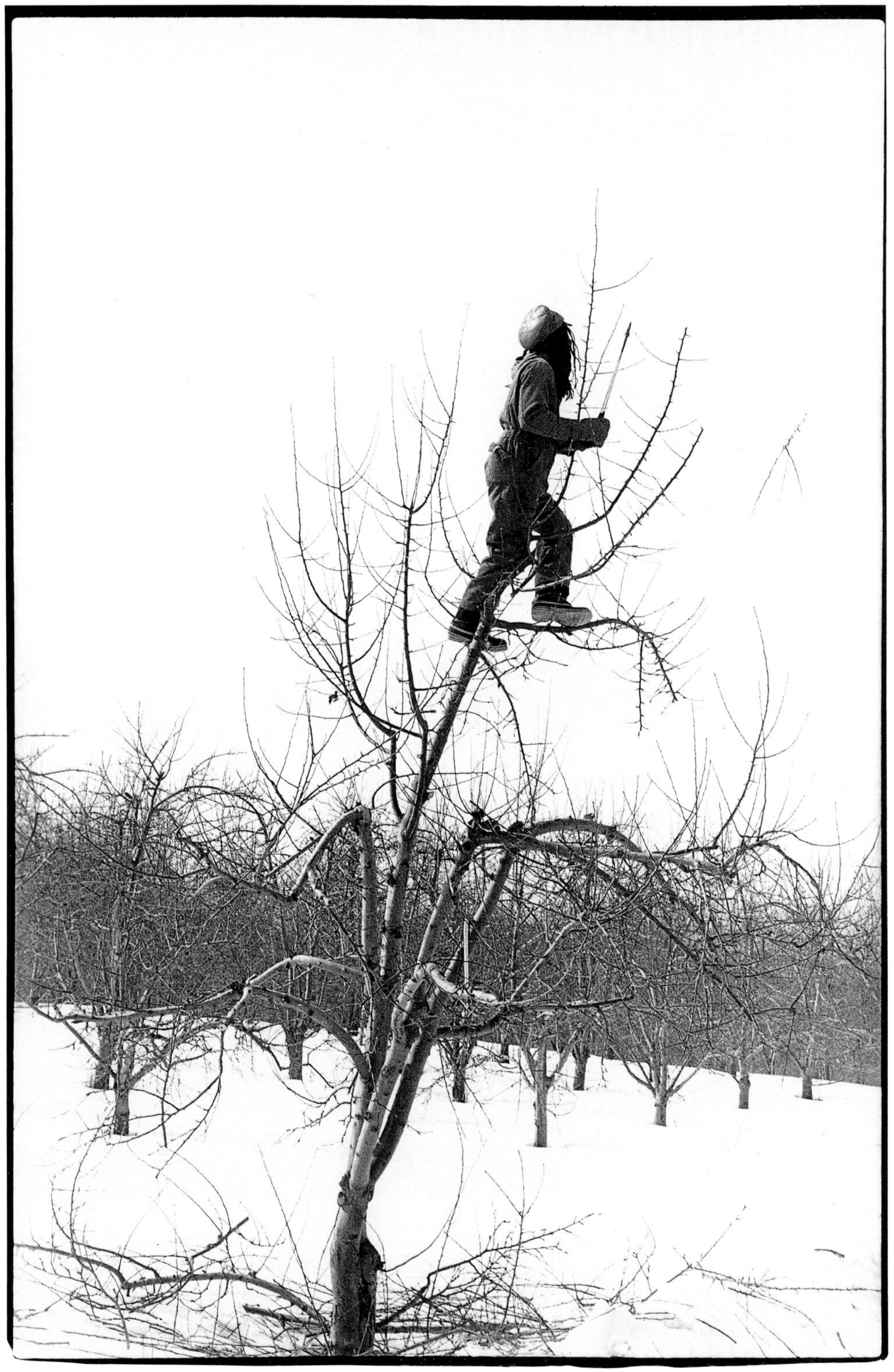

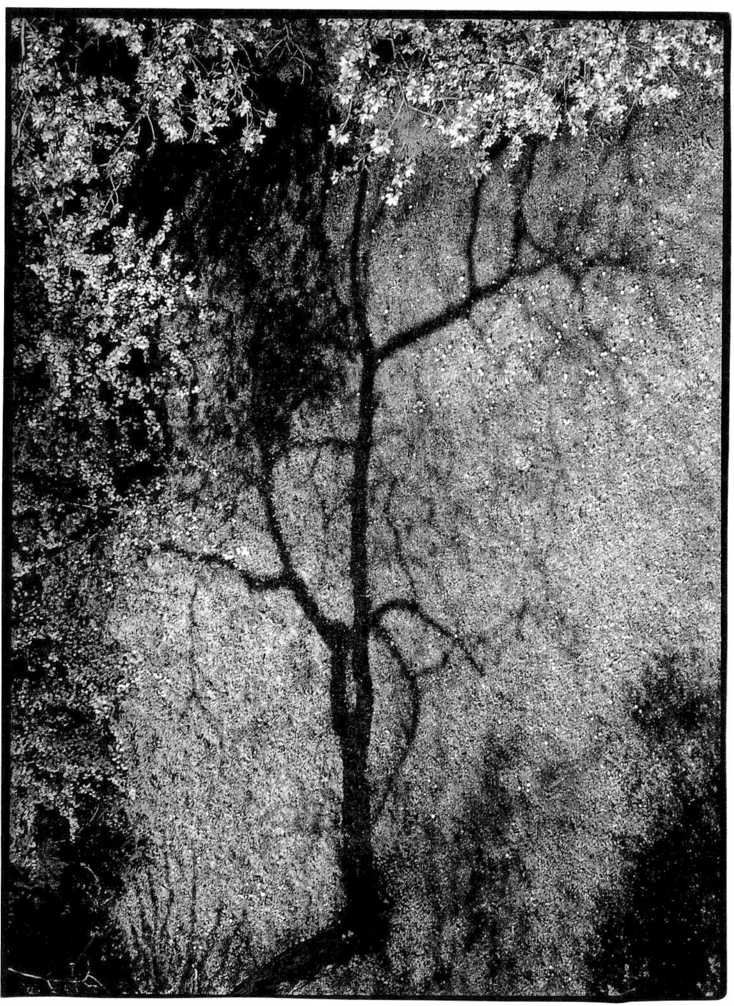

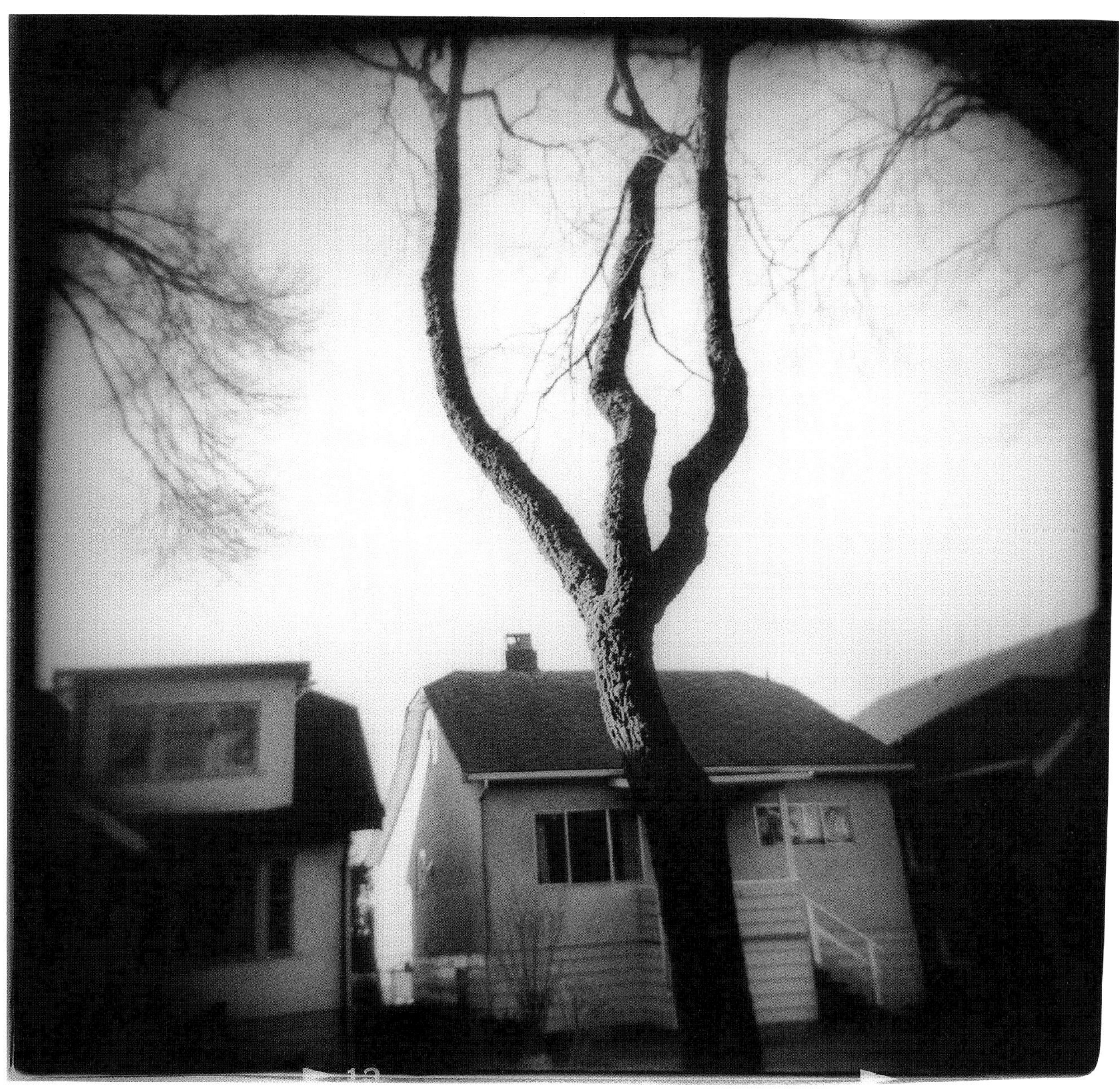

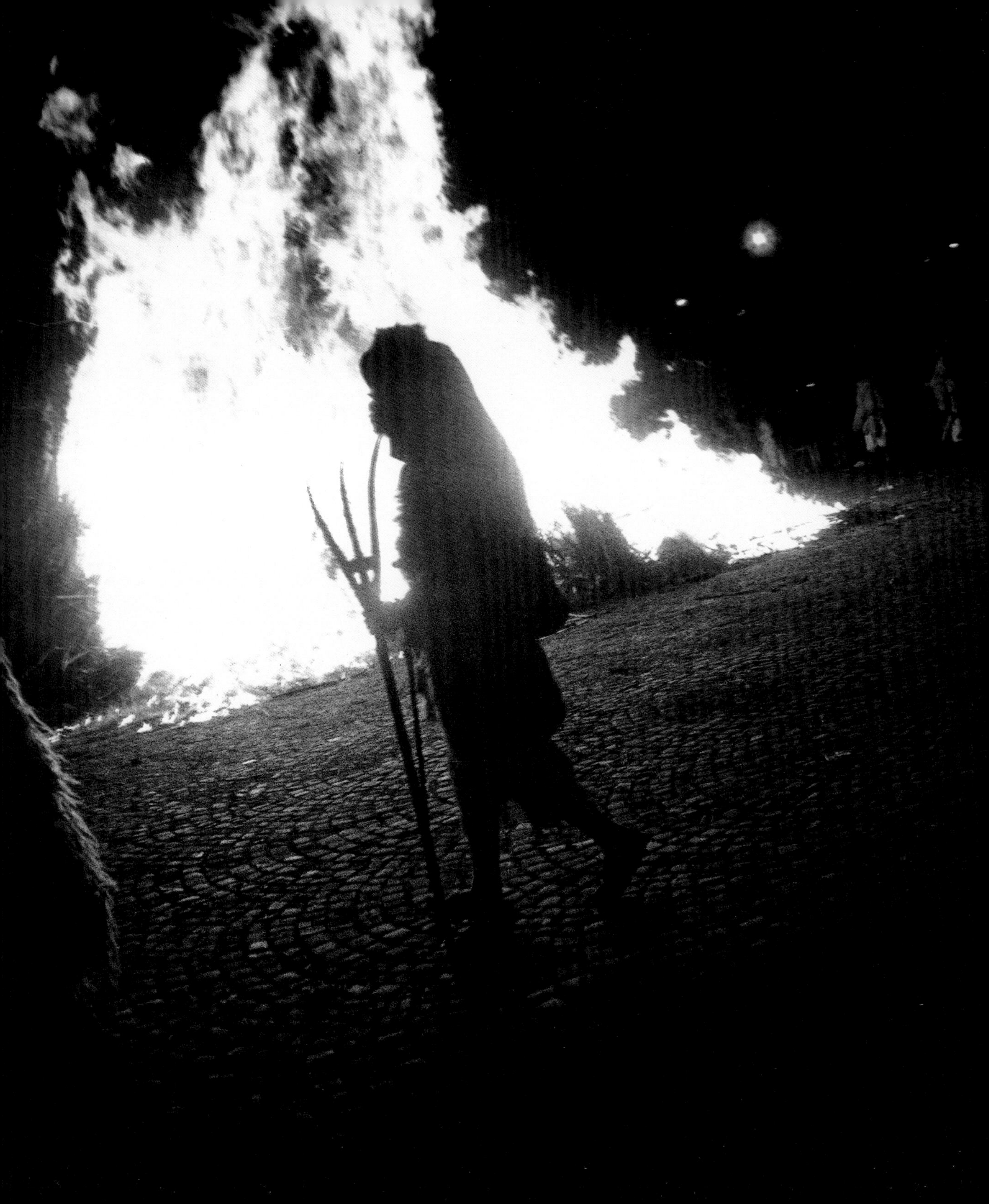

I'd been thinking about forks when the phone rang. "Yes, I found out, you killed my sister with a fork," said a young woman, and hung up. With a jolt I recalled that this tame and graceful dining implement is a descendent of the spear and the trident.

Long before the horrors of Srebrenica and Tuzla, on a 1992 journey between Belgrade and Zagreb, a group of journalists and I stopped at Vukovar. Devastated the year before by bullets and fire, the town stood empty, eerily quiet like a museum installation, a hideous monument to Serb victory.

The road divided. Off to one side was a crucifix riddled with bullets. In the middle of the street, a brand-new sign advertised the only restaurant in town. It featured a cheery drawing of a smug, mustachioed chef holding up a small cow skewered on a fork.

In ordinary times, we would have been amused by a billboard of a happy pig or cow, contentedly offering itself as dinner, but in that setting, among the ruins, it was a diabolical vision.

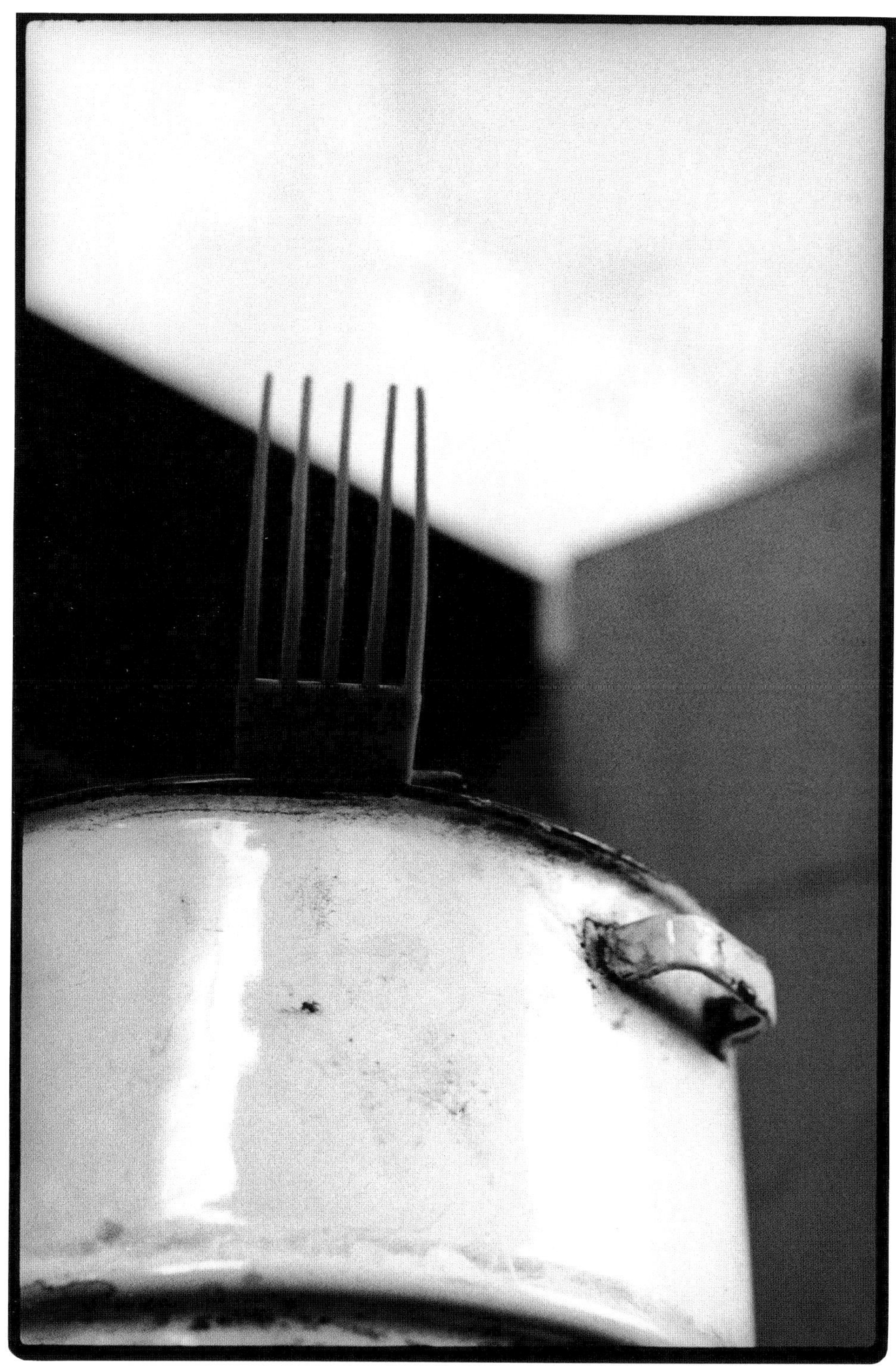

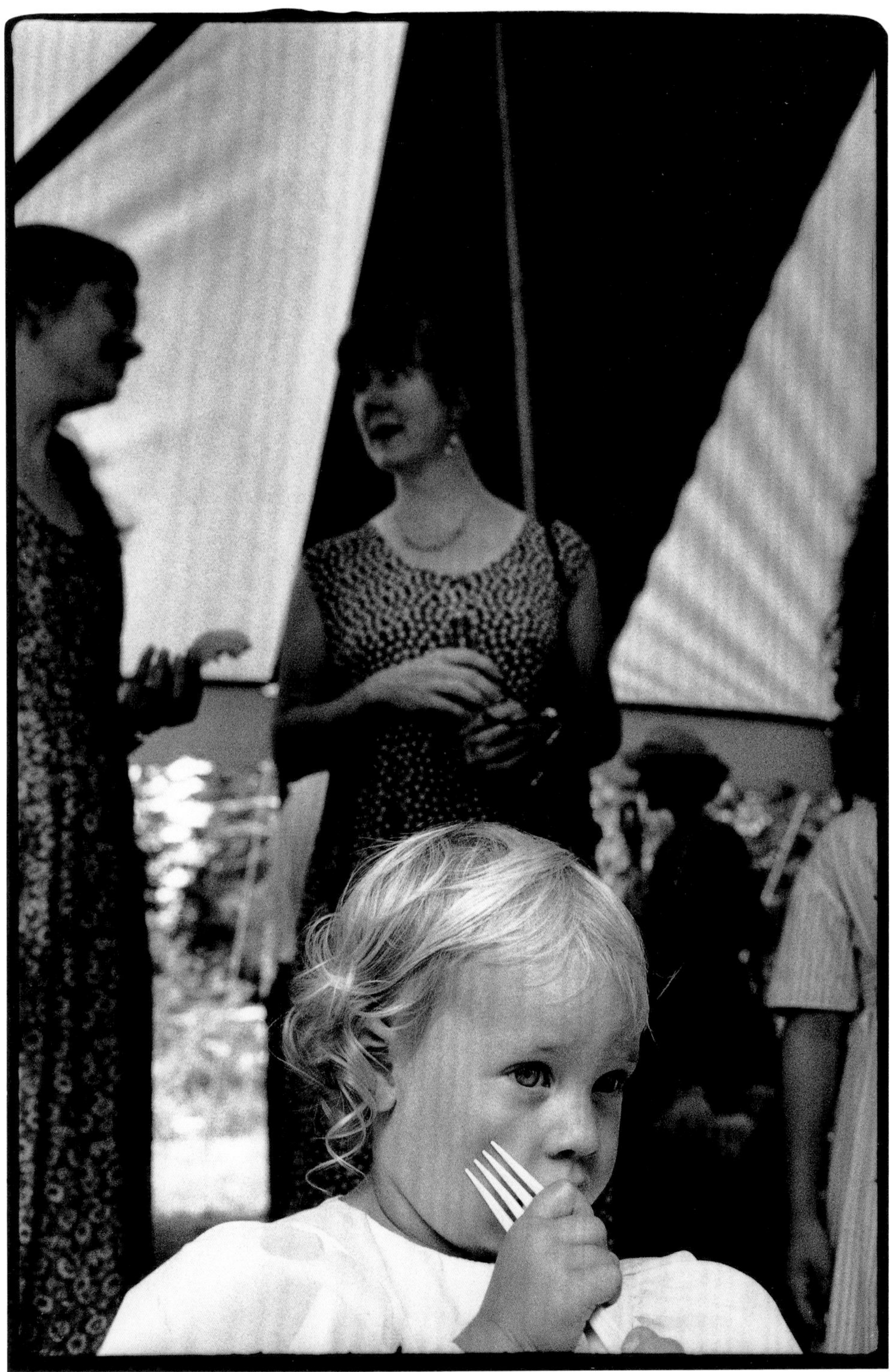

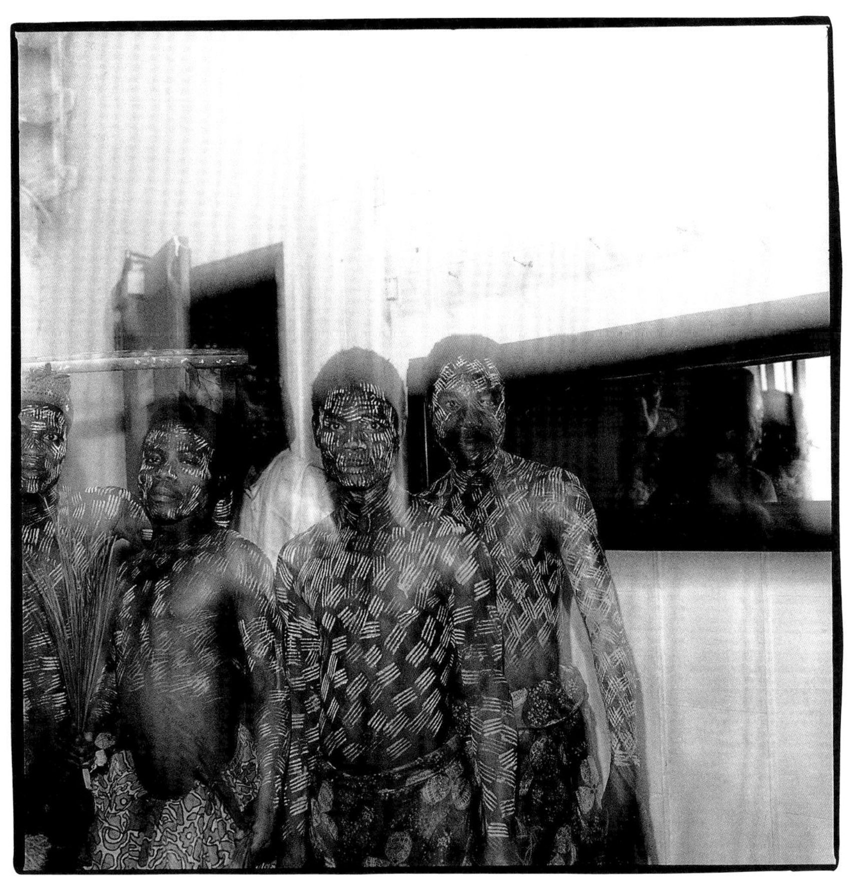

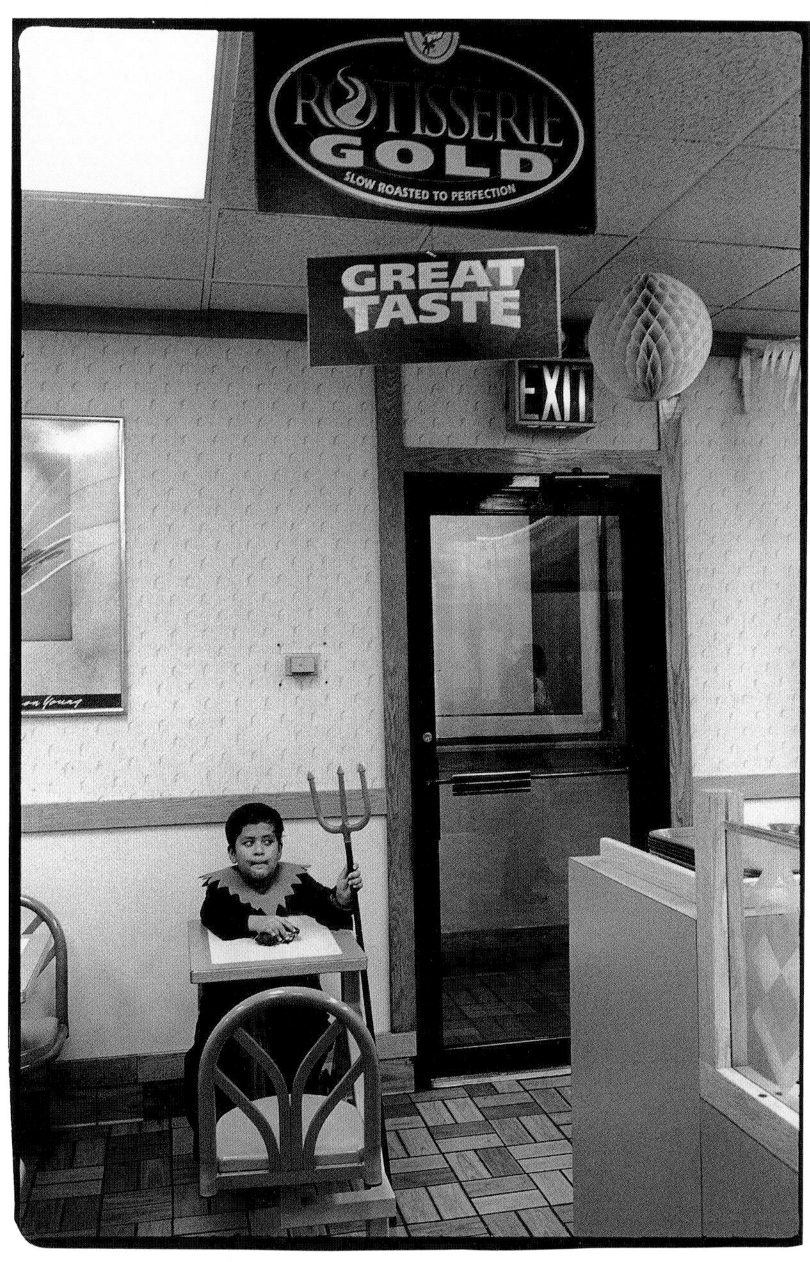
ROTISSERIE
GOLD
SLOW ROASTED TO PERFECTION
GREAT
TASTE
EXIT

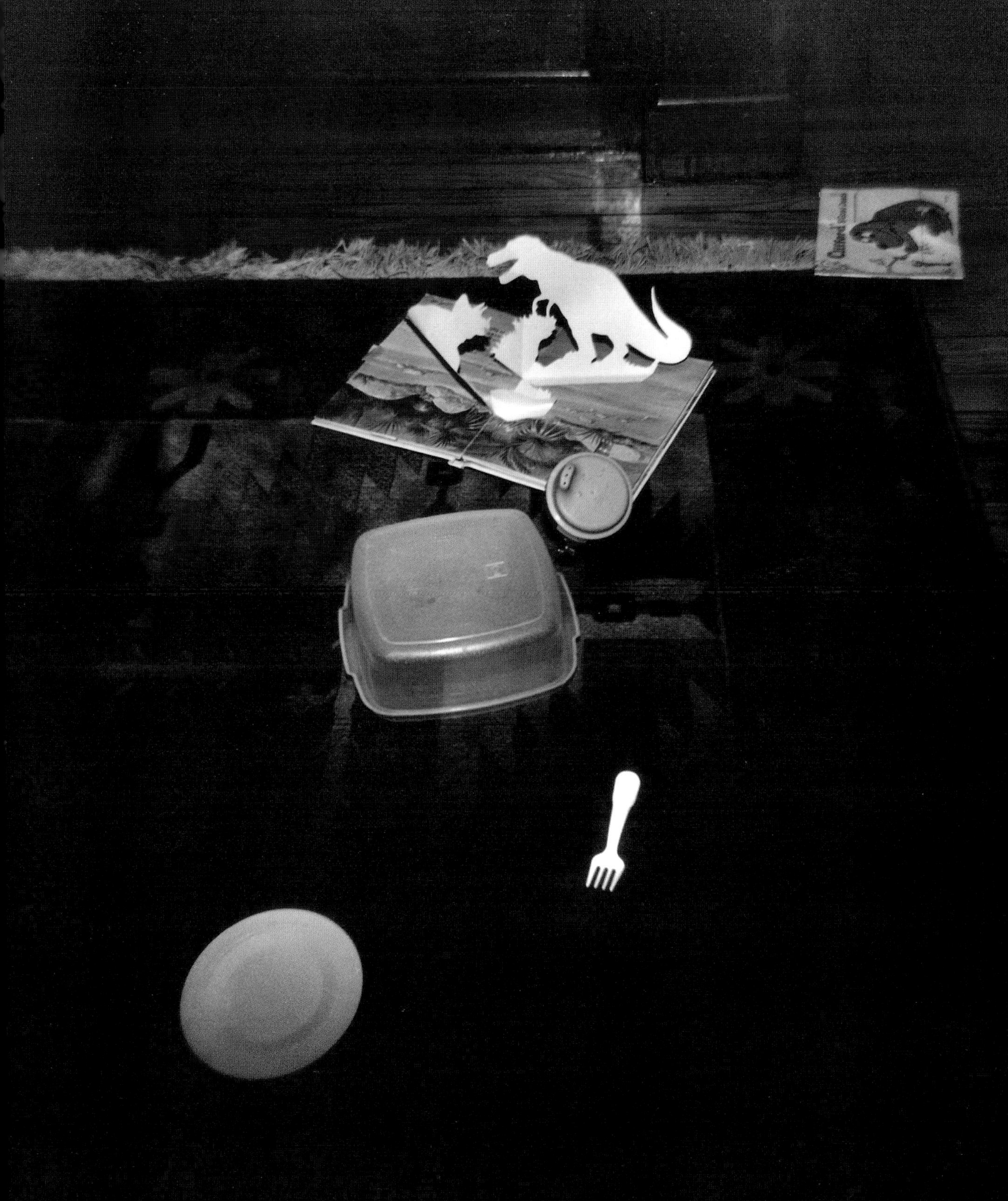

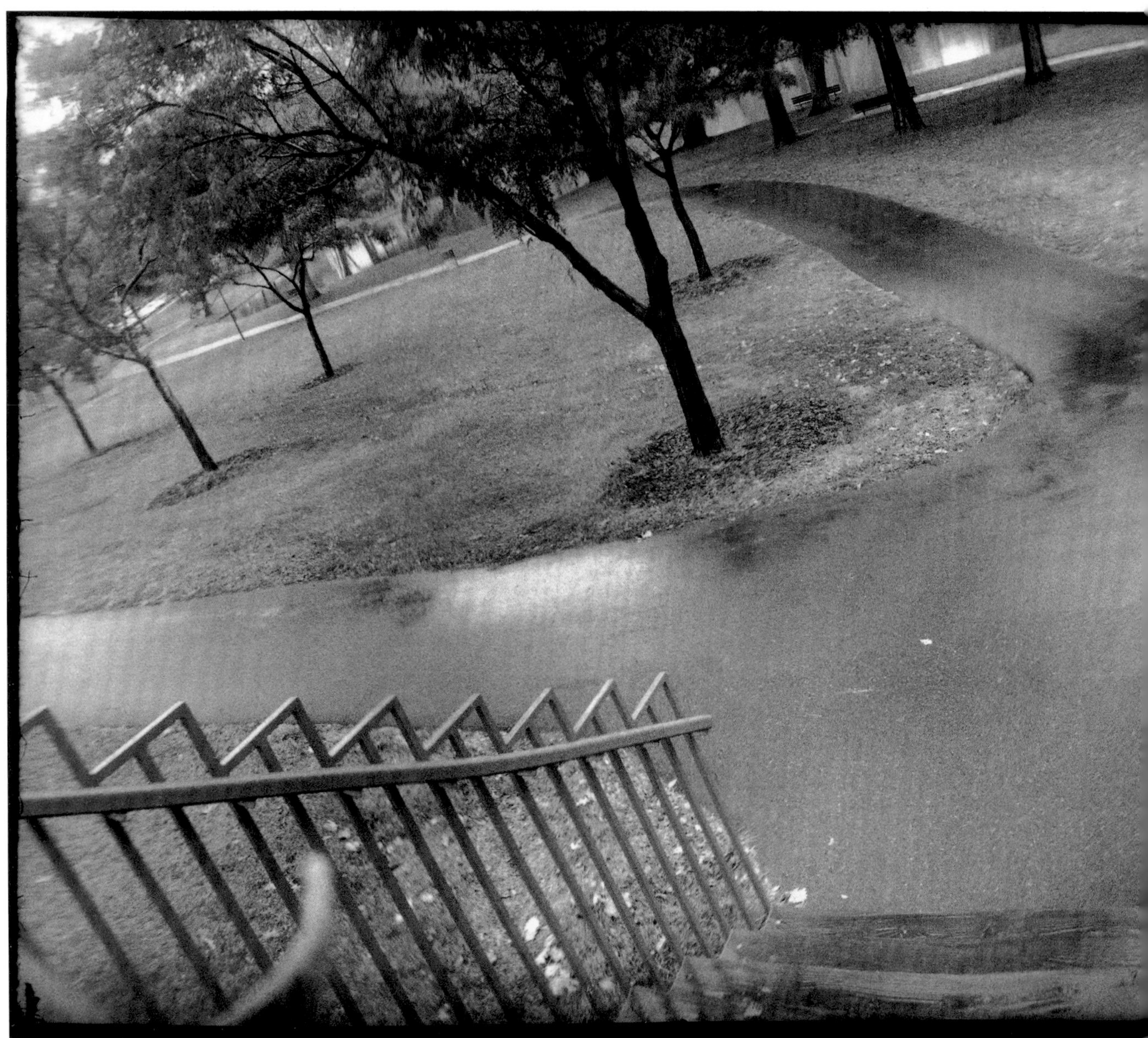

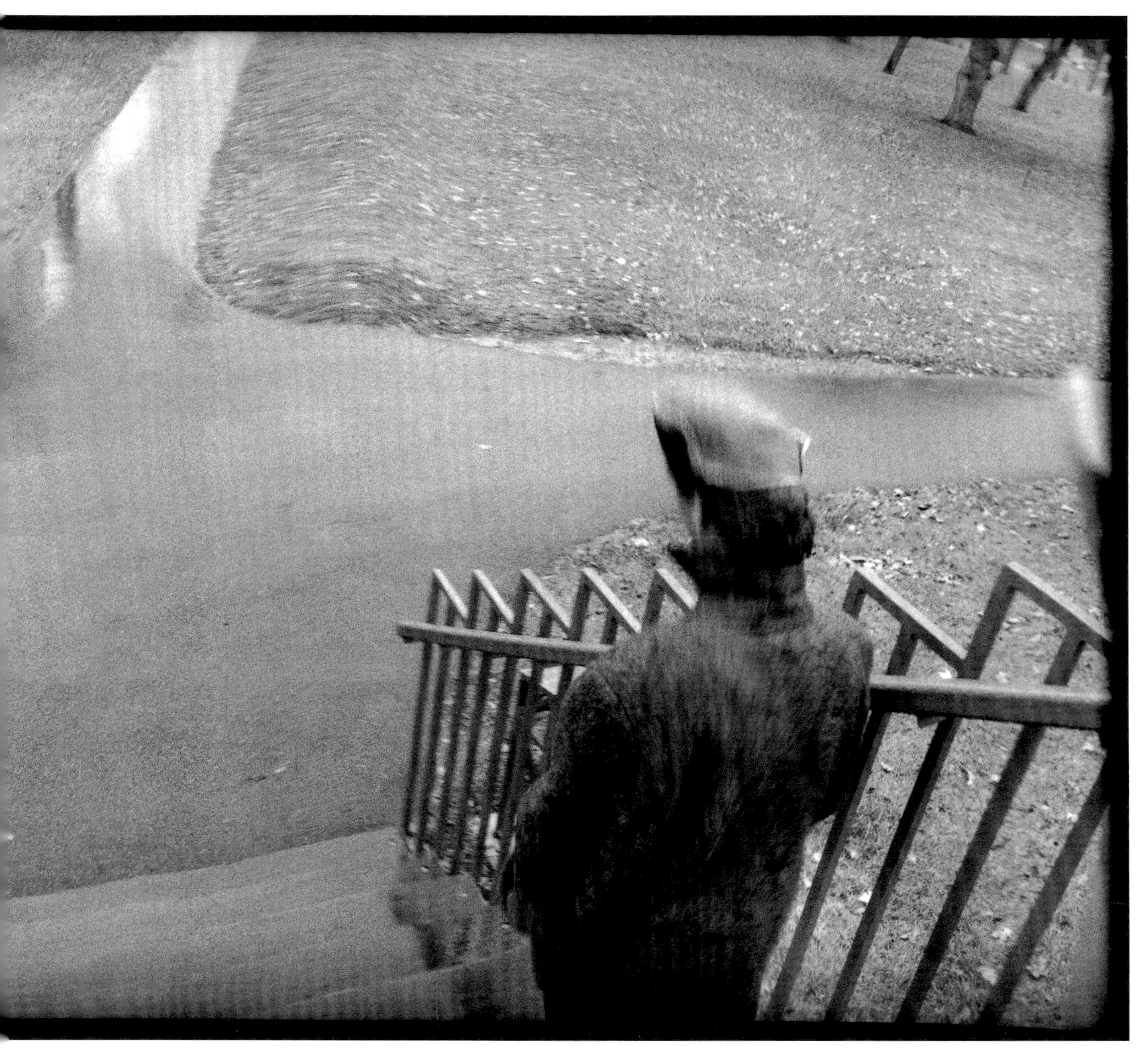

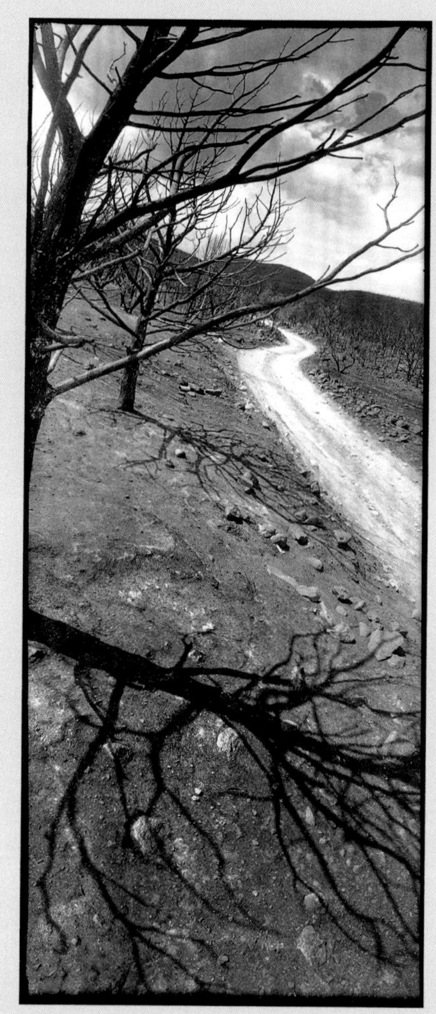

"All roads join in plastic," revealed Elliot one night, sitting up in bed in halfdream and startling me out of sleep.

All roads, yellow-brick and less traveled, are like rivers, never the same. They stretch forward and back, and fade in the distance. As an exile, I regularly retrace my steps to places where a residue of my former self lingers, but as a photographer I follow any road that beckons.

In my dreams, I'm strolling in a brightly lit museum. There are rooms and rooms full of people. There are colorful paintings on the walls. There are guards and benches. It's warm. Suddenly my dog takes off through a door to an as yet unfinished section of the museum that's dim, gray, and cold. I rush after him because I must—I love my dog and the haze of the unknown.

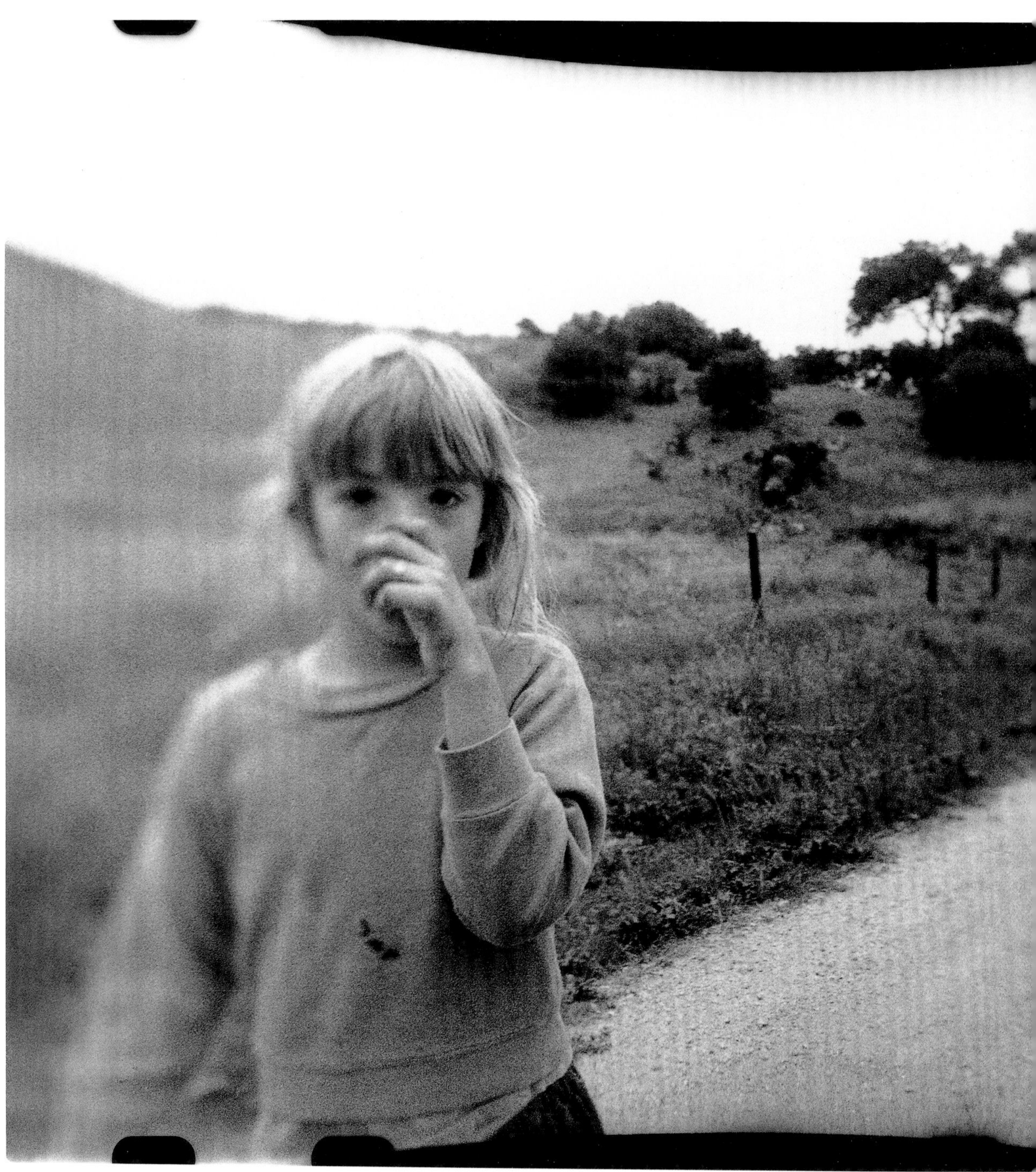

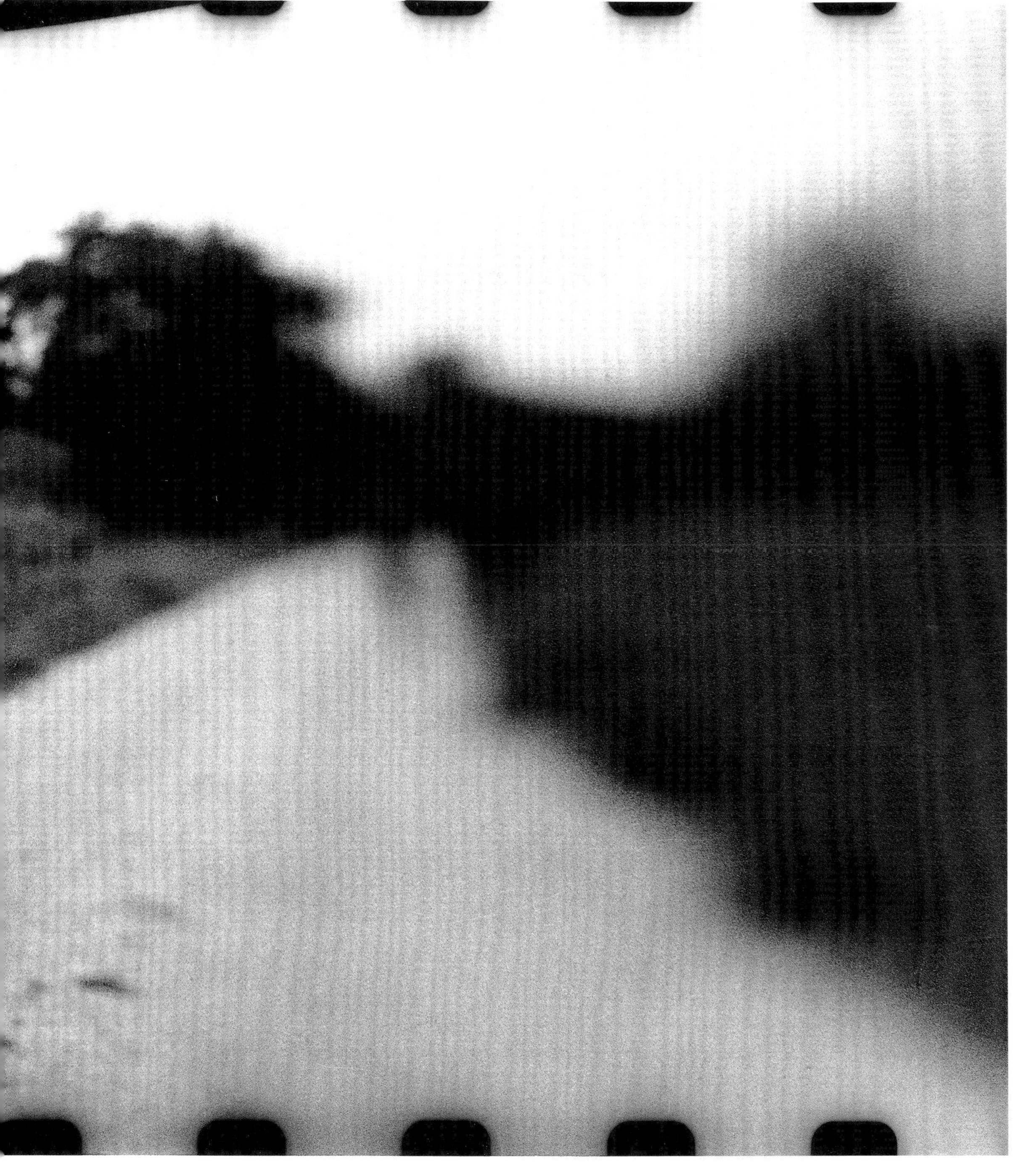

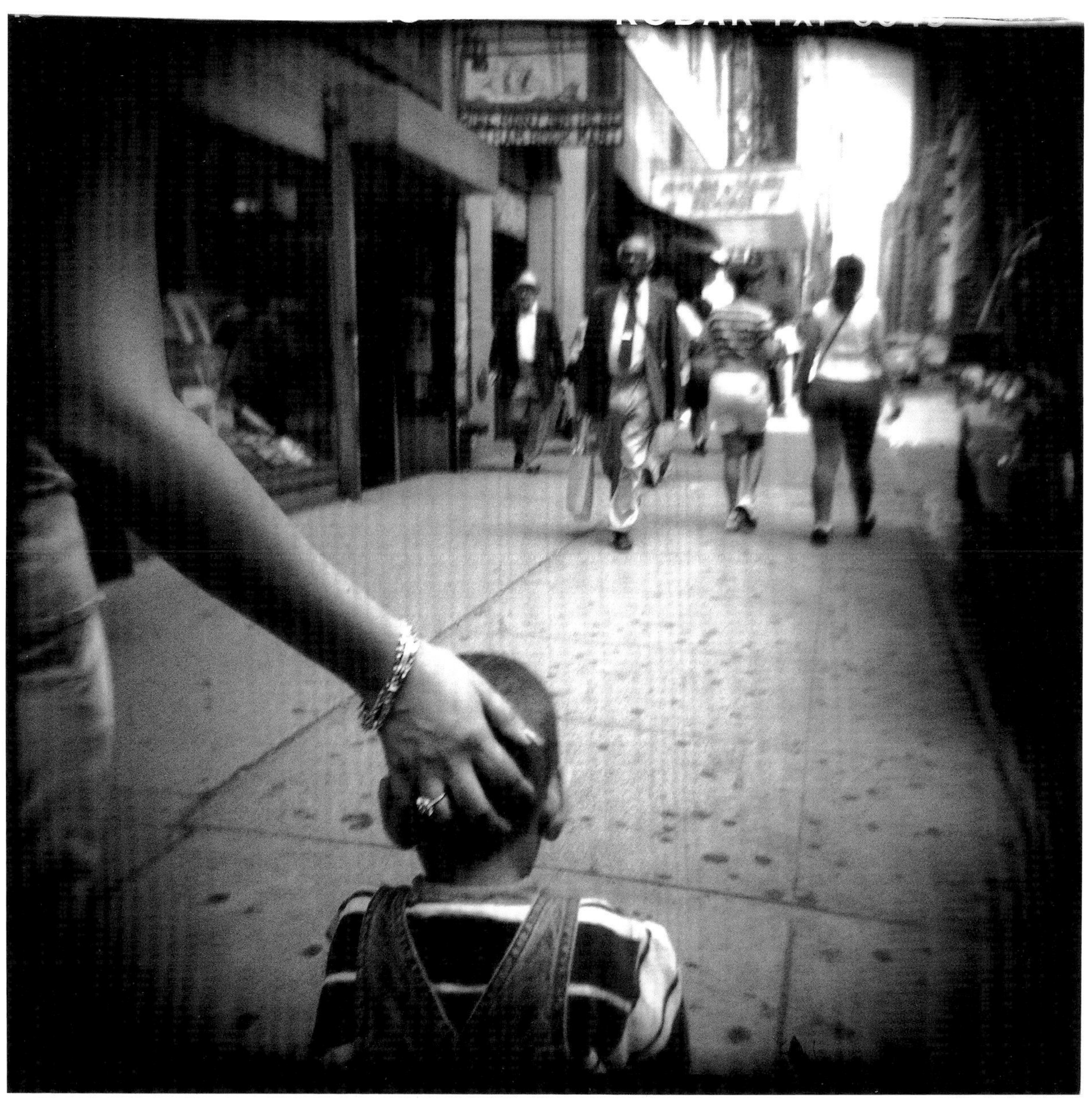

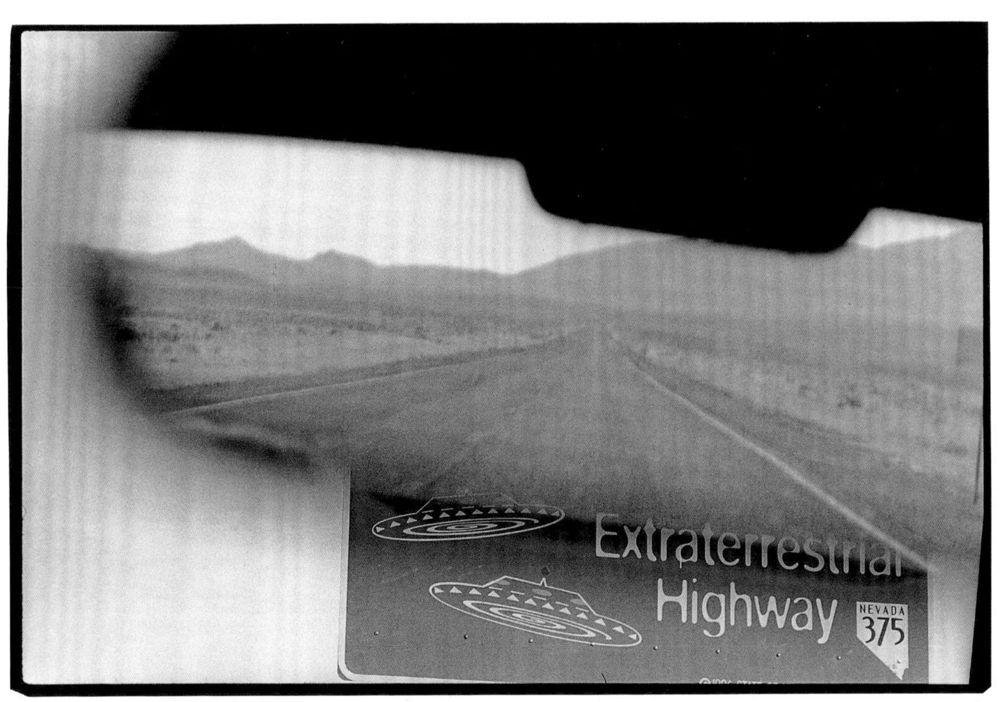
Extraterrestrial
Highway
NEVADA
375

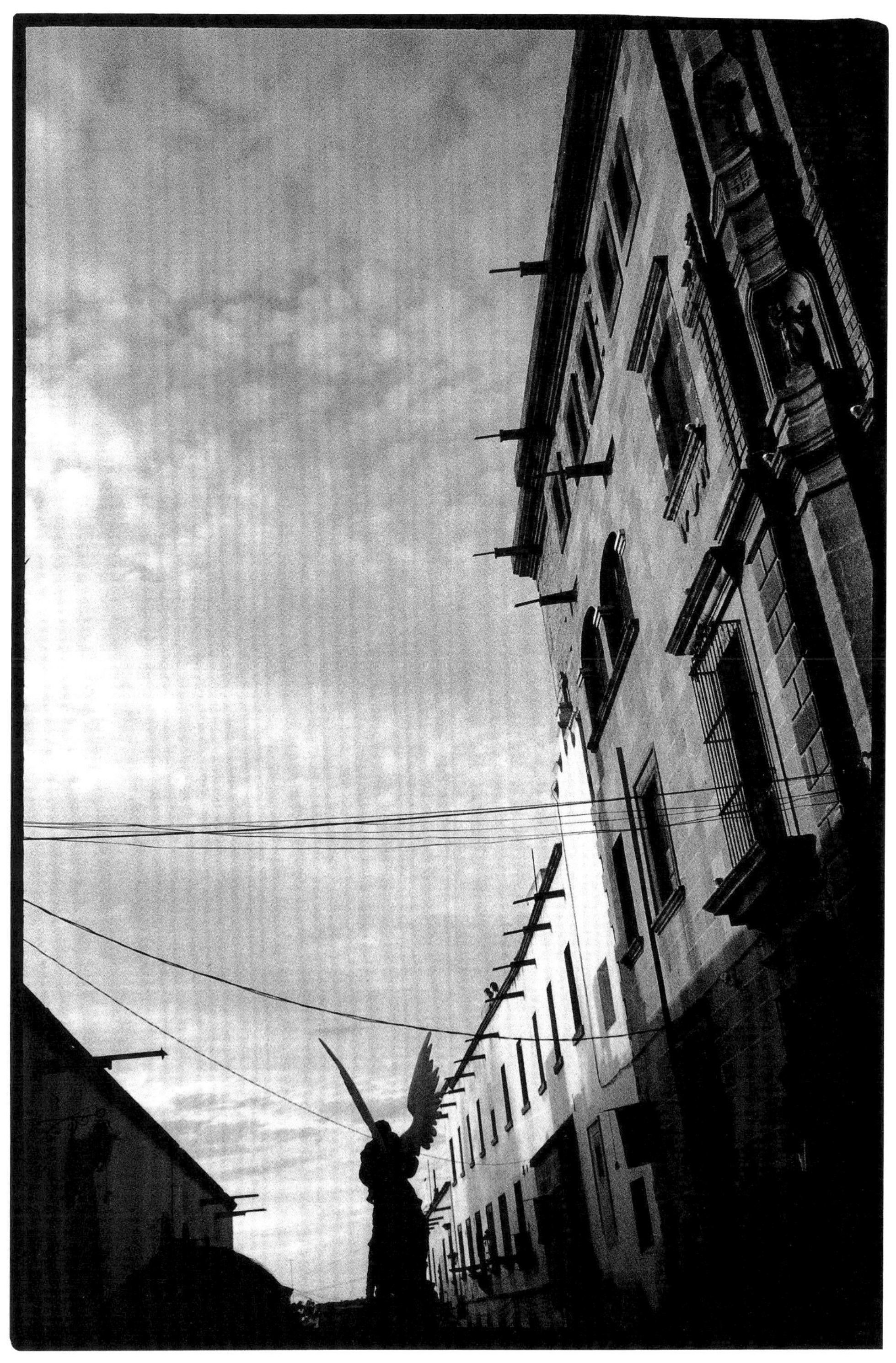

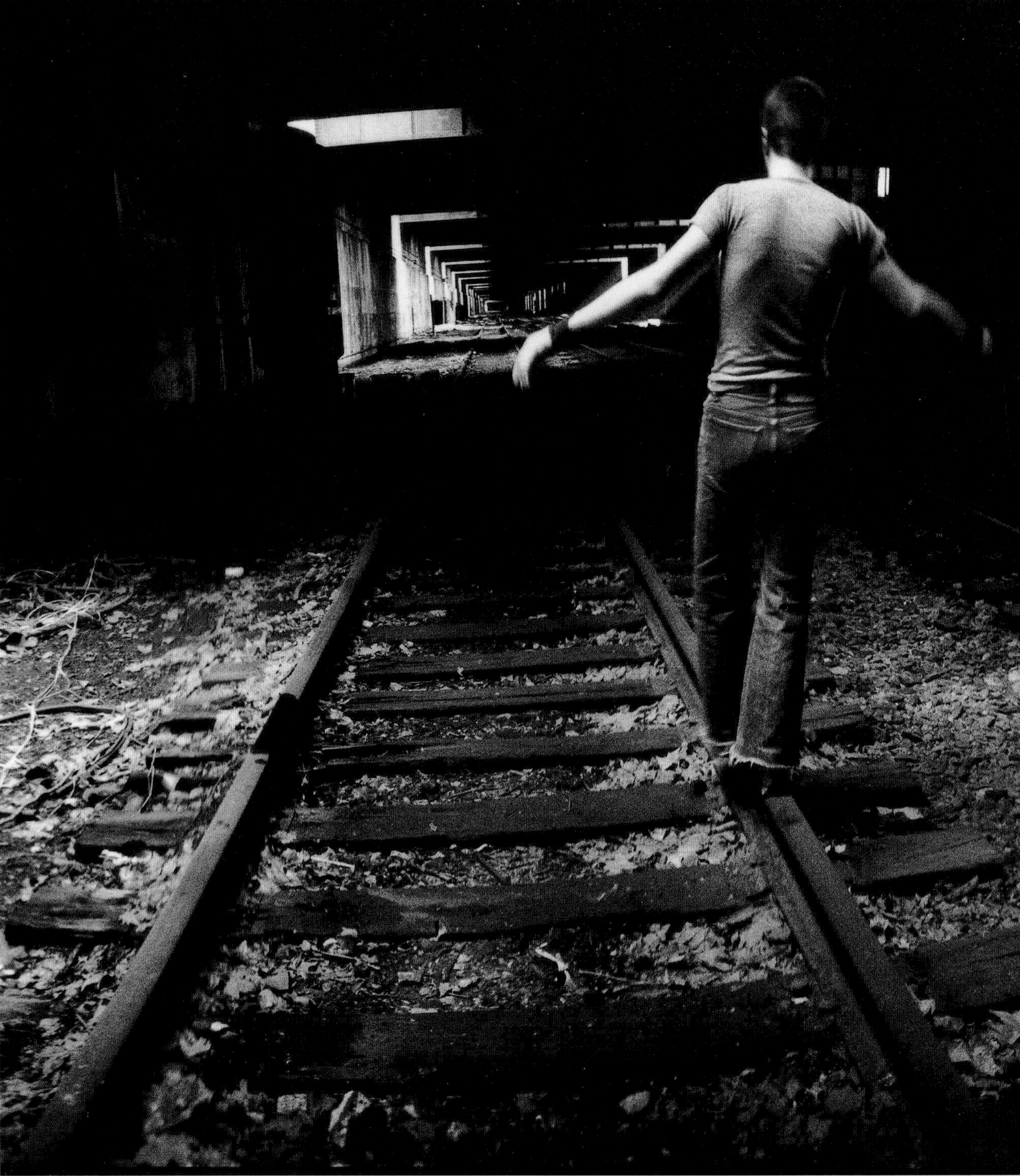

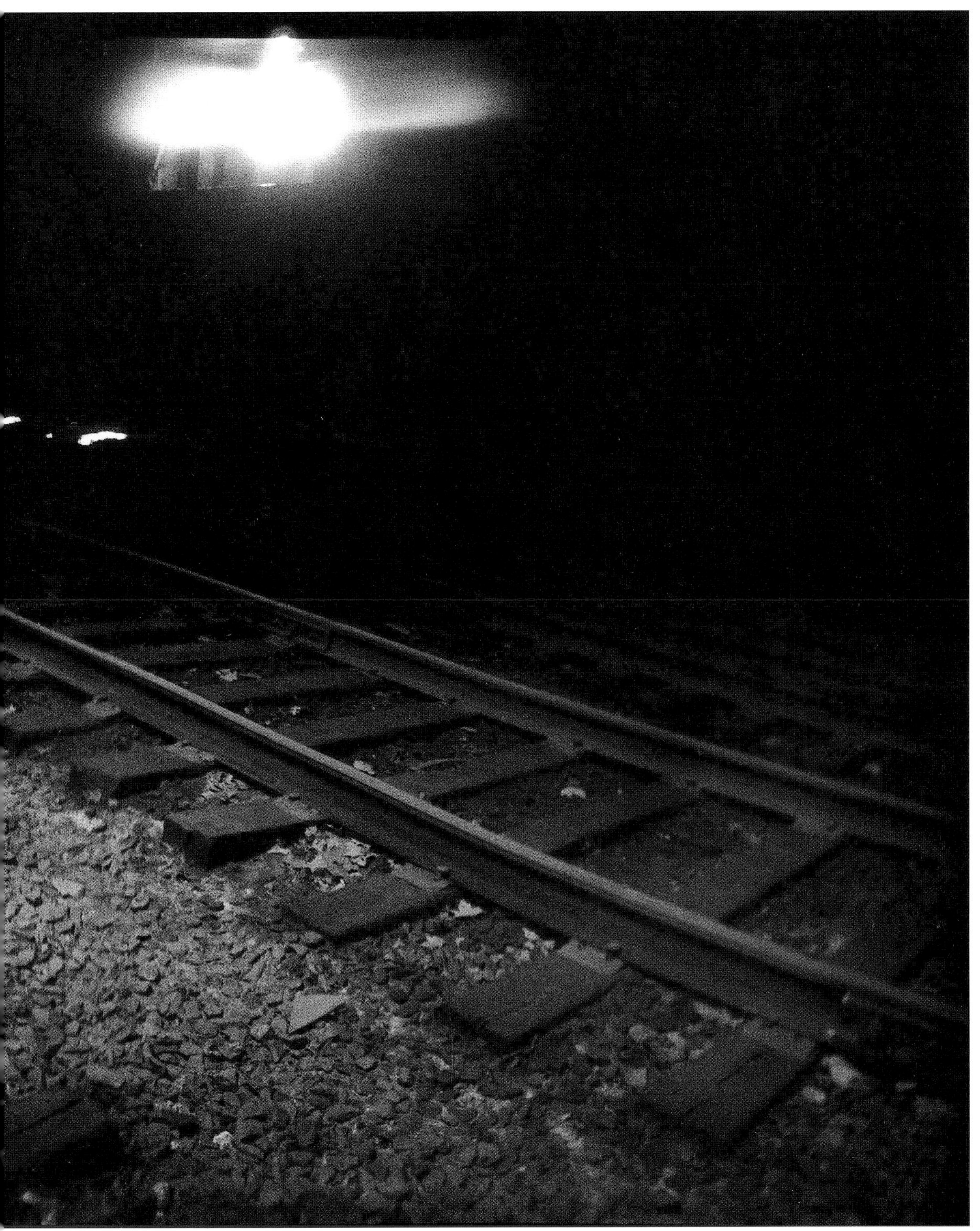

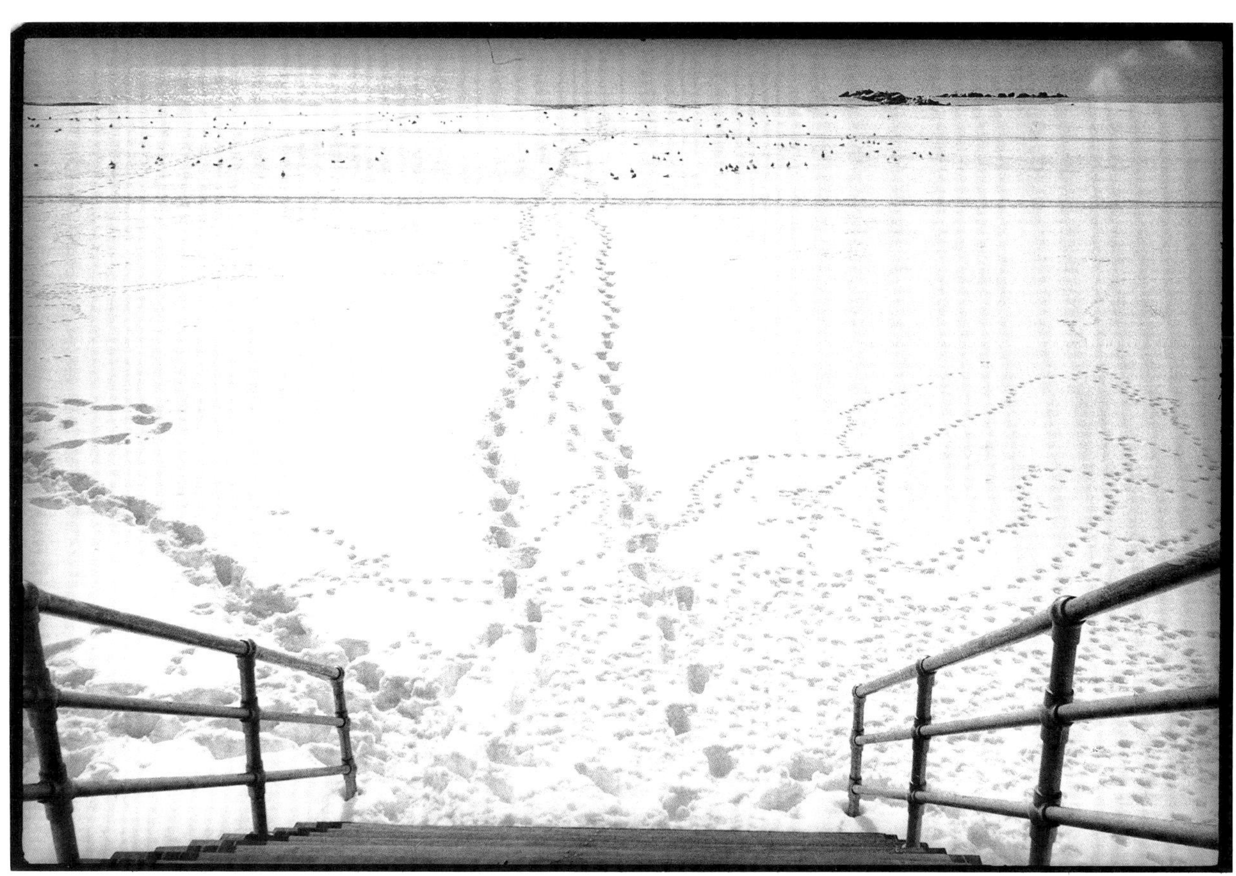

An Art Deco clock with a cracked face was just one of the many cherished objects on my parents' desk. Many years before, who knows how many, it broke, leaving its stiffened hands pointing eternally to six minutes to one.

Revelations seem to tip toe into our line of vision and go BOO! It was like that when I sat vigil with my terminally ill mother. The room was sunny and quiet and she was sleeping. Then suddenly she sighed her last breath. When I looked at my watch, the time was six minutes to one, the same as it had always been on that clock, just a few feet away.

Signs & Relics started as a farewell to my mother. She died in 1993, thirteen years after my father passed away. I wish they were still here: I would ask them about the clock, how they got it, how it broke, and many other things I didn't ask, or didn't know how to ask. If the answer is there, how do we know to look for it if we don't know the question?

These meditations were first sparked by Susan Szenasy, editor of *Metropolis* magazine, and were in part published as columns between April 1994 and December 1996. Later I fidgeted with the words and added new pictures until they were transformed into a book.

I dedicate this book to my parents, who I still sense hovering about. I thank Elliot, my husband and teenage sweetheart, with whom I can "have my cake and eat it too," for his love and his patience; and Mishi, our amazing son, for his rambunctious nature and the joy he gives to us. But how can I thank so many friends, colleagues, kindred spirits, teachers, mentors, and especially the subjects, some whose names I don't even know and who may have been ghosts or even animals, but who shared in making the photographs? Here is a list with some of the names I remember, incomplete, but long, due to my age: Abbie, Alice, Alison, Allen, Aly, Amy, André, Andrea, Anikó, Anna, Anne, Annik, Arthur, Audrey, Bandi, Becky, Ben, Betsy, Bettina, Bill, Bonni, Bruce, Carl, Carole, Charlie, Christine, Clay, Craig, Dan, Daniel, David, Deborah, Delphine, Dick, Dilys, Donna, Dr. Donnenfeld, Dora, Doris, Dorothy, Elisabeth, Eric, Ernesto, Erzsi, Eryl, Esther, Eva, Francene, Francesca, Fred, Gábor, George, Giselle, Grace, Graciella, Guy, Hadas, Henner, Howard, Jane, Janet, Jeff, Jen, Jill, Jim, Joan, Joe, John, Jonas, Judit, Juli, Karcsi, Karen, Karin, Károly, Kate, Kathy, Keith, Kevin, Klári, Larry, Leslie, Lettizia, Liliana, Linda, Lulu, Mareile, Sister Margaret, Margo, Marian, Marika, Marion, Marnie, Marisa, Marty, Mary, Maryanne, Mary Jane, Meg, Melanie, Melissa, Nagyi, Naomi, Neil, Nicole, Panni, Patrick, Peter, Philip, Rae, Ray, Richard, Robert, Roger, Ron, Rui, Sandra, Shelley, Sid, Stephanie, Steve, Sura, Susan, Terry, Thelma, Tom, Trudie, Victoria, Vivien, Will, Wim, Yolanda, and Zsuzsa.

I'm grateful especially to have stumbled into this life of a photographer.

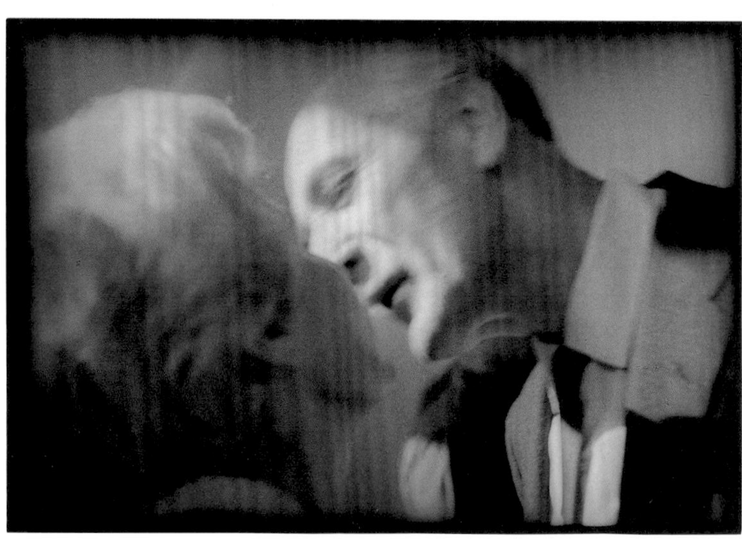